CW00690467

Nationalism, Development and Ethnic Conflict in Sri Lanka

Following the dramatic and violent conclusion of the 26-year old civil war in May 2009, Sri Lanka faces a new 'ground-zero' moment. The defeat of the Liberation Tigers of Tamil Eelam (LTTE) and the weakening of the Tamil nationalist project has meant that attention is now switching firmly back towards its counterpart, Sinhala nationalism, and on the ways in which it is likely to influence the evolution of the post-war, post-Prabhakaran future.

The most pressing challenges for this new post-war future are ethnic reconciliation and economic reconstruction. This book explores the complex and contradictory relationship between these two trajectories in post-colonial Sri Lanka with a view to understanding how they will come to affect the contours of an uncertain future. In doing so, it poses some very fundamental questions: why has the Sri Lankan ethnic conflict been so protracted, and so resistant to solution? What explains the enduring political resilience of Sinhala nationalism, and how is it related to socioeconomic mobility, leftist politics, and market reform policies? How will Sinhala nationalist politics and the role of military employment interact with future generations of market reform and economic growth?

Based on over a decade of research, and drawing on a wide range of qualitative and quantitative evidence from colonial administration reports and household economic surveys to in-depth interviews with contemporary political figures, it asks how Sinhala nationalism has related to the social democratic state in the period of its rise and decline since the mid-1950s. In doing so, this book is informed by and engages closely with recent debates in nationalism, critical development theory, and peacebuilding, and reflects an interdisciplinary reach across history, comparative politics, development economics, conflict theory, human geography, and social anthropology.

Rajesh Venugopal teaches at the Department of International Development at the London School of Economics and Political Science. He works on the political sociology of development and violent conflict, with a special focus on South Asia. He writes on post-conflict reconstruction, development theory, nationalism, and neoliberalism.

SOUTH ASIA IN THE SOCIAL SCIENCES

South Asia has become a laboratory for devising new institutions and practices of modern social life. Forms of capitalist enterprise, providing welfare and social services, the public role of religion, the management of ethnic conflict, popular culture and mass democracy in the countries of the region have shown a marked divergence from known patterns in other parts of the world. South Asia is now being studied for its relevance to the general theoretical understanding of modernity itself.

South Asia in the Social Sciences will feature books that offer innovative research on contemporary South Asia. It will focus on the place of the region in the various global disciplines of the social sciences and highlight research that uses unconventional sources of information and novel research methods. While recognising that most current research is focused on the larger countries, the series will attempt to showcase research on the smaller countries of the region.

General Editor
Partha Chatterjee
Columbia University

Editorial Board
Pranab Bardhan
University of California at Berkeley

Stuart Corbridge
Durham University

Satish Deshpande
University of Delhi

Christophe Jaffrelot
Centre d'etudes et de recherches internationales, Paris

Nivedita Menon
Jawaharlal Nehru University

Other books in the series:
Government as Practice: Democratic Left in a Transforming India,
Dwaipayan Bhattacharyya

Courting the People: Public Interest Litigation in Post-Emergency India,
Anuj Bhuwania

Development after Statism: Industrial Firms and the Political Economy of South Asia,
Adnan Naseemullah

Politics of the Poor: Negotiating Democracy in Contemporary India,
Indrajit Roy

South Asian Governmentalities: Michel Foucault and the Question of Postcolonial Orderings, Stephen Legg and Deana Heath (eds.)

Nationalism, Development and Ethnic Conflict in Sri Lanka

Rajesh Venugopal

CAMBRIDGE
UNIVERSITY PRESS

CAMBRIDGE
UNIVERSITY PRESS

University Printing House, Cambridge CB2 8BS, United Kingdom

One Liberty Plaza, 20th Floor, New York, NY 10006, USA

477 Williamstown Road, Port Melbourne, vic 3207, Australia

314 to 321, 3rd Floor, Plot No.3, Splendor Forum, Jasola District Centre, New Delhi 110025, India

79 Anson Road, #06–04/06, Singapore 079906

Cambridge University Press is part of the University of Cambridge.

It furthers the University's mission by disseminating knowledge in the pursuit of education, learning and research at the highest international levels of excellence.

www.cambridge.org
Information on this title: www.cambridge.org/9781108428798

© Rajesh Venugopal 2018

This publication is in copyright. Subject to statutory exception and to the provisions of relevant collective licensing agreements, no reproduction of any part may take place without the written permission of Cambridge University Press.

First published 2018

Printed in India by Nutech Print Services - India

A catalogue record for this publication is available from the British Library

ISBN 978-1-108-42879-8 Hardback

Cambridge University Press has no responsibility for the persistence or accuracy of URLs for external or third-party internet websites referred to in this publication, and does not guarantee that any content on such websites is, or will remain, accurate or appropriate.

To my parents, Kal and Janaki Venugopal

Contents

Figures

Tables

Preface

This book has its origins in a DPhil thesis at Oxford, submitted in 2008, and has since been much revised, updated, and augmented. It is based on a long period of research and engagement in Sri Lanka which began in 2002, and which continues to the time of writing in 2018. Over the years, I have benefited immensely from the generosity and support of many individuals and institutions, starting with my supervisors, Frances Stewart and David Washbrook, and the examiners, Nandini Gooptu and Jonathan Goodhand. I am very grateful for research funding provided by the Carnegie Corporation and the Wingate Trust, and to the institutional support provided by the University of Oxford, the International Centre for Ethnic Studies, Colombo, the University of York, and the London School of Economics. The Department of International Development at the LSE kindly provided me with sabbatical leave in 2016-17 to complete the manuscript. More importantly, I would like to sincerely thank the many dear friends, colleagues, well-wishers, teachers, librarians, and students, in each of these institutions, who have provided guidance, assistance, and sustenance.

Parts of this book have appeared earlier in different forms. An earlier version of chapter 4 was published as a chapter in Stokke, K. and J. Uyangoda (eds.), *Liberal Peace in Question: Politics of State and Market Reforms in Sri Lanka* (Anthem). Chapter 5 had a previous life as 'The Politics of Market Reform at a Time of Civil War', *Economic and Political Weekly* 46 (49): 67-75. Composite parts drawn from chapters 6 and 7 have formed chapters in Newman, E., R, Paris, and O. Richmond (eds.), *New Perspectives on Liberal Peacebuilding* (UNU Press), and in Raviraman, K., and R. Lipschutz (eds.), *Corporate Social Responsibility: Comparative Critiques* (Palgrave). An older version of chapter 8 was published as 'Sectarian Socialism: The Politics of Sri Lanka's JVP'. *Modern Asian Studies* 44 (3): 567-602. I have drawn on arguments first developed in a 2015 article 'Democracy, Development and the Executive Presidency in Sri Lanka' *Third World Quarterly*, 36 (4): 670-690 in chapters 1, 2, and 9.

The responses I have had from these earlier publications has helped greatly in improving this text, and also in shaping my own intellectual evolution over this period. I must also thank two anonymous reviewers who provided very valuable and thorough comments on the manuscript. Finally, sincere thanks are also due to my publishers at Cambridge: Qudsiya Ahmed, Sohini Ghosh and Aditya Majumdar have been very patient with me, and have been exemplary partners to work with.

I leave the last, the most essential words of gratitude and affection to Ravi, Kiran, and Mohan, who have been my companions in this enterprise from the beginning, and who, despite themselves, have been vital in seeing it through.

1 | Nationalism, Development and Ethnic Conflict in Sri Lanka

Sri Lanka's civil war is over, but the nationalist ideologies that gave rise to it live on, and continue to define the parameters of a post-war future. At the end of the war in 2009, the government of President Mahinda Rajapaksa consciously prioritised economic development in order to rebuild and catch up. But development also served a larger purpose beyond physical reconstruction: economic growth and transformation, it was suggested, would address the underlying drivers of grievance. It would reintegrate the war-torn north and east, rebuild legitimacy for the state through service provision, and create new ground realities that would help to transcend the basis for the resurgence of a violent separatist threat.

At the inauguration of a new expressway in 2011, Rajapaksa explained: 'Separatist tendencies will fade away when we have better road connectivity'.[1] In that sense, post-war development contained not just an economic purpose, but also functioned as a project of ersatz conflict resolution. In lieu of the substantive but difficult tasks of forging reconciliation, redressing past injustices, and negotiating constitutional futures, Rajapaksa instead proposed modern infrastructure, a doubling of the national per capita income, and an eight percent growth rate.

Indeed, much in the name of development did transpire. Beyond the 'dead cat bounce' revival of economic activity after the end of the war, significant strides were made in the restoration of agriculture and fishing, as well as in physical infrastructure. Economic growth increased steadily, and there was a historic reduction in the national incidence of poverty. The Rajapaksa period will, for all its failings, be remembered by posterity for the ornaments to infrastructure that it built – the railways, expressways, bridges, airports and ports, and the urban beautification projects of Colombo.

However, at the end of its nine-year span in power, and five years after the end of the conflict, Rajapaksa's evident record of post-war development had

---

[1] 'Better road connectivity to link all people: MR' Daily Mirror, 27 November 2011.

failed in one important aspect. Sri Lanka, it is common to hear, is post-war, not post-conflict. Far from rendering the ethnic conflict and Tamil grievances superfluous, the economic development approach had, if anything, embittered Tamils more. Even as many evidently benefitted from it, and became complicit in its webs of patronage and affluence, they also resented it , and voted against Rajapaksa in overwhelming numbers when the opportunity arose, bringing about his electoral defeat in 2015.

For those who have sought to label this approach as a peculiarly Sri Lankan or 'illiberal' model of conflict resolution, it is important to bear in mind that the idea of using economic development to address and reverse violent conflict is not an innovation of the Rajapaksa presidency or even peculiar to post-war Sri Lanka. Violent conflict has, since the 1990s, been incorporated as a central problematic of development theory and practice (Duffield 2001), and has been widely explained in academic research and policy practice as a product of under-development. In the course of providing humanitarian relief and implementing poverty alleviation projects, development organisations have found themselves drawn deeper into war-torn regions, working closer with military actors on conflict reversal and prevention. This was very much the case just prior to the Rajapaksa period in Sri Lanka, during the heavily internationalised peace process of 2002–2005. Sriskandarajah describes how, in what became known as the 'Killinochchi consensus', the efforts of aid donors, the LTTE and the government focused on putting the 'development cart' before broaching the contentious 'conflict resolution horse' (2003). In effect, this rested upon the assumption that:

> even the most intractable political disputes can be resolved through the use of economic incentives and levers. Such a view seems informed by a powerful neo-liberal logic that presents a tantalisingly simple message: get the economics right and the politics will fall into place (Sriskandarajah 2003: 32).

Many prominent bilateral foreign aid donors, such as the EU, Canada, Japan, Australia, and the USA incorporated foreign aid as one element of a range of 'carrot and stick' instruments at their disposal to prod the two sides towards negotiations and peace, and to create strong disincentives for a return to war. An unprecedented $4 billion of post-conflict aid was pledged to Sri Lanka at the Tokyo donor conference of June 2003, under the broad assumption that economic incentives would lock the two conflicting parties into a mutually beneficial cycle of development and peace.

Yet, both parties consciously chose to forgo the carrots and endure the sticks. In the course of a slow slide from peace to war from mid-2004 onwards, the domestic dimensions of the conflict confounded the assumptions and expectations of the international actors and overwhelmed their capabilities. By July 2006, war had resumed, ending eventually with an extraordinary bloodbath in May 2009. This historic failure in promoting peace and preventing the resumption of war in Sri Lanka brought about a phase of re-appraisal of the role of development assistance, and of the efficacy of external actors as a whole (Goodhand et al., 2005). One review of donor aid policy, written in the dying days of the peace process lamented that 'aid is not, for the most part, very effective as a vehicle for transformation. It is a relatively minor factor in the politics and mechanics of conflict in Sri Lanka' (Burke and Mulakala 2005: 6).

Indeed, a review of recent Sri Lankan history would suggest that the relationship between socio-economic change and ethnic conflict is even more complex and unusual. Before having become a paradigmatic case of violent third world ethnic conflict, Sri Lanka had paradoxically been considered a model of peaceful decolonisation, ethnic harmony, precocious democracy, and successful social development. Sri Lanka is the oldest and longest running democracy in Asia, having had universal suffrage thrust upon it while it was still the crown colony of Ceylon. The first election in which the masses were invited to participate was held in 1931, a full two decades before it could happen in India. The compulsions of electoral democracy also served to promote a precocious welfarist orientation to the state. Due to a generous measure of public services such as free health-care, that reached deep into the countryside, and the opening up of large tracts of agricultural land under massive irrigation resettlement schemes, Sri Lanka did not experience the kind of rural blight and desperate urban poverty typical of the rest of South Asia (Moore 1992a). Instead, there was the unusual phenomenon of 're-peasantisation' in the 1950s and 1960s, such that the earlier trends of long-term decay of the peasant economy under colonialism were briefly reversed. Alongside Kerala, Sri Lanka became a textbook development case of how low income countries could nevertheless achieve impressive advances in literacy, schooling, infant mortality, and life expectancy.

In a region where decolonisation was marked by the trauma of partition, sectarian massacres, the displacement of millions, war in Kashmir, 'police action' in Hyderabad, insurgency in Malaya, and assassination in Burma, the new dominion of Ceylon stood out as an island of peaceful political transition and harmonious communal co-existence (Ashton 1999). In his Independence

Day speech, the first prime minister, D.S. Senanayake could not but take pride at this achievement: 'there are no refugees crossing Elephant Pass, the Ceylon Light Infantry is organising a party to welcome its Colonel-in Chief, and the only explosions we shall hear will be those of the fireworks' (in Kumarasingham 2013: 125–126). As Donald Horowitz remarks: 'any knowledgeable observer would have predicted that Malaysia (then Malaya) was in for serious, perhaps devastating, Malay-Chinese conflict, while Sri Lanka (then Ceylon) was likely to experience only mild difficulty between Sinhalese and Tamils.' (Horowitz 1989: 18). One such group of reasonably 'knowledgeable' observers were the World Bank's 1951 expert mission to Sri Lanka, whose report was prefaced with a pointed observation on the absence of communal conflict in the island:

> [P]olitical life in Ceylon is not dull ... But their disputes are conducted without physical violence, and there seems little disposition to attempt any major social revolution. There are conflicts and strains between the different racial and religious groups but they have not hitherto led to mass violence (World Bank 1953: 14).

But mass violence did occur, first in periodic 'race riots', and later in the protracted horrors of civil war. Elephant Pass would be crossed back and forth by tens of thousands of people fleeing violence, and become the site of some of the most bloody and consequential battles of the war. It is commonly estimated that 100,000 people were killed, in the five phases of the war between 1983 and 2009, around half of whom were not combatants in any sense.[2] This figure does not include those who died during the Janatha Vimukthi Perumana (JVP) rebellion from 1987–90. It also excludes the missing, and does not adequately account for the civilian death count in the last phase of the war. Many of these civilians who died were not the unintended victims of 'collateral damage', but were deliberate targets of well-planned and carefully executed forms of violence: urban pogroms in the capital, bomb explosions in crowded buses, the execution of humanitarian workers, the hacking to death of villagers in their sleep, or the gunning down of a congregation at prayer.

Over this period, the two and a half million people of the affected areas in the Northern and Eastern provinces suffered extended periods of displacement as well as acute physical and economic insecurity, reflected in the high incidence

---

[2] Based on 23,327 soldiers, and 27,639 LTTE cadres killed as of the end of the war (attributed to a statement by Defence Secretary Gotabhaya Rajapaksa in an interview with state television on 22 May 2009).

of malnutrition, disease, and psychological trauma.[3] A majority of people in the north and east have been displaced from their homes at one point or another during the war, often repeatedly, in many cases, permanently. At one point in the 1990s, almost one million people, or over one-third of the total population of the two provinces were officially registered as internally displaced; while a similar number had fled the country altogether and sought refuge abroad.

By the end of the war, many towns and villages in the north and east were damaged beyond recognition by repeated artillery and aerial bombardment, and had been abandoned and depopulated. Most major roads, railways and other infrastructure such as electricity networks were badly damaged or remained in complete disrepair for over two decades. Large areas of productive farm-land remained uncultivated for years due to land-mines, the designation of 'high security zones', or because they straddled areas of contested military control.

How does one explain the dramatic reversal in Sri Lanka's fortunes? How can the immense suffering, destruction, and the deep ethnic divisions, of a devastating 26 year long civil war be reconciled with an earlier history of democracy, ethnic harmony, and pioneering social development? This book contributes to the understanding of this central question of the evolution of modern Sri Lanka by looking at the interaction of economic development and the ethnic conflict. The questions it raises are two-fold. Firstly, what is the role of economic development, and socio-economic transformation in the genesis of the conflict? Secondly, can an understanding of this relationship help to engineer and direct the political dynamics of the conflict? The book brings these two elements together through a series of studies on the politics of Sinhala nationalism, which has, for much of this period, been the dominant form of political consciousness in the country. The subject matter here, and the broader questions from which it is derived, will be familiar: why has the Sri Lankan ethnic conflict been so protracted, and so resistant to solution? What explains the enduring political significance of Sinhala nationalism? What is the relationship between market reforms, globalisation and the war/ peace processes? What explains the failure of the 2002–06 peace process? How is the Rajapaksa period to be understood?

The topical spread in this book is very diverse, covering peasant agriculture, land scarcity, state employment, party systems, political morality, military employment, business elites, market reforms, development aid, and the executive presidency. This also means that the research into this book has

---

[3] See Somasundaram (1998) and De Jong et al (2002)

had to embrace qualitative and quantitative methods to tackle an eclectic assortment of empirical matter. This includes colonial censuses of population and agriculture from the late 19th century onwards, administration reports from the 1930s and 1940s, newspaper archives of the 1950s–80s, survey data, election statistics, and other primary documents, including a wide range of personal interviews with political actors, corporate elites, trade unions, policy makers, development aid agencies, and nationalist ideologues.

By studying their interactions across diverse settings in space and time, the intention here is to delineate how the ethnic and the economic are imbricated, and are manifest in the making of the political. That is, this book draws on a wide palate of material as the empirical and analytical building blocks that are investigated in themselves, and also because, together, they amount to more than the sum of the parts. These different elements fit together to constitute and illuminate a socio-political matrix that can be termed 'cosmopolitan capitalists and sectarian socialists', capturing the peculiar juxtaposition of class and nation in contemporary Sri Lanka.

It is of course the case that this matrix, and the material presented, refer to Sinhala nationalism, and the politics of the Sinhala south. It does not, for the most part, address Tamil nationalism (Wilson 2000, Gunasingam 1999, Rasaratnam 2016), not because it lacks relevance but simply for economy of space and continuity of thematic focus. This book is not a comprehensive catalogue or history of the ethnic conflict, or nationalism, or even development, in Sri Lanka. Neither does it necessarily provide guidance on how development policy can be better designed, nor should it be read as such. The approach adopted is somewhat indirect, so that there are no neat and direct explanations that emerge to firmly settle the live debates and numerous paradoxes of modern Sri Lanka. The tone and ambition are much more modest and tentative. By studying the interaction of the ethnic and the economic in the making of the political, the intention here is, at best, to provide the basis upon which some of the answers can be better informed.

The Ethnic and Economic Context

As of the last pre-war census, in 1981, Tamils comprised 18 percent of the total population and formed the majority in the north and large parts of the coastal east of the island. The Sinhalese, comprising an overall majority of 74 percent, are concentrated in the south and west (see table 1.1a). But behind this broad statistical generalisation lies a much more diverse picture of spatial-communal dispersion that has significantly complicated the search for a resolution to the ethnic conflict. For example, even prior to the disruptions and refugee flows caused during the war decades, almost half of the Tamil population were settled outside the north and east.

Table 1.1a | Sri Lanka – Demographic Composition by Geographical Region* (1981 Census)

	Sinhalese	S.L. Tamil	Ind. Tamil	Muslim
Northern	3%	86%	6%	5%
Eastern	25%	41%	1%	32%
South total	84%	4%	6%	5%
Total	74%	13%	6%	7%

Table 1.1b | Sri Lanka – Demographic Distribution of Groups Across Regions (1981 Census)

	Sinhalese	S.L. Tamil	Ind. Tamil	Muslim
Northern	0%	51%	8%	5%
Eastern	2%	21%	1%	30%
South total	97%	28%	91%	65%
Total	100%	100%	100%	100%

This includes over 90 percent of the 'Indian' or 'up-country' Tamils – the descendants of plantation labourers who had emigrated from the countryside of southern Tamil Nadu around the present-day districts of Madurai, Thanjavur, and Thirunelveli over the century 1840–1940, and who still remain concentrated in Sri Lanka's south-central districts of Kandy, Nuwara Eliya, and Badulla. The unique geographic, economic, and historical circumstances of the upcountry Tamil community, and their contested citizenship status for most of the post-colonial period, has resulted in the formation of a collective identity that is distinct from the 'native' Sri Lankan Tamils to the island's north and east (Bass 2012, Peebles 2001, Vanden Driesen 1997).

A further dimension of complexity is posed by the fact that, while the north is overwhelmingly Tamil, the east is almost equally divided between Tamils, Sinhalese, and Muslims. Despite being mostly Tamil-speaking, the Muslim community has historically resisted incorporation within an over-arching Tamil identity, and has, for the most part, not participated in the politics of Tamil federalism and separatism (McGilvray 2011, O'Sullivan 1999, Ismail

1995). As with upcountry Tamils, Muslims have remained on the fringes of the conflict in which the Sinhalese majority and the Sri Lankan Tamil minority are the chief protagonists.

The ethnic conflict evolved slowly over the course of the late-colonial and early post-colonial years, but escalated into a sharper antagonism during the mid-1950s, largely as a response to the rise of majoritarian Sinhala nationalism. The issues that animate the conflict are many, but in constitutional terms, its 'irreducible core' relates to the issue of power-sharing and the extent of administrative and political self-government accorded to the historically Tamil-speaking parts of the island's Northern and Eastern provinces. In the 1950s and 1960s, the main currents of Tamil political opinion sought to reform the 'unitary' nature of the post-colonial state towards a more decentralised, federal structure. This was, for the most part, met with outright rejection in the Sinhalese south, where regional self-government and dilution of the unitary powers of the state were viewed as a pathway to separatism, and the balkanisation of the island. This set the stage for decades of fractious negotiations, a deepening ethnicisation of politics, and ultimately, the escalation of Tamil demands, beyond federalism to separatism.

Over this period, there were repeated rounds of negotiations, proposals, and even fully formed agreements on the core issues, starting with the Bandaranaike–Chelvanayakam Pact of 1957. Subsequent engagements include the Dudley Senanayake–Chelvanayakam Pact of 1965, the Thiruchelvam District Councils proposal of 1968, the District Development Councils proposal of 1979, the Annexure 'C' proposal of 1983, the All Party Conference of 1984, the Thimpu Talks of 1985, the Indo-Sri Lankan Accord of 1987, the Mangala Moonesinghe proposals of 1992, the cease-fire negotiations of 1995, the Chandrika Kumaratunga devolution proposals of 1995–2001, the Norwegian mediated Cease-Fire Agreement (CFA) of 2002 and negotiations of 2002–2003, the LTTE's Interim Self-Governing Authority (ISGA) proposals of 2003, and the All Parties Representative Committee (APRC) of 2006–09. Yet each one of these ultimately failed in the face of a conflict that proved resilient and deep-rooted.

By the early 1970s, and particularly in the aftermath of the 1971 Republican constitution, Tamil political opinion had shifted towards a more radical demand for the complete secession of the north and east as a separate state of Tamil Eelam. This shift took place amidst a change of guard in the composition of the Tamil political leadership, which slipped out of the hands of a Colombo-based elite towards the more militant youth-based insurgent groups in the north.

The growing campaign of insurgency and counter-insurgency that took hold in the late 1970s eventually escalated in 1983 to the point where it assumed the proportions of a civil war.

In economic terms, Sri Lanka has a hybrid, many layered structure that reflects the impact of successive generations of economic policy-making, global market influences, and developmental paradigms. As a broad historical summary of the landscape: peasant agriculture, which was the mainstay of the pre-colonial economy and society, was sent into relative decline during the mid- to late 19th century under the impact of large-scale commercial export-agriculture in tea and rubber (Roberts and Wickremaratne 1973; Snodgrass 1966). In the early to mid-20th century, concern over this decline of peasant agriculture, food production, and the welfare of the indigenous peasant population, led the government of the late-imperial and early post-independence period to formulate the first of many development interventions. This involved irrigation and colonisation of under-populated lands in the dry zone (Farmer 1957), to promote food production, as well as provide fresh agricultural land to relieve rural demographic stress. At the same time, there was also a broad expansion of state-led welfare provision, and an increase of the economic role of the state in society, during the 1940s–70s, through the expansion of the public sector and public services such as free health and education.

In the late 1970s, the United National Party government of J.R. Jayewardene initiated a sweeping shift in the policy landscape from a state-led to a market-led development orientation. This resulted in closer integration (or re-integration) of the Sri Lankan economy into the global economy, and the rise of entirely new sectors such as apparel export-manufacturing and tourism, along with the expansion of the service sector in general, including financial services (Athukorala and Jayasuriya 1994). The market reform programme prevailed even after the defeat of the UNP in 1994 by Chandrika Kumaratunga's left-centre People's Alliance (PA) coalition – albeit with a 'human face'.

Finally, the economic landscape was also transformed, beginning in the 1980s, by labour migration and the civil war, both of which occurred at a time of market reform and global integration. The defence budget increased steadily from the 1980s at a time when the role of the state in the economy was being reduced. Military spending created strong vested interests due to the vast procurements and contracts, and also due to the employment it generated (chapter 5). The structural context of the Sri Lankan economy reflects the co-existence of these historically layered and interlocking elements: small-holder agriculture, estate agriculture, irrigation-colony agriculture, the public sector/ public services, garment exports, tourism, services, migration, and the war.

During the 1990s, both the major political parties, the Sri Lanka Freedom Party (SLFP) and the UNP reached a point of greater convergence on two main items of state reforms: ethnic power-sharing and market liberalisation. In themselves, these amounted to a counter-populist reform agenda that was an electoral liability. This convergence created the opportunity for a populist mobilisation to arise in opposition to it, emblematic of which was the extraordinary resurgence of the JVP in the 1995–2004 period. It eventually resulted in the rise of Mahinda Rajapaksa as president in 2005, who embraced a new opposition to market liberalisation, and also a Sinhala nationalist militarism that contributed to the resumption of the last phase of the war (chapter 9).

Concepts and Contexts

Any study of development, nationalism, and ethnic conflict has first to confront the problem that these are ambiguous and heterogeneous terms that contain multiple meanings. Moreover, the terminology available to study this controversial and polarised subject matter is complicated and compromised by the peculiarities of its usage within the very context that it aspires to describe. There is, as a result, a need to not just define meaning carefully, but also to judiciously tip-toe around this lexical mine-field to ensure that one does not convey more than what is intended. Words such as 'ethnicity', 'ethnic conflict', and 'nationalism', which have disciplinary etymologies and associations, have particular meanings in Sri Lanka itself, where it is also referred to as the 'national problem', or even as 'racism' and 'racial conflict'. A more substantial discussion of nationalism is left to chapter 2.

'Development' is a notoriously convoluted concept which has, over the course of its evolution since the 1940s, come to assume a vast array of meanings at a number of different levels. As Serena Tennekoon describes,

> Until nudged into second place by the recent preoccupation with 'national security', development, was the chief priority of the post-colonial state (Tennekoon 1988: 295).

Development often refers, in the abstract, to economic growth and transformation, in contrast to the political, ethnic or cultural categories of reference. At the same time, it has also been confusingly broadened in recent years to refer to non-economic measures of well-being, or indeed, to the vast range of social objectives that development organisations have taken upon themselves. At another level, development also refers to both the 'immanent' process of change and transformation, and the 'intentional', purposive, enterprise of government policy and aid donors seeking to reform, transform, and regulate society (Cowen and Shenton 1996). The term 'development' is deployed in a variety of ways in this book, but what binds these diverse ideas together is not a single set of practices or a common underlying vision. Rather, the rubric of development is employed to shed light on, and to capture, the contradictory processes of the making, unmaking, and re-making of the social democratic state, and in doing so, to illuminate the political effects that are at work, whether intended or otherwise.

Within contemporary Sri Lankan studies, the term 'conflict' is defined almost exclusively with reference to the enduring 'ethnic conflict' between the island's Sinhalese and Tamils. But, while that issue does remain the central concern here, the study of the ethnic conflict also necessarily involves an analytical voyage that goes beyond the ethnic, and beyond the reductive binaries of Sinhala versus Tamil. Due to the phenomenon of 'ethnic over-determination', and the relentless intrusion of the conflict into every sphere of life, the Sri Lankan ethnic conflict presents itself as an object of study within the discursive categories and frames of reference that are self-generated by the conflict itself. As Jonathan Spencer describes:

> Since the mid-1980s, almost all attention has focused on the ethnic crisis and the escalating civil war, and somehow the issue of the distribution of power and resources within the polity have lost their academic urgency (Spencer 2002: 93).

As such, writing on the ethnic conflict is often situated within the confines of a universe where the only actors and identities available are the ethnicities in question, who enter the analysis as fully-formed, timeless, monolithic, pervasive, inescapable, and pre-disposed to mutual confrontation. What follows as a result is that the writing on the ethnic conflict often suffers from a condition, similar to that of Holocaust literature, where 'discussion of guilt masquerades as the analysis of causes' (Bauman 1989: xi).

However, any attempt to bring these subject areas out of an involuted study of their internal narratives and connect them with one another will struggle with the challenge of disciplinary compatibility. Nationalism, conflict, and development fall within distinct theoretical and disciplinary landscapes that have not historically communicated well with one another, and that are separated by a broadening rift of comprehensibility. Development traditionally comes under the purview of economics, while ethnicity, nationalism, and conflict are spread across history, political science, constitutional law, or social anthropology. These disciplinary barriers also generate entirely different frames of reference in posing the relevant questions at hand, and in identifying what constitutes appropriate theory and empirical methods.

Within economics, the study of the ethnic conflict was initially approached as a task of counting the costs of war (Arunatilake et al., 2001, Marga Institute et al., 2001, Grobar and Gnanaselvam 1993). This cost–benefit style understanding of the conflict–development link was influential not just among academic economists, but with national business elites and international aid agencies. It contributed to an economistic rationale for bringing the war to an early end.

A second stream of research, still within development economics, went beyond the costs, and searched for the economic causes of conflict in terms of the familiar categories of development intervention, such as economic growth, poverty, inequality, natural resource dependence, corruption, state capacity, and good governance. However, largely because of its preoccupation with data, technique, and universal generalisability, this literature is also noteworthy for being context insensitive, politically naïve, historically uninformed, clumsy with the conceptual terminology, and unable to engage with non-quantitative literature. While it has been successful in illuminating many broad empirical regularities at work, it is also limited to that level of generality; it struggles, for example, to provide insights into how exactly an economic correlate such as poverty connects causally to political outcomes such as violent conflict. In the specific case of Sri Lanka, the main factors that are identified by this literature – natural resources, geography, poverty, or relative deprivation – provide few meaningful insights into understanding the dynamics of conflict. This is not to suggest that economic factors are unimportant in Sri Lanka, but the way in which they are modelled, measured, and analysed in the quantitative 'civil wars' literature, has largely proven to be crude and misleading.[4]

Beyond the problems with this particular literature, the idea that the ethnic conflict is fundamentally rooted in socio-economic causes has a long intellectual

---

[4] Paul Collier's work on 'greed and grievance' is often cited as a reference case in point, but the critique applies more broadly to the civil wars literature in economics and quantitative political science. For a comprehensive summary of that literature, see Blattman and Miguel (2010).

history within Sri Lanka. The rise of radical anti-state insurgencies in both the Tamil and Sinhala communities has been widely identified as a problem of deep rooted social problems and economic deprivations based on poverty, geographic marginalisation, and caste. Economic categories and formations such as class have been used productively as a lens to understand how ethnicity is constituted and politically deployed. That is, the rational, objective categories and motivations that can be boxed in within economic terms are meant to help explain the supposed irrational aspects of ethnicity, war and violence better. Moreover, the idea that the conflict can be seen in terms of economic categories is significant because it naturally leads to the conclusion that its solutions are in the economic realm. On the one hand, it points to cross-ethnic, class-based consciousness and political mobilisation as a way of overcoming the twin evils of capitalism and ethnic division. On the other hand, for those within the policy realm, it provides the framework within which conflict prevention and ethnic reconciliation can be cognitively framed and mainstreamed into the language, modalities, and funding priorities of economic policy and foreign aid.

In contrast to this economic and technocratic understanding of the conflict, there is another tradition which is distinctly anti-technocratic, and which offers a sharply different approach to the relationship of economic development to ethnic conflict. This explanation steps outside the confines of development's inner technical modes of evaluation, and argues that failure is not due to dysfuntionality at all, but quite the contrary. As Benedikt Korf's research on an aid project in eastern Sri Lanka describes:

> [D]evelopment is not part of the solution, but part of the problem; political violence has been nurtured, not countered, through development interventions. Development in Sri Lanka has often been used to 'rule and divide' rather than 'build and unite'. (Korf 2006: 50)

Indeed, at its point of delivery, development is not neutral to politics, nationalism and conflict, but is quite explicitly political in terms of its rationale, and also in terms of how it is presented, justified, and perceived. Serena Tennekoon's pioneering study of the Mahaweli project (1988) described the intricate way in which this massive complex of development was, in its inspiration and implementation, infused with a deep nationalist significance. Caitryn Lynch (1999) describes a similar logic in the 200 Garment Factory Programme of the early 1990s, as does James Brow (1988) of a government housing project in Anuradhapura in 1978, and Michael Woost (1993) of a village irrigation project in Moneragala in the 1990s. In this reading, the failure of post-war development of the Rajapaksa period to win over the Tamils of the north and east would be seen as a foregone conclusion, because its real objective was ultimately to consolidate a triumphalist Sinhala nationalist project. Development was, alongside an expansive regime of militarised governance, used to demographically transform the north and east, and to monitor, control, and dominate its population.

Moreover, the idea of development as an assertion of power became more widely apparent in the intense politicisation of development interventions in this period. Development organisations, and, in particular, NGOs working at a community level in the north and east, were subject to constant scrutiny and surveillance, and were viewed as subversive agents of hostile western powers who served the separatist agenda. Many western aid donors who were critical of the government on human rights and the conduct of the war scaled down their projects and funding. In their place, India and China emerged as important sources of finance, and their rivalry for influence in Sri Lanka became manifest through the types of projects that they promoted.

The idea of development as a political project finds it most systematic elaboration in the critical anthropology of development (Escobar 1995, Ferguson 1994, Li 2007), where it is the dominant approach. This literature departs entirely from any presumption about the stated economic intentions of the development industry, and views its failure as functional and subservient to a deeper, concealed, self-serving ambition. Moreover, it casts the technocratic rendering as not just inaccurate, but as a component, complicit element of this enterprise. In this context, development is no longer seen as separate from, or antagonistic to nationalism, but as a vehicle for its promotion. It is in effect the projection of a Sinhala nationalist agenda to recreate society in its own image, and to enshrine its hegemonic ideological hold.

In summary, there are two radically divergent views of the relationship between development, nationalism and conflict. These are separated not just by a vast disciplinary and epistemological chasm, but also by a tendency to mutual reductionism. That is, one approach suggests that economic development can mitigate the politics of nationalist conflict, which it understands as a product of, and thus reducible to, economic grievances. Economic development is both the means to end conflict, and also the end in itself, while nationalist politics and conflict are obstacles to achieving this end. Nationalism and conflict are seen, at best, as epiphenomenal, and even superficial, manifestations of what is at heart, an economic failing. The other approach instead argues the converse – it is economic development and the technicalities which are the illusion, behind which lies the real substance, which is of nationalism, power and domination. While the first is informed by the idea that the social world can be explained by economic development and its lack thereof, the second is largely concerned with revealing the hidden operation of politics and power.[5]

Both of these approaches are valuable and have provided a series of very rich insights into the relationship of development to nationalist conflict. There are, however, also grounds for caution and to recognise their limitations; the study of the politics of development should neither be naïve to the effects of power, and nor mesmerised by it. As the chapters in this book demonstrate, development and nationalism are indeed closely imbricated in their socio-economic background, ideological construction, and political consequences. Development is connected to the production of Sinhala nationalism, but not in the way that is usually asserted. The relationship between them is far more complex, so that the causal chains involved are multi-pronged second or third order linkages that are unanticipated, contingent on a variety of other factors, and lacking in conscious intentionality. Moreover, the relationship varies considerably from one context to another, so that there is no comforting over-arching connection that can be drawn between their different encounters; no grand unifying framework can be constructed in support of either of the two approaches.

The analytical stance, theoretical orientation, and conceptual vocabulary that guides this book are based on what can be termed an extended political economy approach, within which there are three broad components. Firstly, it is historically informed, and draws on the longer trajectories of socio-economic evolution in order to situate the present. Secondly, it is sensitive to the role of class, and to economic factors, in explaining social realities and outcomes. Thirdly, it places great emphasis on understanding the nature of the state, the structure of political competition, and the way that power is constituted and sustained, particularly by economic and political elites. The strength of this approach is that it bridges the complex inter-disciplinary divides described above, and creates the possibility of folding in diverse forms of evidence. It also makes it possible to situate this work within the broad currents of Marxian scholarship, which has been very influential in Sri Lanka, providing it with conceptual parameters and critical sensibility, as well as an implicit ethical underpinning.

Having said that, it will also be evident that the material in this book struggles to work within this approach, strays from its conceptual parameters,

---

[5] On the critique of the critique of development, see Venkatesan and Yarrow 2012.

and ultimately exposes some of its inadequacies. This is evident at one level from the presence of concepts and dynamics that are traditionally outside this milieu, such as the 'inner world' of nationalist subjectivity, political morality, and the idea that these govern and regulate political conduct (chapter 2). At another level, it is evident in the way that the evidence and analysis presented in this book challenge many of the traditional political economy causal links that have entered into received wisdom in the Sri Lankan context. The most important of these are in the relationship of economic liberalisation to the ethnic conflict (chapters 4–5), the idea of elite instrumentalism, or even in the adequacy of the concept of hegemony (chapter 2). These, and other positions that I have advanced elsewhere, for example on neoliberalism (Venugopal 2015), are not intended as hostile assaults against the edifice of political economy analysis, but are critical points of engagement from a sympathetic insider, designed to expand and strengthen it.

The different parts of the book are, to some extent, self-contained, and engage with debates that are often quite specific to the periods in question and to the thematic issues at stake, calling upon distinct forms of empirical evidence, and employing different methods of data analysis. This is not to say that the book is agnostic or hostile to theory or to coherence of purpose, but just that those larger debates and concepts are not the protagonists in this book, but the props. What is ultimately at stake is to pursue the study of contemporary Sri Lanka in itself and for itself, not in terms of the ill-fitting categories drawn from elsewhere, and not as a one-country case study that bears mention only insofar as it can provide empirical fodder to feed a comparative debate. While this is inevitably the fate of scholarship about smaller countries, the ambition here is to resist that pressure, drawing on that larger body of theory and comparative work to illuminate the study of contemporary Sri Lanka rather than the reverse.

Structure of the Book

Chapter 2 situates the context, dynamics, and framework of contemporary Sinhala nationalism. It starts by exploring the debate over modernism versus primordialism in Sri Lanka, and the politics of studying Sinhala nationalism. The chapter then moves on to delineate the political operation of Sinhala nationalism in terms of five pillars. Firstly, nationalist politics takes shape as an explicit political project of majoritarian domination, or Sinhalisation, and this is the intuitive and self-evident way in which Sinhala nationalism appears in the outer world. Secondly, there is, beyond this evident politics of the outer world, an inner world of Sinhala nationalism evident as a cognitive moral framework. That is, Sinhala nationalism provides the basis on which people can judge what is legitimate from illegitimate, regulating the dangerous realm of electoral politics. Thirdly, this moral framework is the basis on which Sinhala nationalism forms the argot of instrumental political discourse between people, and between people and state. In other words, it is the language of political communication and performance. Fourthly, Sinhala nationalism constitutes a form of class consciousness against Sri Lanka's westernised post-colonial elites, and in that sense, needs to be situated within the history of that elite–mass dynamic. Fifthly, Sinhala nationalism structures the party system in what is described as an inverted left–right axis.

Chapter 3 draws on a modified version of the socio-economic framework drawn by Ernest Gellner (1964, 1983) to examine the impact of agricultural change, welfare policies, and government employment in the making of Sinhala nationalism during the 1950s. Drawing extensively upon historical statistical data on agricultural land, education, examination results, population growth, civil service employment, and unemployment, it describes the inter-generational class transition from peasants to clerks. This transition became particularly acute during the 1950s, and played an important role in catalysing the growth of Sinhala nationalism from its intellectual phase to a mass political force.

Chapters 4 and 5 are about the relationship between market reform policies and the prosecution of the civil war over the period 1977–2000. They dwell on the complex and unanticipated ways in which the market reform agenda, and particularly the political acceptability of those reforms became inter-twined with the prosecution of the war. Chapter 4 examines the role of J.R. Jayewardene and the UNP in promoting a new counter-populist politics and strategy of state reform. In a significant re-interpretation of that period that draws on a variety of primary and secondary material, the chapter articulates how Jayewardene created a more authoritarian institutional structure, promoted Buddhist religiosity, and expanded state development programmes manifold in the strategic politics of subverting Sinhala nationalism. As a result of the unforeseen and uncontrollable consequences of his policies, the UNP exacerbated the ethnic conflict, and triggered its escalation to civil war. In seeking to counter the moral dilemmas posed by the reform agenda and by their defensive compulsion to seize control of the mantle of Sinhala nationalism, the UNP found itself contributing to the radicalisation of Tamil political opinion, aggravating the conflict that they had sought to control and minimise.

Chapter 5 examines how the war has perversely been a source of economic and political stability, through the mechanism of military fiscalism. Drawing on quantitative data, particularly a large household survey dataset collected in 1999/2000, it argues that military employment had, by the mid-1990s, become a significant source of poverty alleviation and upward mobility for the rural Sinhalese hinterland. Contrary to the conventional view that the war has had negative economic repercussions, the vast growth in military employment mitigated the negative economic effects of growing inequality and agricultural stagnation under the reform period. While civilian-sector state employment fell due to market reforms in the 1980s and 1990s, the war effectively compensated for this by propping up state employment in the military, so that the war and destruction in the north perversely, and in unexpected ways, promoted stability and well-being for the poor in the south.

The third part of the book is about the December 2001 – April 2004 period, when a short-lived cease-fire agreement and peace process came into effect. This section is based on documents and personal interviews gathered from 2002 to 2007. Chapter 6 starts by examining the circumstances of the peace process and its failure, and analyses the role of the Sinhala Buddhist vote in the April 2004 elections. In examining the failure of the peace process, this section counterposes the politics of 'cosmopolitan capitalism' under the UNP-led United National Front (UNF) government, which promoted the peace-with-reforms agenda, against the 'sectarian socialism' of the opposition JVP, which led the opposition to both the peace process and the market reforms.

Chapter 7 examines the ideological, political, and financial emergence of the peace agenda under the UNP while in opposition during the late 1990s, particularly with respect to the role of the Sri Lankan business community and the aid donors in its articulation and implementation. The main thrust of this chapter is that Sri Lanka's peace process failed because it was tightly bound to an aggressive and controversial programme of market reforms. The peace agenda effectively came into being as part of the articulation and realisation of the material interests of Sri Lanka's corporate sector, who by the late 1990s increasingly found the war to be an expensive and futile indulgence.

The corporate lobby was one of the most influential constituencies demanding an end to the war, but they did so by couching the peace agenda within a larger package of rapid market reforms and private-sector led development. The embeddedness of the peace process within such an economic rationale and the social constituency of its inspiration and sponsorship had important fatal consequences for its sustainability. The government's heavily market-reform laden economic agenda enjoyed a very narrow social constituency of support; and widespread opposition to market reforms dragged the peace agenda down with it.

Chapter 8 explores the role of the Janatha Vimukthi Peramuna (JVP) in the collapse of Sri Lanka's 2001–2004 peace process. In doing so, it is divided into two parts: the first focuses on the evolution of the JVP in the post-1994 period culminating in the peace process during 2001-2004; the second seeks to situate the JVP's actions during the peace process through a more historical and analytical exploration of the JVP phenomenon. The fundamental analytical enigma of the JVP lies in explaining its hybrid Marxist-nationalist ideo-political agenda, which permitted it to craft a highly effective double-barrelled campaign of opposition to the pro-market, pro-peace UNP government on both fronts. The chapter provides an elaboration of the JVP's ideology and politics in the context of the left movement in Sri Lanka, and the socio-economic base that it represents.

Chapter 9, the final chapter in this book, examines the implications of the framework in understanding the Rajapaksa period (2005–14), and the executive presidency introduced in the 1978 constitution. It puts forward an argument that Sri Lanka's executive presidency was a project of cosmopolitan capitalism to recalibrate elite–mass relations (in favour of elites). By creating a more stable, centralised, and authoritarian political structure to overcome and reverse the negative effects of populist electoral democracy, its framers sought a vehicle to push through state reforms on the economy and ethnic relations which were otherwise electorally unfeasible. This project succeeded on its own terms in its early years when the president had command of a dependable legislature, but lost momentum as populist electoral pressure found strength and became manifest in parliament. The power of the presidency was eventually restored under Mahinda Rajapaksa during 2005–14, but only because the president openly championed the very populist positions that the presidency was formed to resist.

2 | Sinhala Nationalism

Sinhala nationalism is the dominant form of political consciousness in contemporary Sri Lanka. As what might easily be characterised as an illiberal 'ethnic' nationalism of the east rather than the western 'civic' ideal[1], it is also widely identified as a serious challenge to the functioning of liberal democratic institutions, and to multi-ethnic coexistence. Sinhala nationalism features as a central element in the literature on contemporary Sri Lankan politics, and in particular, on the ethnic conflict. Understanding Sinhala nationalism is thus of critical significance, and this imperative has inspired an extensive and sophisticated literature.

This includes the historicity of Sinhala identity (Gunawardena 1985, Dharmadasa 1992, Roberts 2004), the Buddhist revival and colonialism (Malalgoda 1976, Bond 1992, Tambiah 1992, Blackburn 2010, Rogers 1994), the *Mahavamsa* (Kemper 1991), colonial forms of knowledge (Rogers 2004, Kemper 1991), the State Council, Olcott and Dharmapala (Seneviratne 1999, Amunugama 1985, Roberts 1997, Kemper 2015), archaeology, the rediscovery of Anuradhapura and the Sinhala Buddhist past (Nissan 1989, Kemper 1991, Jeganathan 1995, De Silva 2013), the evolution of 'protestant' and post-protestant Buddhism (Obeyesekere 1970, Gombrich and Obeyesekere 1988), the changing role of monks (Seneviratne 1999, Kemper 1980, Bartholomeusz 2005, Kent 2015), temperance, the 1915 riots, language and literature (Coperahewa 2012, Rambukwella 2012, Field 2014), the transformation of village society, politics, and religious practices (Spencer 1990, Brow 1997, Woost 1994), the discourse of peasant preservation, and development projects (Brow 1997, Tennekoon 1988), the nationalist upsurge of 1956 (Kearney 1967), and the constitution (Schonthal 2016, Wijeyeratne 2013).

---

[1] On Hans Kohn's (1961) distinction, and the critiques of it (to which I am sympathetic), see Kymlicka (2001), Brubaker (1999), Yack (1996).

But despite the large amount of historical and anthropological literature, there is surprisingly little research available on the actual insinuation and operation of nationalism in the contemporary political sphere. Sinhala nationalism is widely deployed as an independent variable to explain political outcomes and as an explanatory prop. It is often thought of as a bubbling cauldron, a dormant evil genie, or some base instinct in the masses that is awakened by irresponsible politicians. But being seen as a self-evident evil in this way, nationalism itself is under-explained and its political operation is obscured.

Succinct, abstract definitions of nationalism are often found wanting and inadequate, in part, because the task is complex: it involves creating a generalisable, universally applicable, comparable category out of something inherently very particular. It requires an assumption that the set of phenomena delineated and deemed to comprise 'Sinhala' nationalism bear more than just a family resemblance, but have core commonalities with a generalised abstraction of nationalism drawn from elsewhere. But even when working just within the peculiarities of Sinhala nationalism, definition still involves the challenging task of capturing the range of connected manifestations that operate at very different levels, and compressing them all within a single moniker.

Nationalist politics is manifest at one level in its visible and vocal advocates such as former president Mahinda Rajapaksa, its ideologues such as Nalin De Silva or Gunadasa Amarasekara, the *Jathika Hela Urumaya*, or the assertive monks of the *Bodu Bala Sena*. The content of this overt and manifest outer world of nationalism has taken the form of campaigns to assert the primacy of Sinhala Buddhists in Sri Lanka vis-à-vis a range of other groups, ranging from Catholics, Tamils, Evangelical Christians, and Muslims. But nationalism is also immanent beyond these often ephemeral nationalist groups and individuals, so that another level of analysis would seek out the ways in which it has suffused the broader political realm, is instituted as a project of *Sinhalisation* of the state, or is instrumentalised, and appeased by elite actors seeking power through 'ethnic outbidding'. While each of these approaches provide insights into the larger phenomenon, they are in themselves not answers as much as components, or entry points, into the study of the profound and complex ways in which Sinhala nationalism is constituted and exerts influence in the political realm at different levels.

This chapter provides an outline of the political operation of Sinhala nationalism in terms of five features. Firstly, nationalism has its outer life in the project of Sinhalisation, the grand politics of ethno-nationalist conflict and as an agenda of ethnic domination. Secondly, the political significance of nationalism also has an inner life in framing subjectivities and forming the world view that situates and guides individuals in the political realm with moral parameters. In this way, it regulates and governs the turbulent world of electoral politics. Thirdly, nationalism is also inscribed in the structure of political communication and performance, so that all manner of political agendas – even those which are clearly venal, divisive, and contrary to the ethic of nationalism – must perforce be dressed in the language of nationalist righteousness. Fourthly, this element of communication and performance is particularly significant because the political project of nationalism has a distinctly anti-elite character, and deeply influences the nature of the elite–mass political relationship. Finally, nationalism structures Sri Lanka's political party system in a distinct, inverted left–right axis in terms of economic policy and ethnic relations.

The Study of Sinhala Nationalism

In approaching the study of Sinhala nationalism, there are a number of important issues that need to be engaged with. Firstly, any work on nationalism bears the burden of having to address the existing debate on modernity versus primordialism. Is Sinhala nationalism, and the Sinhala 'nation' as ancient as its own internal narratives claim, or is it, instead, of relatively recent construction and imagination? Despite specific idiosyncracies with the Sri Lankan case, the parameters of this debate are largely predictable, and follow the literature on comparative nationalism featuring the canonical work of Ernest Gellner (1983), Anthony Smith (1991), Benedict Anderson (1983), Tom Nairn (1977), and many others.

Rogers Brubaker remarks that primordialism is 'a long dead horse that writers on ethnicity and nationalism continue to flog' (Brubaker 1996: 15). In fact, the polemical thrust of modernist, constructivist, and instrumentalist theories of identity and nationalism is not directed at the dwindling and often mis-identified academic defenders of primordialism, but at the inner primordialism of nationalist narratives. In many respects, this grand divide in studies of nationalism mirrors the divide in development studies between the positivist versus the critical approach. That is, the debate is ultimately about whether the claims and narratives of nationalism or development are to be taken at face value or whether they are to be viewed with suspicion as ephemeral or as a veil behind which lurks some deeper enterprise.

In Sri Lanka, the weight of scholarly opinion since the 1970s has been firmly on the side of the modernist position (Spencer 1990, Nissan and Stirrat 1990). This is in fact also the case beyond Sri Lanka, where, as Anthony Smith notes 'by the 1960s and 1970s, the 'modernist' perspective had become the established orthodoxy' (Smith 2009: 6). In this rendering, Sinhala nationalism is identified as a product of economic, social, and political transformations that took place in the late-colonial and early post-colonial periods. The Buddhist revival, colonial racial classifications, the spread of literacy, print capitalism, the education system, and electoral democracy are all critical elements in the modernist understanding.

In contrast, a small but significant counter-view has prevailed to argue that a strong pre-colonial Sinhala group identity and self-consciousness has existed, and that these have enduring relevance in understanding the contours of contemporary Sinhala nationalism (Dharmadasa 1992, Strathern 2007, Roberts 2004). Michael Roberts, in particular, has argued at length that, by viewing nationalism as epiphenomenal to stages of development or print capitalism, the modernist position fails to account for its substantial pre-existing, pre-colonial building blocks and the resilience of its deeper narratives.

Given that the thrust of this book is on economic development, it is intrinsically sympathetic to and linked to the modernist position, and flows from it as an epilogue that extrapolates that historical literature into a more contemporary setting. Nevertheless, the purpose here is not to launch into a defence of the modernist position, and neither is it necessarily productive any more to engage in that debate or to take it as a point of departure. The debate about modernism versus primordialism or perennialism in Sri Lanka (and indeed more broadly) has largely exhausted itself, both because it is overworked, and also because it increasingly appears contrived. In many cases, the debate circles around differences that are relative rather than absolute, that are exaggerated for the sake of emphasis, or else that result from different definitions of the key terminology, including the very concept of nationalism itself.

Secondly, there is the issue of the positionality and politics of the scholar. What is the purpose of studying Sinhala nationalism? What attitude have scholars brought to this task, and how does that relate to the kind of knowledge that has been produced? It is impossible to be agnostic and detached about a phenomenon as politically vivid, so that to study it is inevitably to identify and position oneself not just with respect to its claims over the past, but with its present day politics and future consequences. In the academic writings on Sinhala nationalism, stretching from history and anthropology to political economy and constitutional law, this attitude is inevitably one of concern and even antagonism. At times the purpose of scholarship is explicitly subversive and hostile towards nationalism, as with the programmatic declaration that introduces Pradeep Jeganathan and Qadri Ismail's book *Unmaking the Nation*:

> We suspect the nation ... we are not enamored by the possibilities of the nation and nationalism, rather we are deeply suspicious of its claims and consequences ...the contributors to this book come together in the belief that the inclusive pretences of the nation must be exposed, that not just its inadequacies but its very superfluousness must be called into question. (Jeganathan and Ismail 1995: 2–3).

Similarly, Kumari Jayawardena writes 'Careful historiographical analysis is needed to unravel the constituent elements of this consciousness and to expose the myths, falsehoods and misinterpretations that have become embedded in it' (Jayawardena 2003: 114).

With this often explicitly-stated purpose in mind, it is not surprising that nationalist narratives, practices, and politics are, when held up to academic scrutiny, found to be not just false, invented, or derivative, but also dangerous. More often than not, they are identified as complicit in some troubling system of domination such as patriarchy, caste, or class. But even where there is no such manifest agenda, the very act of bringing Sinhala nationalism under the scrutiny of critical historical and social science investigation involves a certain performance of intellectually encircling, overwhelming, and subjugating it.

By unearthing the historical evolution, belief structures, mundane practices, and moral parameters of a phenomenon held in such widespread awe by millions, academic research is unmistakably a project of *dispelling* that awe. This point requires a certain emphasis because many of the dispellers draw inspiration from Said and Foucault on knowledge as power, and on the colonial construction of Indology. Much as modern science might be used to unmask witch doctors, the full armoury of modern critical social science and historical scholarship has been unleashed to overpower and demystify Sinhala nationalism, wielding scholarship as a weapon with which to expose this false doctrine, refute its texts, ridicule its followers, and shatter its idols.

We have reliably learnt as a result that Sinhala nationalism is not ancient, but modern, not pristine but produced, not anti-Christian, but modelled on Christian missionary practices, not anti-colonial, but derived from colonial discourses and forms of knowledge. These are, on the face of it, devastating attacks on Sinhala nationalism, which, if it depended on the academic robustness of these claims alone, should by now have succumbed and shriveled into irrelevance. But it goes without saying that this has not happened. The academic assault on Sinhala nationalism has done little to diminish the influence of its ideas or its political salience. Indeed, as the reaction to Stanley Tambiah's book *Buddhism Betrayed* (1992) in the early 1990s showed, the attempts to confront power through challenging its forms of knowledge served to strengthen, not weaken that power.

Academic scholarship on Sinhala nationalism, including, for that matter, this book, speaks from a milieu, and to an audience, dominated by a cosmopolitan left-liberal ethic committed to multi-ethnic coexistence, and that is deeply hostile to the nationalist project. Many scholars of Sinhala nationalism are, as Michael Roberts describes, 'liberal humanists at the coalface' of the struggle against ethnic chauvinism (Roberts 2001: 1). The frankness with which many texts on nationalism explain their political leanings and purpose is refreshing and even admirable for its transparency.

But there are also obvious concerns and shortcomings with turning academic writing into tracts that are engaged in explicit political advocacy. Yoking research to a clear ideo-political and moral end-position explicitly pre-determines the outcome, and suggests that it amounts to cherry-picking evidence to validate one's prejudices. This is not to suggest that it is possible to depoliticise the scholarship on Sinhala nationalism or even to pretend that scholars can (or should) transcend their own politics to produce some pure and positivist rendering. There is, however, a compelling case for greater reflection and consideration of the purpose and value of this enterprise, and more willingness to let the evidence lead to the conclusions, rather than vice versa. Even if this is a futile task, and amounts to a fiction, it is nevertheless a useful fiction to project.

A third issue that has to be addressed is that Sinhala nationalism has come to be approached and understood as an ideology of extremism and violence. There are certainly connections to be drawn between nationalism and a range of violent outcomes, and this is perhaps an understandable concern given the magnitude of what has transpired in Sri Lanka. But how far is this appropriate, and what kind of knowledge about nationalism does this approach generate (Jeganathan 1998)? Perhaps the most influential and extensively argued work in this regard is of Bruce Kapferer and his thesis on the relationship between the ethnic violence of 1983 and the Sinhala Buddhist cosmological ordering of person, community (nation), and state. What Kapferer suggests is that within the corpus of Sinhala Buddhist thought and practices is a mechanism that lends it prone not just to imbue culturally specific meaning to acts of violence, but to a culturally determined capacity to enact symbolically meaningful acts of violence. As he describes:

> [T]here is a relation between the passion of sorcery and the furious passion of ethnic violence. Both, I suggest, find their force in ideologically driven concerns, founded in a Sinhalese Buddhist ontology of the state, of the person, and of evil (Kapferer 2011: 32).

Kapferer's work is pioneering, and often deeply impressive, not least for its intellectual range. It is also unusual and important for its 'ontological' approach, into the inner life of nationalist subjectivity. But it is also the subject of concern and critique, much of it warranted (Spencer 1990, Scott and Geertz 1990). The problems are, in brief, two-fold. Firstly, Kapferer's approach fetishises violence, and accords it a position of exaggerated centrality and uniqueness in the landscape of Sinhala Buddhist consciousness. Violence in other words, is presumed to be such a defining feature of Sinhala nationalism, that it sets it apart. Moreover, it suggests that violence forms an appropriate entry point to studying the broader landscape of nationalist consciousness. Decoding the specific forms of violence and the way it is enacted could thus presumably reveal essential features of nationalism's ontological core.

The problem, of course, is that there is much more to nationalism than violence. As Michael Billig (1995) points out, the everyday life of nationalism is not about spectacular violence, but is borne out and internalised in a variety of routine, banal forms. That is, the inner cognitive essence of nationalism contains not just the possibility of enacting symbolically meaningful acts of regenerative violence, but a more expansive range of mundane behaviour. Analyzing nationalism through the lens of its most extreme and violent consequences not only diminishes the understanding of nationalism, but it also limits the frame of study to a narrow and even marginal range of manifest experiences and consequences. Conversely, there is much more to violence than nationalism. Nationalism is invariably an important factor in explaining certain types of manifest violence in Sri Lanka, but the link from one to the other is complex and diffuse, involving a sequence of highly contingent causal steps. These synapses that connect nationalist subjectivity to the extraordinary violence that it inspires cannot be minimised as they are, in many cases, the determining factors at stake.

Fourthly, and of more direct relevance to the ambit of this book, how are class and ethnicity interposed in Sinhala nationalism? Class as a category, and class-related analysis has faded from the analytical frame over the years, both because of the broader intellectual trend in this direction, and also because of the evident displacement of class politics with ethnic politics in Sri Lanka. This is, however, not to suggest that class is absent, or even that class analysis has not been deployed productively in the past. Kumari Jayawardena's work on trade union movements and class politics documents the long history of its interaction with Sinhala nationalism (Jayawardena 2003). This is manifest not only in the hybrid Marxist-nationalist politics of the Janatha Vimukthi Peramuna (chapter 8), but beyond that in the 'old left' parties, who steadily compromised with Sinhala nationalism in the 1960s and 1970s. One of the more original and influential ways in which class analysis has been articulated is in Newton Gunasinghe's explanation of the connection between the open economy and the 1983 riots. Gunasinghe explains that market liberalisation benefited externally connected Tamil merchants at the expense of Sinhala businessmen who had emerged under state patronage and regulation (1984 chapter 4). Violence was in that sense, motivated by underlying economic motives and grievances that were widely shared.

Valuable and significant as this literature is, there is often a sense that it dwells in the realm of the 'terrible postal error' that Ernest Gellner famously described (Gellner 2006: 124). That is, it is a literature that struggles – often with itself – to come to terms with the question of why nationalism triumphed as it did, and why the promise of class did not materialise. Nationalism thus enters the frame not as a real world phenomenon which requires explanation in itself, but as part of the explanation for why some other anticipated outcome did not transpire. Class is indeed a very significant component in understanding Sinhala nationalism, not in the static sense, but more in terms of the way Ernest Gellner deploys it to explain the formation of vernacular intellectuals and horizontally immobile clerks (chapter 3).

A different strand of literature has explored the idea that the deeply hierarchical nature of Asian societies creates nationalisms that are themselves hierarchical rather than egalitarian. Asian nationalisms may thus be fundamentally different from the European prototype (Tonnesson and Antlov 1996). Interestingly, Bruce Kapferer's work on the hierarchical ontology of Sinhala nationalism is specifically cited as an emblematic case in point of the peculiarities of Asia. This is however, not just a fundamental misreading of

Kapferer, but is also in itself just inaccurate in its characterisation of Sinhala nationalism. The hierarchies that Kapferer describes are in the realm of cosmology, and relate to the ordering of the person, nation, and state, rather than internal social hierarchies within the nation. That is, it relates to the hierarchical encompassment of the Sinhala Buddhist person by the state rather than the social hierarchies of class, caste or gender within Sinhala Buddhists.

Where social hierarchies are present in Kapferer's work, they imply not the class hierarchies that would support an Asian exceptionalism, but the hierarchical standing of different ethnic groups within this ontology, that places the Sinhala Buddhists at its apex. As he explains, 'The hierarchical ideology of Sinhalese nationalism stresses the internal unity of Sinhalese in themselves ... It is in the encompassment of the Sinhalese Buddhist state wherein Sinhalese as a nation are in a hierarchical relation of domination to others that the unity of Sinhalese qua Sinhalese is determined' (Kapferer 2011: 214) .

That is, Sinhala nationalism contains a world-view in which the majority Sinhala Buddhist 'nation' has a special connection to the state, and has a superior claim on it to the minorities. Extracted from the cosmological framework and idiom that Kapferer uses, what it amounts to is not particularly different from the way majoritarian nationalisms operate elsewhere in the world, including Europe. But even beyond Kapferer, the idea that Asian nationalisms or that Sinhala nationalism in particular is embedded with an anti-egalitarian, hierarchical core that distinguishes it as a case apart, is quite simply mistaken, for much the opposite is borne out.

Sinhalisation

The 'outer' politics of Sinhala nationalism is manifest in the political realm through a project of ethnic domination, or 'Sinhalisation'. In substance, Sinhalisation takes as its axiomatic starting point the idea that the indigenous Sinhala Buddhist majority is due a rightful position of primacy that is not adequately recognised by the post-colonial state. This project of state reform consists of advancing and prioritising the material, spiritual, and cultural interests of the Sinhala Buddhist people with a view to enhancing and enshrining their predominance in society. Citizenship rights and all claims on the state are viewed in terms of an ethnic hierarchy, with the Sinhala Buddhists due the highest position and priority. The minorities are accorded their due share, and are tolerated, as long as they recognise and respect this dispensation and behave in an appropriately demure manner. As Sri Lanka's army commander, Sarath Fonseka clarified in the final months of the war:

> I strongly believe that this country belongs to the Sinhalese but there are minority communities and we treat them like our people ... We being the majority of the country, 75%, we will never give in and we have the right to protect this country ... They can live in this country with us. But they must not try to, under the pretext of being a minority, demand undue things (National Post 23 September 2008).

Importantly, the project of Sinhalisation does not understand itself or base its actions on the idea of imposing the brute force of the majority, but on the notion that it is a righteous obligation, bears legitimacy, and is the exercise of justice. That is, the Sinhala Buddhists' claim to predominance flows from idea of *dhamma-dweepa*, which relates the Sinhala Buddhist people to a unique historical-religious-territorial destiny and responsibility to protect the Buddhist religion in the island of Lanka. This in turn is based on the legitimacy of the Sinhala Buddhist claim to primacy because of indigeneity, historical evidence of habitation in the entire island, and the democratic principle of majority rule. Sinhalisation is also based on the idea of redressing a grave historical injustice done to the indigenous community by centuries of European-Christian colonial rule, cultural-religious persecution, and economic dispossession. Related to this last point is the redressal of the undue historical advantages that accrued to minority groups such as Tamils under colonialism.

In comparative terms, there is much that the project of Sinhalisation and the Sinhalised state bears in common with what Sammy Smooha (2002) describes as an 'ethnic democracy ', or even the more severe concept of an ethnocracy by Oren Yiftachel (2006) – both originally modelled on Israel. As Smooha explains, the dominant nation appropriates the state, and shapes the symbols and laws, to benefit itself. Outsiders to this dominant nation have citizenship rights, but are viewed as a security threat to the dominant nation and as such, enjoy distinctly inferior rights. State measures to avert the risk from minorities affects their equal status, as well as the broader rule of law and democracy. Similarly, Yiftachel and Ghanem describe ethnocracy as a 'regime facilitating the expansion, ethnicisation and control of contested territory and state by a dominant ethnic nation. The dominant ethnic nation appropriates the state apparatus and shapes the political system, public institutions, geography, economy, and culture, so as to expand and deepen its control over state and territory' (2004: 649).

In both versions, liberal democratic features of government co-exist uneasily, and are undermined by the assertive dominance of a majority ethnic group that gains control over state power. To that extent, many elements of these archetypes are clearly resonant with the Sri Lankan experience, and indeed in subsequent work, Sri Lanka is explicitly identified as an illustrative case study of ethnocracy (Yiftachel and Ghanem 2004). Uyangoda further expands on the specificities of the ethnocratic state in Sri Lanka as 'a specific form of democracy that privileges ethno-nationalism as the dominant framework of political imagination, competition, and mobilisation' (Uyangoda 2011: 4).

There are three broad components to the Sinhalisation agenda. Firstly, there is a cultural and symbolic agenda of infusing the state with a Sinhala Buddhist aura. This agenda operates at a number of different levels and includes the incorporation of distinctly Sinhala Buddhist symbols within the state's majestic presence such as the national flag, and the national emblem. It involves enshrining the formality of official status for the Sinhala language, or according the 'foremost' place for the Buddhist religion. There is also a de facto Sinhalisation that takes place through everyday practices such as the presence of official sign-boards in Sinhala only, the appearance of Buddhist symbols, practices, and monks in government offices and public functions, or the staffing of entire government bureaus or police stations with ethnic Sinhalese personnel. Through these processes from above and below, the Sri Lankan state has acquired a distinctly Sinhala Buddhist quality to it.

Secondly, Sinhalisation is an agenda of economic advancement; that is, the prioritisation of the material interests of Sinhala Buddhists. This signifies directing state resources and influence towards employment opportunities, economic development projects, and commercial enterprises in ways that benefit the majority community. State employment, previously dominated by minorities such as Jaffna Tamils, Sinhala Christians, and Burghers, became increasingly dominated by Sinhala Buddhists through the 1960s and 1970s. The political economy of Sinhalisation is also inflected by the association of peasant agriculture with a quintessential Sinhala Buddhist authenticity, so that Sinhalisation is also about providing for the indigenous peasant.

Thirdly, Sinhalisation is a territorial agenda of expanding the spatial reach and control of the dominant nation, and of containing the territorial claims of minorities. This involves expanding the frontier of Sinhala Buddhist populated areas of the island, and opening new areas through irrigation resettlement colonies (Tennekoon 1988, Korf 2009, Klem 2014). It also involves preserving the unitary nature of the state and to limit, fragment, or complicate the territorial claims to political decentralisation or separation by the minorities.

In this way, the politics of Sinhala nationalism is an agenda of constituting and capturing the sources of public authority – including the state – and wielding it to effect the predominance of the Sinhala Buddhist community. The motor engine driving this process was the grip that Sinhala nationalism as an ideology had on the majority of the electorate, and the role that this framework came to play in governing the larger political space. Indeed, this political dominance is of an extent that it transcends party competition and constitutes a Gramscian 'common sense', that is the conformist consensus widely accepted across the mainstream political spectrum. Through the inexorable pressure of the ballot box, all of the ostensibly national parliamentary parties in Sri Lanka: the United National Party (UNP), the Sri Lanka Freedom Party (SLFP), and the Janatha Vimukthi Peramuna (JVP) have at some point advanced a Sinhala nationalist agenda. At times they have done so implicitly and through obfuscation – that is, by pandering, collaborating, and compromising. At other times it has been more explicit, openly championing Sinhalisation through the dynamics that DeVotta (2005) describes as 'ethnic outbidding'.

A Moral Framework of Regulating Electoral Politics

Behind the 'common sense' consensus of Sinhala nationalism, and its outer life as a manifest political project, is an inner life, buried in individual subjectivities, 'deeper' discourses, and what Michael Billig describes as banal, mundane practices. Nationalism on the public stage rests on widely shared understandings and aspirations of the political world and how it should be constituted. As Liah Greenfeld describes, nationalism is

> a form of social consciousness, a way of cognitive and moral organisation of reality. As such it represents the foundation of the moral order of modern society, the source of its values, the framework of its characteristic – national – identity and the basis of social integration in it. (Greenfeld 2001: 24)

It establishes the framework, tenor, and vocabulary that people use to engage, evaluate and accept the authority of the state. Nationalism is the cognitive framework that allows individuals to situate themselves vis-a-vis a larger community, and to acquire a historically contextualised, symbolically meaningful, framework of the present. That is, it draws fluidly on a social imaginary (Taylor 2003) and an inner cultural edifice of Sinhala Buddhist principles, traditions, narratives, symbols, cosmology, and historical memory. From this, it identifies and establishes a set of transcendental objects and values of supreme veneration that have widespread collective resonance, and against which political actors and political action, including those of the state and other sources of public authority, can be judged. These include, but are not limited to, three widely cited, interlocking symbolic elements: the land, the people, the faith (*rata, jathiya, agama*), corresponding to the territorial homeland of Sri Lanka, the community of Sinhala Buddhist people, and the Buddhist faith.

This cultural edifice and these objects of supreme veneration constitute moral beacons that illuminate electoral politics, rendering it comprehensible and navigable, identifying what is valuable, and distinguishing what is legitimate and permissible from that which is not so. The idea of nationalism as a moral framework is derived and inspired from E.P. Thompson (1971) on the moral economy. Thompson argued that 18th century English bread riots and peasant revolts were triggered not by hunger or exploitation in the abstract, but only at the point when this breached a trigger point determined by customary norms. In contrast to the modernist view of nationalism, which argues that the superficially cultural phenomenon that is understood as nationalist 'tradition' is in reality the product of modern economic forces, the moral economy finds the converse. That is, what superficially appears as an economically determined phenomenon (bread riots) is in reality governed by factors that are more cultural and 'traditional' in their character.

Thompson unnecessarily confines the idea of the moral economy to the circumstances of 18th century England (Gotz 2015), but it can be extended well beyond, and be re-deployed to the broader framework and language of governmentality and regulation. That is, the moral economy regulates the dangerous and potentially harmful world of economic activity, which is guided by self-interested human venality, so that it functions in the public interest. The basis of this regulation is a subjectively held, but widely shared notion of what constitutes legitimate economic behaviour. As an institution, morality thus constitutes rules, policing, and punishment, so that a bread riot is not about violence and theft by a hunger-crazed mob. It has an entirely different meaning and rationale of causation in terms of the dispensation of justice to those found guilty of having breached the moral code. As Thompson (1971: 108) describes, justice was not a rash descent into pillage, but was about restoring prices to a just level: 'What is remarkable about these "insurrections" ... is not the sack of granaries and the pilfering of grain or flour but the action of "setting the price".'

Sinhala nationalism effectively constitutes something that resembles a moral economy. The expansion of welfarism under a nascent electoral democracy in the 1940s meant that the state had become the most important economic actor in society. Sinhala nationalism thus inscribes customary economic rights and expectations that citizens can expect from the state. James Brow describes Sinhala nationalism along these lines as a 'dominant code of moral regulation ... The ideal image of the social order in nationalist rhetoric is one that recognises the responsibility of government to ensure the welfare of the common people, particularly the peasantry' (Brow 1990b: 13). It is in the course of being demonstrably moral that people engage, evaluate, and accept the authority and good standing of those in the political realm.

For this reason, it is perhaps more appropriate to view nationalism as broader than a mechanism for economic regulation, but one that regulates and governs political conduct and political relationships, including that of citizens vis-à-vis the state. Regulation in this sense refers both to the self-control that comes from the exercise of conscience and an individual code of ethical self-conduct, but also in terms of judging how others, and particularly those in positions of authority *ought* to behave, and what Sinhala Buddhist people can rightfully expect from them.

As Charles Taylor (2004: 7–8) describes of social imaginaries and moral orders, there is a 'founding contract' – a 'hermeneutic of legitimation' that outlines the reciprocal arrangement – but this can also be prescriptive in dealing with a breach of this contract and justify serious consequences. Breaches of these customary rights due from the state, or of unethical, immoral political behavior by any actor in the political landscape can, as with the transgression of the moral economy, invite extraordinary and demonstrative acts of collective disapproval and punishment. Depending on the institutional and organisational ways they are channeled, these can take the form of votes, *hartals* and demonstrations. Moral transgression is also the basis upon which acts of violence, such as riots, assassinations, or even insurgency, can become viewed as publicly legitimate, and hence tolerated.

This relationship between nationalism and the political behavior it regulates is illustrated well in an episode from Jonathan Spencer's ethnography of a village in Sabaragamuwa. Spencer describes how one of his informants carefully distinguishes between *desapalanaya*, or politics, and *jatika prasnaya*, or the national question (Spencer 2008: 611). The emphatic way in which these spheres are viewed as separate bears scrutiny, not because it reflects an underlying reality, but because it describes the way in which they are cognitively organised and seen to relate to one another. Politics is the sordid, cut-throat, real-life business of pursuing political power. Nationalism on the other hand is the code of conduct by which this dangerous practice is to be managed and controlled in the collective interest. Drawing deeply on an available wealth of concepts, symbols, images, and stories, nationalism constructs a vision of unity, harmony, and righteousness that has significance and bears constant repetition, so that it self-evidently contrasts against the disunity, greed, and conflict of the real world of politics. In other words, the categorical separation of these two spheres that informants are eager to assert has validity, although the two are in reality interlocking, inter-dependent components that have significance with respect to one another.

Elites and Masses

The role of Sinhala nationalism in the political relationship between the rulers and ruled needs to be traced back to the late 1920s and the hearings of the Donoughmore Commission (Barron 1988). Political reforms had, since the 1880s, gradually expanded the quantity and quality of native representation within the colonial government, and the nascent Ceylonese elite that had been thus drawn in, expected and lobbied for further such gradual reforms. However, the Donoughmore Commission, which arrived in Ceylon in 1927 had more ambitious ideas in mind. They proposed a significant expansion in self-government, but linked this to an even more significant expansion of the franchise. Voting had hitherto been restricted to men of education and property, but the Commissioners made the radical proposal of extending it to all men and women aged 21 and over (Kumarasingham 2006, 2014).

Ceylon's native political elite, composed entirely of wealthy, educated, westernised men, were aghast at this idea. Almost unanimously, they opposed the extension of the vote to those they considered manifestly unsuited and unprepared for it.[2] Their most senior and respected personality, Sir Ponnambalam Ramanathan, wrote in outrage that it was 'an utter stupidity' to 'transfer political power to a dangerous mob'.[3] Yet it went ahead. Under the Donoughmore constitution (1931–47), the crown colony of Ceylon – not even a dominion yet – was the first country in Asia, and the first 'non-white' unit of the empire, to be granted such extensive self-government, and also the first to have universal suffrage.

---

[2] Manor (1989:78) lists the only three people who advocated universal franchise in Ceylon as a trade unionist A.E.Goonesinha and two British residents.
[3] Cited in Russell (1982:18).

The elite in early post-colonial Sri Lanka typically refers to the Colombo-based, English-speaking classes that had emerged during the nineteenth century, and who were linked either to the plantation economy or to the modern professions. For the most part, they were low-country Sinhalese and Jaffna Tamils in origin. But they were set apart from the rural majority of both communities by virtue of their wealth, English education, and by their adoption of a lifestyle and outlook that was markedly westernised and even Christianised (Roberts 1973, Roberts 1974, Fernando 1973, Singer 1964, Oberst 1985, Jayawardena 2000, Spencer 2002). Indeed, a disproportionately large share of the Sinhalese and Tamil elite were actually members of the Protestant church.

The 'mass' in question – and as with elites, this is an unavoidably sweeping generalisation – consists of the overwhelming majority of the population; predominantly the peasantry, but also the urban working class, and the urban lower middle class. This last section includes the majority of the salariat, but also their more precarious counterparts in the urban and rural informal sector. The composition of these elites and masses in question has a clear basis in class, although for analytical and descriptive purposes, the less rigid and more fluid, albeit less conceptually rigorous, categories of elites and masses are more appropriate and functional.

Elites are an important part of understanding Sinhala nationalism, and the elite–mass distinction gives it a significance that complicates the familiar narratives of Sinhalisation. James Manor had in the late 1970s asserted that the 'elite/mass discontinuity, rather than the Sinhalese/Tamil discontinuity, is the principal cleavage in the polity of Sri Lanka' (Manor 1978: 22) and this remains an important theme in the study of the conflict. The role of elites in relation to Sinhala nationalism has taken shape in the literature largely through the idea of elite instrumentalism (Stokke 1998, Bush 2003). In this rendering, Sinhala nationalism is an ideology that is constructed, promoted, and exploited by a manipulative elite seeking to achieve, retain and legitimise economic and political power. Elite instrumentalism is also compatible with the idea of Sinhala nationalism as the hegemonic ideology of a ruling class imposed on society in order to rule and exploit by consent rather than dominance.[4]

In attempting to transcend the ethnic, and to situate the politics of Sinhala nationalism beyond 'Sinhalisation', elite instrumentalism and hegemony have

---

[4] See in particular the work of James Brow and Michael Woost.

great relevance. Elites have presided over the worst excesses of Sinhalisation, starting with D. S. Senanayake's disenfranchisement of upcountry Tamils immediately after independence, and S. W. R. D. Bandaranaike's 'Sinhala only' campaign. Their periodic affectation of Sinhala nationalism was often transparently feigned, exploitative and opportunistic. There is much that elites can be held culpable for, both in their actions and inactions. But to what extent does culpability, in terms of that which enters into the historical record, amount to causality in the analytical sense?

As with the moral polity framework, hegemony is an explanation that seeks to challenge economic determinism, and it similarly finds that the pathway from economic impulse to political outcome is mediated and constrained by the way legitimacy is constructed and collectively internalised. There are however important differences between them in the way they understand power and ideology to operate. That is, in the moral polity explanation, nationalist consciousness serves to regulate and contain the pursuit of power by political operatives. This means that it operates to protect the community (the nation) against the excesses of its rulers. Hegemony instead finds that nationalist consciousness serves not to limit power, but to legitimise it and render it acceptable. As such, it does the reverse, protecting rulers against their subjects.

There are elements and fragments of hegemony that are borne out by the evidence in this book. In particular, exaggerated performances of Sinhala nationalism are often used to legitimise what is otherwise illegitimate. But beyond this, the Gramscian idea of hegemony suggests that the ideological mechanism that dulls the hegemonised masses into a consensual relationship of subservience is one that is of, and for, the ruling elite. That is, the model implies that Sinhala nationalism is the ideology that emanates from, and is 'owned' by the ruling capitalist elite, and is projected by them onto the masses. This is however, not the case in Sri Lanka. Sinhala nationalist ideology was evidently not the expression of the material or symbolic values of the Donoughmore or Soulbury era post-colonial elites. Although they quickly adjusted and learned to cope with the new nationalist dispensation, and have even presided over it, their relationship to nationalism has always been ambivalent and uneasy. Rather, nationalism is deeply anti-elite in its moral formation, and has constantly provided the basis for continued anti-elite mobilisation, including the violent insurgencies of the JVP. There is, as a consequence, a need to reconsider whether Gramsci's hegemony provides an adequate guide to model this relationship between ideology and social hierarchy.

The Language of Political Communication

The political enfranchisement of the entire adult population quickly changed the calculus that guided the behaviour of state elites. On the one hand, it led to the precocious social development that Sri Lanka became known for. By the mid-1940s, the government had initiated a range of transformative social welfare schemes such as subsidised food, free education, and free public health, which changed life for the better for the large majority that had hitherto been deprived of these (Jayasuriya 2013). As a result, by the early 1960s, Sri Lanka was being described as an unusual and precocious miracle of social development.

But beyond providing for their new constituents through policy, universal franchise also forced political elites to cultivate, engage and relate to their new rural voters in symbolically resonant forms of vernacular communication. Given the social, cultural, economic, geographic, and even linguistic gulf that separated this elite from the electorate, this was an unusual and challenging task that required great effort. In establishing this new relationship between the voters and the voted, electoral politics generated a special vocabulary and rhetorics: a synthetic patois that would be employed in this emerging realm. This new template of communication drew upon ideas of rights and righteousness that had resonance and were meaningful to the newly enfranchised rural masses, relating them to the political circumstances of citizenship, elections, and the relationship between rulers and subjects that was being forged.

As such, the template of political morality that constitutes Sinhala nationalism is in practice, deployed as the morally laden language of formal political communication. Citizens, political actors, and the state itself approach, conduct, negotiate, and resolve their problems with one another in the rhetorics of nationalist righteousness.[5] In James Brow's ethnography of a *Vedda* village in Anuradhapura in the late 1970s, he describes how the nationalist cosmos is widely understood and resonates well with the received cultural rhythms, life experience, and worldview of the residents themselves. But nationalist rhetoric is also viewed by his respondents as a stylised, synthetic jargon of collectivity, rights and morality that villagers switch to when engaging with politicians and state officials in the course of seeking access to material benefits. He describes:

---

[5] Of note, Spencer (1993: 103) makes the observation that notions of fairness are directed towards access to state resources, not the redistribution of existing resources from the wealthy.

[T]he villagers could indeed employ the discourse of nationalism when its adoption promised advantages, as in attempts to acquire benefits controlled by politicians and officials, but when engaged in their own internal affairs they reverted to a local idiom which was their own and which, despite the similarities and connections, was only marginally infused with specifically nationalist themes (Brow 1990a: 141–142).

These rhetorical performances of nationalism were required not just of the rural poor, but also, more demandingly so, of their rulers, who were defensive of their authenticity, and as such, perpetually forced to demonstrate and perform it. At its extreme, it led to the phenomenon of the 'Donoughmore Buddhist', the elite Sinhalese Christian born politician who converted to Buddhism after the introduction of universal franchise in order to gain in electoral appeal.[6] But it also led to an established practice of everyday instrumentalisation of nationalism as the necessary performance that elites had to pass through on their path to power. Elite performances of nationalism are significant in understanding the nature of elite–mass interaction, and to the strategies of elite counter-populism that gained momentum in the 1970s.

A Matter of Dignity

Liah Greenfeld describes how 'national identity is fundamentally a matter of dignity', (Greenfeld 1992 : 487) and this has relevance not just with respect to the outside world: that is, in fighting for the dignity of the Sinhala Buddhist people, language, and religion. Of relevance here is also what Jayadeva Uyangoda calls the 'inner courtyard' (Uyangoda 2000). Whereas all other forms of social identity in the context of Sinhala Buddhist society involve explicit status hierarchies of wealth, caste, occupation or gender, nationalism reconstitutes identity on the basis of a community of homogenous, equal people of Sinhala Buddhist heritage. The collective claims that Sinhala nationalism makes on the Sri Lankan state are the patrimony of the whole nation, membership in which elevates and liberates its nationals from the humiliating identities of explicit inferiority that burden them in every other sphere of life.

---

[6] It is extraordinary to note that the assassin of Sri Lanka's most famous Donoughmore Buddhist, S.W.R.D. Bandaranaike, was a Buddhist monk who performed the reverse journey, and converted to Christianity in jail prior to his execution in 1962.

This capacity that Sinhala nationalist identity bears for social emancipation, even as it remains embedded in a deeply hierarchical and unequal world, needs further elaboration.

Firstly, it means that Sinhala nationalism has much more than just an 'ethnic' personality, and amounts to more than a political project of Sinhalisation. It also bears an anti-elite dimension that is critical in understanding its evolution and contemporary operation. Sinhala nationalism emerges from and is produced in the context of the social, cultural, economic and geographic distance that separates the rich from the poor, English from Sinhala, the urban from the rural. Within these circumstances of multiple exclusion, and where the elite itself bears a distinctly cosmopolitan character, the politics of class consciousness and resistance spontaneously takes shape through Sinhala nationalism: an assertion of rights based on equal membership in a community of the indigenous majority.

Secondly, Sinhala nationalism became associated with antagonism to commerce and capitalist enterprise (Moore 1998). The traditional economic left-wing agenda of redistribution, welfarism, and state socialism gained a fundamentally Sinhala nationalist colouring, particularly from the mid-1950s onwards. As Mick Moore writes, 'The extent of "nationalism" has thus correlated crudely with leftism' (Moore 1992a: 37). Gunadasa Amarasekera, an important Sinhala nationalist ideologue of the generation of 1956 explained pithily: 'in the west, the protestant ethic worked for the spread of capitalism. The Buddhist ethic works for the spread of socialism.'[7]

At the time of its catalysis into the popular realm in the mid-1950s, Sinhala nationalism was sedimented upon a recent and concurrent history of populist, anti-elite, anti-UNP mobilisation by the Marxist left. Despite the doctrinal differences between Marxism and Sinhala nationalism, these two ideo-political currents have in terms of practice often shared many elements of rhetorical, analytical and programmatic overlap such that the popular discourse of political legitimacy, electoral competition, and lay intellectualism frequently featured an eclectic mix of themes drawn from both currents such as social justice, the

---

[7] Interview, Gunadasa Amarasekera, 7 April 2007. For an extended commentary on Gunadasa Amarasekera and his views on Marx, Weber, and Buddhism, see also Rambukwella (2008). See Seneviratne (1999), chapter 7, and Tambiah (1973) for a discussion of Buddhism and Weber. Of note here is also Southwold-Llewelyn's interviews with farmers on the 'mudalali myth', and their attitudes to traders, who are widely as outsiders in terms of community and morality (Southwold-Llewelyn 1994: 177). See also Weeratunga (2010).

alleviation of poverty, the protection of the (Sinhala) peasant, the promotion of indigenous culture, and a broad antipathy towards the neo-colonial cultural and economic domination of the Euro-American 'west'.

Thirdly, it posited a strong set of welfarist obligations on the Sri Lankan state that oriented its economic policy in this direction during the 1940s–70s, and that has continued in many ways even after the market reforms of 1977. It means more broadly that as a result of the circumstances of its insertion into mass politics, the political morality inherent in Sinhala nationalism is not confined to territory, language, culture, ethnicity, and religion, but extends beyond that to a broader set of referents on social justice. The moral framework of nationalism establishes a strong set of paternalistic obligations on the part of the state to promote the welfare and improvement of the people, and to cultivate what might broadly be termed as a Sinhala Buddhist-centric social democratic welfare state.

The protection and advancement of public services such as free education and health, the provision of public employment, the protection of peasant agriculture and rural life against the pressures of internal capitalist expansion and international price pressures, the alleviation of poverty and social inequalities, together with the promotion of the Sinhalisation agenda had over this period come to comprise a set of customary rights. They formed the moral parameters within which the very legitimacy and stability of the government and indeed the broader political system was hinged. Stanley Tambiah describes this in terms of its Buddhist foundations:

> [T]he majority of monk ideologues who formulate a theory of Buddhist politics read in the Buddhist canon and in later Buddhist chronicles a clear endorsement of welfare politics and state planning and redistribution. They also interpret Buddhism as being against 'self interested action' which leads to greed, competition and even exploitation, and therefore as being against capitalism, which leads to inequality. This is a critical parameter of a type of modern interpretation of the relevance of Buddhist norms for life today (Tambiah 1992: 118).

It is tempting to read into this explanation something of Max Weber's well known writings on the ascetic other-worldliness of Buddhism (Weber 1978: 627–630). But the hostility that nationalism bears for commerce relates more directly to its social origins in de-peasantised intellectuals, to the late-colonial romanticist narratives of the immiseration of the indigenous peasantry at the hands of the capitalist plantation economy, and to the influence of Marxism in its formation.

The relationship between the public morality of politics, notions of popular social justice, and Sinhala nationalism framed here is resonant with James Brow's description: 'The ideal image of the social order in nationalist rhetoric is one that recognises the responsibility of government to ensure the welfare of the common people, particularly the peasantry' (Brow 1990b: 13). It also has similarities with Jani De Silva's (1997) description of how the concept of a 'just society' forms a fundamental premise that structures the discursive field of electoral politics, and is captured within the signature slogans advanced by the main electoral parties – such as the UNP's *dharmistha samajaya*, (righteous society) the SLFP's *samajavadhi samajaya* (socialist society), the LSSP's *sama samajaya* (equal society), or the insurgent JVP's *sadharana lova* (just world).

Stanley Tambiah describes the way in which the moral imagination of an ideal Sinhala Buddhist dominated, welfarist-social democratic state is reflected in the contemporary writings of Buddhist monk-ideologues of the 1950s–80s. The historical-political work of one prominent monk-ideologue, Henpitagedera Gnanasiha, he describes, invoked a

> vision of a utopian past invoked as a vision of a utopian future [which embodies] precedents for instituting a welfare state and a social and economic egalitarianism in a noncompetitive agricultural society of villages. … Gnanasiha paints the regime of Parakrama Bahu I of Polonnaruwa as a collective welfare oriented dispensation, indeed as a kind of 'socialist welfare society' where the monarch was the chief holder, developer and distributor of land, resources and rewards to all people, while at the same time, a liberal supporter and protector of the sangha and a propagator of Dhammic virtues (Tambiah 1992: 106–107).

An Inverted Left–Right Party System

This moral structure and the widespread power it acquired in regulating and structuring the political landscape is manifest in the particular alignment of political competition that it has given rise to. At independence in 1948, the party system had briefly and ephemerally been defined by a conventional left–right axis that resembled a European style division between a pro-business UNP and pro-labour Marxist left. But this was transformed by the nationalist ascendancy of 1956, which established economic redistributive justice and Sinhalisation as the structural pillars of popular electoral mobilisation. This transformed the electoral terrain with a powerful incentive structure, and consequently, gave birth to a new configuration of Sri Lanka's 'national' level political party system (outside the Tamil-speaking north and east or the central plantation districts).

That is, it is defined on the one hand by a classic economic left–right axis, based on a traditional party of business, the UNP on the right and the Sri Lanka Freedom Party (SLFP) on the centre-left, and the Marxist parties on the far-left. The other axis that defines the party system is that of Sinhala majoritarian nationalism, along which the UNP is the furthest to the (liberal)-left, while the SLFP and more extreme Sinhala nationalist parties are further to the right. In other words, there is an inversion of the familiar left–right layout with respect to these two axes, so that the party furthest to the right on economic issues is to the left on issues of minority rights, and vice versa. This is an unconventional arrangement of the left–right axes compared to the rest of South Asia, where, as with the Awami League in Bangladesh, Pakistan People's Party (PPP) in Pakistan, or the Indian National Congress in India, national political systems were anchored by a party of economic populism that was also identified with ethnic or religious minority rights.

Figure 2.1 | The Left–Right Political Spectrum Defined by Economic Policy Versus Majoritarian Nationalism

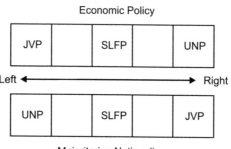

Sri Lanka's unusual party system where cosmopolitan capitalism confronts sectarian socialism is not a temporary aberration, as this alignment has been resilient, and forms a natural ordering of the party political system since then, and to which it has reverted on numerous occasions since 1956. Political elites, particularly of the UNP have found that this alignment places them at a position of particular disadvantage vis-à-vis the two axes of political morality and electoral populism that animate Sinhala nationalism. In subsequent decades, Sinhala nationalist sentiment has been aggravated and acquired a particularly sharp edge on every occasion when a ruling UNP government found itself the subject of a repeat of the alignment of 1956: that is, when it confronted both economic and ethnic populism. This occurred most vividly in 1987, when simmering anger at the UNP's market reforms fused together with the widespread outrage at Indian military intervention, sparking an extraordinarily violent insurgency. It occurred again in 2004, as the Ranil Wickremasinghe government's two-track policy of market reform and negotiations with the LTTE aroused a combined resistance from trade unionists, left parties, and Sinhala nationalists.

The Politics of Sinhala Nationalism

In conclusion, this chapter has served to introduce, contextualise, and provide historical background for many of the themes that are explored in greater depth in subsequent chapters. It deals primarily with the political circumstances, insinuation and effects of Sinhala nationalism, and has provided five different ways in which this occurs.

Firstly, nationalist politics takes shape as an explicit political project of majoritarian domination, or Sinhalisation. It contains the strong idea that Sinhala Buddhists have a righteous claim to primacy, and that the state must recognise and reflect this. It is in this sense that Sinhala nationalism fuels ethnic polarity and the conflict.

Secondly, Sinhala nationalism provides the cognitive structure through which popular conceptions of political morality are conceived, and suffuses the matrix of criteria against which the state and political actors can be accorded legitimacy or the lack thereof. It constitutes a moral subjectivity that situates voters in the realm of modern electoral politics. In doing so, it serves to regulate that sphere, tempering the cut-throat and divisive world of electoral politics with an ethic of unity and community.

Thirdly, Sinhala nationalism gives rise to the specialised technical jargon drawn upon when people engage in political discourse and make claims on the state. That is, it provides the template for political interaction, communication, and performance. This includes the frequent performances of nationalist authenticity by elites that are either entirely expedient, or else born of insecurity and defensiveness at their lack of popular credentials.

Fourthly, Sinhala nationalism must be seen within a dynamic of elite–mass confrontation, so that it is an expression of class consciousness. In this sense, it contains an anti-capitalist sentiment of 'Buddhist socialism', in which the legitimacy of the state is connected to the pursuit of social justice and welfarism.

Sinhala nationalism has thus emerged as the ideology of an ethnicised social welfare state. This state is seen as having deep moral obligations towards the welfare of society in general, and towards the material, spiritual, and cultural needs of the Sinhala Buddhists in particular.

Fifthly, Sinhala nationalism structures the party system in a peculiar order, with its polarity determined by two rival historical meta-projects. This consists on the one hand, of a populist agenda of left-wing Sinhalisation, and on the other, of an elite-driven agenda of market-based economic reform together with ethnic conflict resolution based on concessions to the Tamils.

3 | Kulaks to Clerks

In 1954, Sir Ivor Jennings, Vice Chancellor of the University of Ceylon and a key figure in the decolonisation period, described a new political phenomenon that he had identified: an 'undercurrent of opinion which has no direct political representation':

> It is aggressively nationalist and aggressively Buddhist. In language policy it is anti-English; in religion it is anti-Christian; in foreign policy it is anti-Western; and in economic policy it is both anti-capitalist and anti-socialist. Socially it might be described as anti-Colombo, because it consists primarily of English educated young men from the provinces, the sons of small cultivators, minor officials, shop-keepers, and the lower middle-class groups generally (Jennings 1954: 344).

Jennings's brief sketch of this group of young educated lower-middle class men from the provinces is a historical freeze-frame of a social avalanche in the making. What was an 'undercurrent of opinion' without political representation in 1954 had just two years later, gained enormous momentum, and went on to dominate and permanently transform Sri Lanka's nascent electoral politics.

The first phase of the nationalist project as Miroslav Hroch describes it, is a time when a small group of intellectual activists initiate scholarly inquiry on linguistic, historical and cultural attributes of the nation (Hroch 1985). In a second phase, these ideas gain some circulation among intellectual circles, but have little political influence before they reach the third stage of mass nationalism. This early cultural nationalist phase of Sinhala nationalism took place roughly over the span of a century from 1850–1950, under the Buddhist revivalist movement, and over the intellectual life-span of Sinhala nationalism's iconic founding father, Anagarika Dharmapala (Seneviratne 1999, Kemper 2015). After a century of incubation in the cultural nationalist phase, Sinhala nationalism was transformed into a contemporary mass nationalism in a moment of explosive political transformation in the mid-1950s, and the angry young men that Jennings describes were the main protagonists.

The trigger factor that catalysed the Sinhala nationalist mobilisation of the time was over the official status of the Sinhala language. The necessity to promote the vernacular languages in place of English had featured as a pending item on the political agenda since at least the early 1940s. Given that the administration and a significant part of the education infrastructure was in English, that significant numbers of government officials could not function effectively in Sinhala, and that almost one third of the population spoke Tamil, it was broadly assumed that the transition would be gradual, and that it would involve the parallel promotion of both Tamil and Sinhala in place of English.[1] But by 1954, the debate over national language was overwhelmed by a new groundswell of opinion demanding that the gradual transition to Sinhala and Tamil be abandoned in place of a more immediate transition to 'Sinhala only'. At village council meetings, Sinhala cultural organisations, lay Buddhist associations, and Buddhist religious meetings, the dominant themes of the debates and speeches of the time reflected a newly invigorated nationalist consciousness that had fired the imagination of the Sinhala-educated intelligentsia, and that was being transmitted by them to society at large. As one prominent monk, Narada Maha Thero argued at a Buddhist Sunday school in September 1955: 'For every nation there is a language. Sinhalese is the language of the Ceylonese and it is imperative that it should be adopted as the national language of this country'.[2]

Buddhist monks, lay Buddhist leaders, and monks' organisations such as the *Eksath Bhikku Peramuna* comprised another critical element of the vernacular intelligentsia that pressed not just for the adoption of Sinhala as official language, but also for the explicit (re)-establishment of state patronage and promotion of the Buddhist religion. Baddegama Wimalawamsa, another well known activist-monk described it to a Buddhist Sunday school audience in March 1955:

> We must all admit that the life-blood of the Sinhalese nation is Buddhism. Buddhism and Buddhists are in a declining condition today. If this continues further it will lead to the destruction of the nation.[3]

---

[1] See Kearney (1967), chapters 3–4 for a thorough summary of the language dispute.

[2] CDN 8 September 1955 'Thero Calls for One State Language': remarks of Narada Maha Thero, speaking at Sunday Dhamma Buddhist School, Moratuwa.

[3] CDN 10 March 1955, 'Decline of Buddhism must be Stopped': remarks of Baddegama Wimalawansa Thero, principal of Sri Lanka Vidyalaya, Colombo at a meeting of the Dharmadeeptha Sunday School, Udahamulla (Maharagama).

In their content, there was a rhetoric of desperation and the very deeply held concern that the language, culture, and religion of the majority community faced extinction in its own homeland, at the hands of a government, and a deracinated ruling elite that was indifferent and even hostile to this imminent threat. English was not only the language imposed by an alien coloniser, but signified the dividing line between the elite and masses, the rulers and the ruled. English was the language of the westernised ruling elite, while Sinhala was the language of the indigenous and authentic, but deprived majority. As a union official of the *Lanka Jatika Guru Sangmaya*, a Sinhalese vernacular teachers' association described in the early months of the language campaign:

> Our mother-tongue is in danger of being destroyed ... It is said that we are now free and that we are living in a democracy. If so, I should like to ask why the language of the majority is set aside and a language spoken by the few is given preference. We made a mistake in selecting our rulers who do not know their mother tongue and who don't care for the Sinhalese culture.[4]

In 1955, the language campaign gained political representation and leadership in the newly formed Sri Lanka Freedom Party (SLFP) of S.W.R.D. Bandaranaike. In the 1956 elections, Bandaranaike made a campaign promise to implement a 'Sinhala-only' law within 24 hours of coming to power. On this basis, the SLFP won a resounding election victory against the ruling United National Party (UNP) of Sir John Kotelawala, albeit one that was greatly magnified by the iniquities of the Westminster electoral system.

Robert Kearney's political history of the period describes how the SLFP's captaincy of the language campaign and their historic electoral victory in 1956 took place in the context of links forged between the SLFP and a rising group of sub-elites in village and local level bodies. These comprised small village traders, teachers, minor landowners and ayurvedic physicians who 'had begun to challenge the dominance of the prominent families' in local government bodies, and who formed the basis of the SLFP's surge in 1956 (Kearney 1967: 81–82).[5] In the political lore of the era, the SLFP attracted widespread support from the so-called *Pancha Maha Balavegaya*, the 'five

---

[4] CDN 3 December 1954 'Teachers want Swabhasha in the SSC': remarks by Mr. T.R.P. Premawardena, president, Ambalangoda branch of the *Lanka Jatika Guru Sangmaya*, (Sinhalese vernacular teachers union).

[5] The use of the term 'elite' to describe the village level protagonists of 1956 also deserves caution as Spencer (2002) notes.

great forces', consisting of Buddhist monks, teachers, farmers, traditional (ayurvedic) physicians and workers. Over the course of the first four months of 1956, the SLFP's election campaign effectively fused with the 'Sinhala only' language campaign, gaining in the process thousands of lay political activists from these groups and generating an unprecedented level of political energy and excitement.

Unlike other election campaigns, there was something transformative and permanent about the Sinhala nationalist mobilisation of 1956, and the SLFP's election victory. As Stanley Tambiah describes, this febrile moment of nationalist political triumph became 'the climactic and singular moment in twentieth century political life' (Tambiah 1992: 44–45). It represented the ascendancy not just of a political party but of nationalism itself over the entire political landscape.[6] Even more than the formality of independence in 1948, it was the rise of Sinhala nationalism and the emblematic election of 1956 that became the defining, watershed moment in the socio-political evolution of modern Sri Lanka. It instituted Sinhala nationalism as the central political driving factor in contemporary Sri Lankan politics.

What explains this extraordinary political moment, and the transformation? Why did this 'rural middle class', or the 'nativist petit bourgeoisie' activate themselves at this particular historical moment? While the rise of popular democracy, universal franchise, and the over-heated atmosphere of the 1956 general elections are clearly critical elements of the explanation, it is not clear why this impulse remained dormant until 1956. Sri Lanka has had universal franchise since 1931, so why did Sinhala nationalism emerge to the fore only in the fifth general election, when it might equally have done so in the prior elections of 1931, 1936, 1947, or 1952?

One economic explanation that frequently features in the literature is relative deprivation, and the purportedly superior economic position of the Tamils relative to the Sinhalese. To use Donald Horowitz's terminology, Tamils are supposed to have been an 'advanced group' from a 'backward region' eliciting the envious hostility of the Sinhalese (Horowitz 1989). But confusingly, the available data on income and wealth shows that Tamils were as a group not particularly over-privileged. Depending on what definition of community group is used, various others such as Eurasians, Protestants and even Muslims were clearly wealthier in comparison. In average terms, (and the use of such

---

[6] On 1956, there is a vast literature. See among others, Wriggins (1960: chapter 9), Weerawardana (1960), Kearney (1967), Roberts (1989b), Roberts (1979).

averages is of course questionable) Sri Lankan Tamils were at comparable levels of income and wealth to low-country Sinhalese, and both were in a considerably better position than Kandyan Sinhalese or 'Indian' Tamils.[7]

Indeed, Sri Lankan Tamils were often considerably under-represented in terms of their participation either directly or indirectly, in the prosperous plantation economy, or in the distribution of good agricultural land, access to state power and patronage, proximity to the main centres of economic development, or any other major source of economic advancement. The notion that Jaffna Tamils were an 'advanced group' relies not on averages of wealth or income, but on the fact that they had an identifiably disproportionate – presence in government employment, the urban professions, and university education – all critical avenues for upward mobility in circumstances where the stagnant peasant economy was the path only to a life of hardship and poverty.

Chelvadurai Manogaran, for example, describes how the over-representation of Jaffna in government employment was reversed when various forms of discrimination in favour of the Sinhalese occurred in the post-colonial period. In terms of education, 'Sri Lankan Tamils, who constituted 10 percent of the population, were over-represented in 1948 when they held 31 percent of the places in the university, but this percentage had dropped to less than 16 percent by 1970'. In terms of employment, he reports: 'prior to independence, 30 percent of those employed in the government service in Sri Lanka were Tamils, but by 1975 the figure had dipped to nearly 6 percent' (Manogaran 1987: 119).

Samarasinghe similarly offers the poor agricultural economy and the surfeit of English secondary school in the peninsula as reasons for the preponderance of Jaffnese in government service:

> There was a relatively unfavourable man-land ratio in Jaffna district ... [where] ... climate and other environmental and physical factors are less favourable than anywhere else in the country for agricultural production. (Samarasinghe 1984: 175)

But there has actually been surprisingly little careful investigation of this 'man-land' ratio in Jaffna compared to other parts of the country. What

---

[7] See Sriskandarajah (2005) for an exhaustive review of data from the Consumer Finance Surveys of the 1950s–70s.

data exists often starts only at 1946, includes considerable non-peasant land and population, and has not thus far been disaggregated to the extent that the available data permits. This is not to suggest that the assertion about agriculture in Jaffna is wrong per se, but that it can be misleading if it is not historically contextualised within a trajectory of changing economic and social circumstances. And there are more puzzling issues to be considered – Jaffna Tamils had a disproportionate share of government jobs since at least the 1920s and probably even before that. If ethnic imbalances are to be considered a cause of conflict *ipso facto*, then it remains to be fully explained why this sharp, prolonged imbalance triggered conflict only in the mid-1950s?

Furthermore, the focus on disproportionality and ethnic percentages obscures the fact that the actual number of government jobs under discussion at various points in time was quite small. For example, Samarasinghe finds that in 1948, Tamils were heavily over-represented in various segments such as the government accountants (46%) and irrigation department engineers (40%) (Samarasinghe 1984: 178). Important as these percentages are, it is also important to note that there were only a grand total of 61 such accountants and 46 engineers in each of these departments. In other words, the magnitude of disproportionality at stake was as trivial as 20 surplus Tamil accountants and 10 surplus Tamil engineers. Even if government employment in the 1940s had been corrected to scrupulously match ethnic population percentages, the number of jobs to change hands would have been of the magnitude of a few hundred one way or another – an entirely inconsequential amount considering that the total workforce numbered almost three million people, the vast majority of whom earned livelihoods from plantation agriculture, peasant farming, petty manufacturing and commerce.

Much the same can be said for the highly controversial issue of university 'standardisation' in the early 1970s, through which university entrance marks were re-scaled on a regional basis in order to reduce the over-representation of certain areas such as Jaffna, particularly in heavily sought-after fields such as medicine (De Silva 1984, Gunawardena 1979). A dispassionate analysis of the hard numbers involved would suggest that this policy could not have affected the careers and lives of more than a few hundred out of a total population of 1.5 million Sri Lankan Tamils, and was limited to middle-class Jaffna, as the re-scaling was to the benefit of Batticaloa. But it nevertheless had a very serious, radicalising effect, and is routinely cited as the final straw that led Tamil youth of the 1970s down the path of separatism and militancy. This is of course not to deny the existence of ethnic inequalities in the making of the conflict, or to trivialise the very palpable fears of discrimination that thousands of young Tamils perceived and experienced. But even a passing acquaintance with the numbers would clearly show that the demand for university places and jobs far outstripped supply, so that it is the making of those larger economic circumstances rather than disproportionality that bears attention.

This chapter sets out a case that the social genesis of Sinhala nationalism of the 1950s occurred in the course of a grand social and structural transformation in which public education, structural economic transformation, and clerical employment were critical. In doing so, it also provides the context within which issues of ethnic proportionality can be placed in better historical and socio-economic perspective. The nature of this explanation and its reliance on a structural economic transformation has clear resonance with the work of Ernest Gellner, who situates nationalism as a product of the transition from agro-literate to industrial societies. In Gellner's (1983) framework the two central institutional elements in the production and mass diffusion of nationalism are centralised vernacular public education systems, and horizontally immobile clerkdom. These are also important pillars in the history of Sinhala nationalism, although the circumstances of their role itself requires further explanation.

The structure of colonial Ceylon's economy in the 1930s was divided into two fairly distinct spheres. On the one hand, there was the modern sector, dominated by the plantations or estates, owned and managed mostly by Europeans, worked almost entirely by a massive immigrant labour force, and closely dependent on international export markets and prices. On the other hand, the large majority of the non-estate rural population was tied to smallholder, semi-subsistence peasant agriculture, typically on very small plots and with low levels of productivity. There were in general very few nodes of linkage between these two sectors, and they remained broadly untouched by one other in a dualistic economic structure that had evolved over the previous century (Karunatilake 1987, Snodgrass 1966).

By the 1930s, there were signs that both these sectors had reached critical points of crisis and transition. At the same time, a new generation of social and economic policy was in the making as a result of universal franchise and constitutional changes that had handed over considerable powers of domestic decision-making into the hands of elected Ceylonese ministers. The coincidence of these three factors in the early 1930s gave rise to a complex series of very rapid social, demographic, and economic transformations over the next three decades, and this period can as a result be described as the critical point of transition when colonial Ceylon began to give way to modern Sri Lanka.

It is in the circumstances of these changes that the social basis for Sinhala nationalism emerged. In the context of rapid demographic growth and the ensuing land scarcity during the 1930s, the rapid expansion of free education, and the equally rapid eradication of malaria in the 1940s caused an explosive increase in the annual cohorts of educated rural youth of peasant backgrounds emerging with vernacular secondary school leaving credentials in the 1950s. Most such educated rural youth followed their predecessors in terms of aspirations to upward mobility, and sought to leave agriculture for the far more prestigious and comfortable life of a government clerk or school teacher. This path of social transition from the ranks of the middle peasantry to the middle levels of the bureaucracy occurred across different parts of the island, with strong implications for ethnic imbalances and the spread of nationalist politics.

The main sources of data used here are government publications of the period 1898–1971, particularly the successive rounds of the census, annual administration reports of various government departments (particularly education), parliamentary sessional papers, statistical abstracts (after 1949), parliamentary papers, census of agriculture, and various other occasional survey and census reports published. In addition, there are two very useful statistical compilations: those by Snodgrass (1966), and Peebles (1982) which provide summary data using these sources on a wide variety of topics.

Peasant and Plantation Agriculture in Crisis

While the expansion of colonial Ceylon's plantation economy during the coffee (1840–1870) and tea (1870–1900) booms did not in itself have very serious consequences for the peasant economy at the time, this situation had changed by the time of the rubber boom of the first decades of the 20th century. As the peasant population steadily increased, there was, by the closing years of the rubber boom in the 1920s, a sharp scarcity of land that had appeared in both the highland and lowland areas of the south.

With peasant villages and their lands proverbially 'hemmed in' (Meyer 1992) by massive plantations on all sides, the growing rural population was forced to subsist on an inadequate base of agricultural land. The available quantum of land was not entirely static as such, and it did actually increase through these years with the extension of the cultivated frontier – but it did so at a rate incommensurate with that of the population growth. Consequently, the average plot sizes on which families subsisted shrank down to levels that in many cases became uneconomical.

The extent of land scarcity in the 1930s is substantiated and better elaborated by the available data on population to land ratios, rural population growth, the absolute size of the peasant sector, and emigration during the first half of the 20th century. Snodgrass provides nationally aggregated estimates to show that land concentration in the peasant sector rose relatively slowly over 1901–21, subsequently accelerating to a much higher rate over the period 1921–46 (Snodgrass 1966). But the national-level trends on rural land-pressure give little indication of how these trends varied over different parts of the island, where there exist at least eight distinct zones corresponding to different densities of population, ethnic clusters, and agro-climatic conditions.[8]

This chapter features a new index of peasant land concentration at the level of administrative districts (as they were in 1946), drawn from estimates of the rural non-estate population and from derived estimates of cultivated land in the peasant sector. Table 3.1, which summarises the results, shows that by 1946 there were very high levels of peasant land concentration in Jaffna, the coastal south-west (Colombo, Kalutara, Galle and Matara), and the hill districts of Kandy and Nuwara-Eliya. These continued to increase sharply over 1946–71.

In 1901 and 1921, land concentration in Jaffna was already much higher than that of the most crowded coastal south-west districts such as Kalutara and Galle, and the south-central hill districts such as Kandy. Secondly, it shows how the population growth in these districts outstripped the growth of cultivable land at an accelerated rate through 1921–46, such that they had caught up with Jaffna's high concentration rates by mid-century. Figure 3.1 plots the index of concentration in Jaffna compared to composite indices of the coastal south-west (Colombo, Kalutara, Galle, Matara) and hilly south-central (Kandy, Nuwara-Eliya, Badulla) districts. It shows that these two regions surpassed Jaffna around the early to mid-1950s, so that by 1971, both had extremely dense population to land ratios.

---

[8] These consist approximately of (i) the coastal south west; (ii) the highland south-central, (iii) the Jaffna peninsula, (iv) the north-west 'coconut triangle', (v) the north-central dry zone, (vi) the Batticaloa-Amparai rice belt, (vii) the southern dry zone, (viii) the inland south-western 'rubber belt' districts.

Table 3.1 | Peasant Sector Land Concentration Index by District (1901–71).

	1901	*1921*	*1946*	*1971*
Jaffna	2.32	2.15	2.67	3.32
Colombo	1.26	1.67	2.64	3.06
Galle	1.70	1.73	2.46	2.87
Kandy	1.29	1.54	2.44	3.74
Kalutara	1.46	1.96	2.32	2.82
Matara	1.26	1.42	1.89	2.72
Nuwara Eliya	1.29	1.25	1.86	3.26
Badulla	1.15	1.41	1.83	2.09
Sri Lanka	1.21	1.36	1.82	2.23
Kegalla	0.71	1.06	1.81	2.73
Ratnapura	0.49	0.85	1.80	2.14
Puttalam	2.31	1.81	1.73	1.64
Trincomalee	1.21	1.11	1.57	1.56
Batticaloa	1.39	1.40	1.28	1.83
Hambantota	1.11	1.27	1.20	1.79
Kurunegala	1.00	0.91	1.18	1.61
Matale	0.89	0.89	1.07	2.11
Mannar	2.16	1.11	0.98	1.58
Anuradhapura	1.63	0.98	0.87	1.33
Vavuniya	1.10	0.82	0.79	0.95

Source: Author's calculations, based on Census 1901–71, Blue Books 1898–1928, Census of Agriculture 1946, 1971.

Figure 3.1 | Index of Peasant Land Concentration by Region

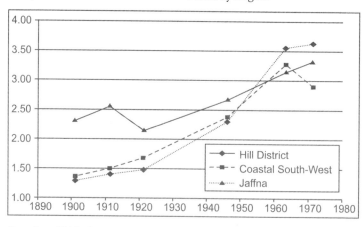

Source: Data from Table 3.1

The severe land fragmentation and land poverty that emerged in farming households naturally led to pressure to escape this environment. For those that had the requisite means, the most attractive path out of an increasingly difficult life on the land lay in financing the cost of an English-language secondary education, and becoming qualified for employment as a clerk in a government office.

This pathway from the farm to the clerical office was well under way in land-scarce Jaffna from the late 19th century. By the turn of the century, Jaffna was exporting clerks in such large numbers that they were forced to look much further afield than Colombo for employment. As the commentary in the 1911 census describes 'One of the most remarkable features of the past ten years has been the steady flow of Jaffnese to the Straits Settlements and the Federated Malay States.' The retired *Maniagar* (hereditary headman) of Jaffna town is quoted as describing how:

> Thousands of our boys are educated in the Jaffna colleges and English schools, and when they get out of them the vast majority of the English-educated Jaffnese find employment in those countries [...] 'There is not a village in the Jaffna District which is not benefited by the employment of its inhabitants abroad (Census of Ceylon 1911: 67).

The 1921 census similarly describes how

> emigration is heaviest from the Jaffna peninsula, and consists largely of educated young men, who, on account of their native astuteness, combined with superior educational facilities provided originally by the American and other missions, have been successful in securing clerical and other posts in the other districts of Ceylon and in Straits Settlements and the Malay States (Census of Ceylon 1921: 111).

The Jaffna farmer's obsession with turning his sons into government clerks was so widely known that it became the topic of policy discussion and official reports. For example, a report by the Education Department on the failure of vocational education in the north explained:

> Even now it is difficult to get the Jaffna parent interested in our rural scheme of education. He prefers his son to try for work under Government than to follow in his footsteps as a farmer. He is probably right in wishing his son to be freed from the hard work of a small farmer with its inadequate return for all the labour and patience that are required (Administration Report of the Director of Education 1942: A5).

Of course, what these comments omit to mention is that this particular form of emigration via education was not the preserve of the population at large, but of the upper and middle strata of the peasant economy and caste hierarchy. As Rohan Bastin notes:

> [M]embers of the large dominant caste of Jaffna who had been for a long time involved with colonial cash economies found themselves in difficulties as landowning farmers in the nineteenth century. This resulted in large-scale movement into schools and the expanding bureaucracy of the colonial regime (Bastin 1997: 409).

In summary then, the data on peasant land concentration, rural population growth rates, industry attachment, and migration help to build a picture of the severity of the crisis in Jaffna's rural economy in the early 20th century. This was not a peculiarity of Jaffna but fits in within a welling tide of demographic pressure and land scarcity that have been slowly in the making in many different parts of the island. Very similar economic pressures erupted across rural Ceylon at different rates in different regions, resulting in a staggered process of emigration and social class transition. During the period 1921–46, the peasant economy of the Sinhalese south-central and south-western districts, containing the majority of the island's population, had reached conditions similar to that which Jaffna had experienced several decades prior. It triggered pressures among landed groups in the rural south to undergo the same forms of social transition that were already well underway in Jaffna for half a century.

Welfare Policy and Education

The issue of rural poverty and the apparent disintegration of peasant society became a central and enduring feature of political discourse from the 1920s onwards, and the upliftment of the peasantry and the preservation of peasant society became critical components of the ideological and institutional formation of the post-colonial state (Farmer 1957, Samaraweera 1973, Peiris 1996a, and Peiris 1996b: chapter 13).

Emblematic of the changes of the period was the expansion of public health and education in the mid-1940s, which transformed the lives of a significant portion of the population in a very short space of time (Wickremeratne 1973). Public education and literacy in Ceylon was relatively widespread since the late 19th century with an abundance of vernacular language primary schools. Among Sinhalese and Sri Lankan Tamils, primary school attendance levels grew from 55% to 75% (of school-age children) over 1900–1945.[9] But free public education was largely restricted to the vernacular primary level. Secondary education was dominated by a small number of fee-paying, missionary-run English medium schools that prepared students for external examinations such as the London Matric or Senior Cambridge, which were essential requirements for employment in the colonial government or further education (Jayaweera 1973, Jayasuriya 1969). A secondary education in Sinhala or Tamil was considered clearly inferior in status, and prepared candidates for a local examination that offered a far more restricted set of less prestigious and less remunerative employment opportunities. Consequently, at the eve of the free education reforms in 1944, only about one in ten students in the vernacular channel proceeded from the primary to secondary level. As the Director of Education described:

> [O]nly a very small proportion of the country's school going population is receiving a post-primary education, and that there is a considerable amount of educational wastage. ... The existence in the Island of social and economic conditions which render a post-primary education in Sinhalese and Tamil profitless largely explains this situation (Administration Report of the Director of Education 1944: A8).

In effect, there was a two-track system that segregated the entire population from an early age. The wealthy, the professional middle classes, and those who aspired to join their ranks pursued an English-medium education at the secondary or higher level that qualified them for the different grades of white collar occupation. Meanwhile, the large majority of the rural non-estate population attended a few years of Sinhala or Tamil medium primary school that offered them few prospects for social mobility. There was, additionally, a third segment of the population, comprising primarily the estate Tamils, the poorest rural and urban strata, and a small but significant section of the female population, who received little or no schooling whatsoever. The English-medium secondary school performed an important institutional function in socialising, consolidating, and reproducing an aspiring native elite. But this was not an entirely closed system, and such schools also served as the effective

---

[9] Derived from census tables on literacy by age – Census of Ceylon, 1953, section 5, table 20. This was in sharp contrast to the estate-based Indian Tamils who had literacy levels half that of the rest of the population (compare, for example, literacy figures for Tamils in Nuwara Eliya versus Jaffna).

conduits through which a small but steady stream of the rural population was skimmed off the top and absorbed into an English-proficient middle class.

All this was to change very quickly by the mid-1940s, when the segregated schooling system became the target of sweeping reforms that effectively removed the formal iniquities between these two levels, and at a stroke expanded secondary education manifold. Fig. 3.2 gives an indication of the increase of the school population through the late 19th and early 20th centuries, and shows how this accelerated sharply immediately following the reforms of the mid-1940s. In the fifteen years 1945–60, the school population almost tripled as the existing church-based English secondary schools were effectively absorbed into the free, state-run vernacular system at the same time as numerous new government secondary schools were established in under-served rural areas.

Figure 3.2 | School Population, 1852–1963, Highlighting Pre-1944 Versus Post-1944 Trajectories

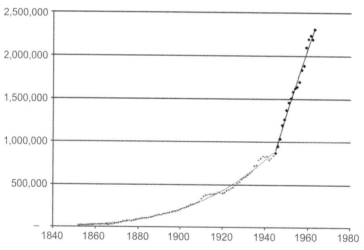

Source: Peebles (1982).

Fresh segments of rural society, hitherto restricted to a decidedly inferior primary education, responded enthusiastically to the reforms and swelled the ranks of secondary schools each year. But, while the school system was previously divided between distinct English and vernacular streams, the new educational system that emerged by the late 1950s was one divided into separate streams of Sinhala and Tamil vernacular medium students.

The demographic effects of the expansion in education were accentuated by an unprecedented improvement in public health during the mid-to late 1940s, most notably through the use of DDT spraying, which caused Ceylon to become a world-leading success story in malaria eradication. Indeed the statistical evidence of the precipitous drop in mortality statistics over the space of a few years is spectacular. Infant mortality, which stood at 141 per 1,000 live births in 1945, dropped to 82 in 1950 and 57 in 1960.[10] In that interim phase in the demographic transition between the drop in mortality and fertility, the rate of population increased sharply in the 1950s and 1960s, creating a 'baby boom': a demographic bubble of infant survivors born between the mid-1940s and mid-1960s, who subsequently worked their way through the newly expanded school system in the 1950s and began entering the labour market in the late 1960s.

Figure 3.3 | Annual Number of Students Completing Secondary Education, 1924–69

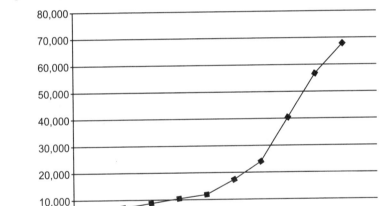

Source: Table 3.2 below.

The combined effects of free education and the malaria-survivor generation after 1945 had important consequences for the rural population. As increased population growth rates threatened to worsen an already critical problem of peasant land fragmentation, the availability of free secondary education appeared to hasten the way out of an emerging trap of lower living standards and backward mobility. With the financial barriers to secondary education

---

[10] Statistical Abstract (various years).

removed, there was now the prospect and indeed the expectation among a much larger group of people that occupational mobility (particularly out of small-holder agriculture) and economic betterment was, if not inevitable, then not entirely out of their grasp. Fig. 3.4 shows that the number of students who completed secondary school grew slowly from the mid-1920s to mid-1940s, then at an increased rate for the next decade, and then at much higher rates from the mid-1950s onwards.

Table 3.2 Education Level by Annual Cohort of 20 Year Old Population in Absolute Numbers and as Percentage of Total Cohort. Selected Years 1924–69.

	Cohort Size	Illiterate	Some School	Completed Secondary	(of which SSC Pass)	(of which higher)
1924	92,000	40,000	49,000	2,900	(2,200)	(1,300)
1929	98,000	40,000	54,000	4,200	(3,000)	(1,900)
1934	107,000	40,000	62,000	5,500	(4,000)	(2,400)
1939	117,000	38,000	72,000	7,000	(5,000)	(2,600)
1944	128,000	39,000	80,000	8,000	(6,000)	(2,900)
1949	138,000	36,000	90,000	13,000	(9,000)	(3,700)
1954	152,000	40,000	95,000	18,000	(11,000)	(3,800)
1959	177,000	32,000	112,000	33,000	(19,000)	(5,000)
1964	197,000	31,000	119,000	48,000	(25,000)	(6,000)
1969	221,000	29,000	133,000	59,000	(25,000)	(3,000)
	Cohort Size	Illiterate	Some school	Completed Secondary	(of which SSC Pass)	(of which higher)
1924	100%	44%	53%	3%	(2%)	(1%)
1929	100%	41%	55%	4%	(3%)	(2%)
1934	100%	37%	58%	5%	(4%)	(2%)
1939	100%	32%	62%	6%	(4%)	(2%)
1944	100%	31%	63%	6%	(5%)	(2%)
1949	100%	26%	65%	9%	(6%)	(3%)
1954	100%	26%	62%	12%	(7%)	(3%)
1959	100%	18%	63%	19%	(11%)	(3%)
1964	100%	16%	60%	24%	(12%)	(3%)
1969	100%	13%	60%	27%	(11%)	(1%)

Source: Author's calculations from a variety of sources.

Table 3.4, on which the above figure is based, presents estimates of the changing educational profile of Ceylon based on annual population cohort levels of age 20 from the mid-1920s to the late 1960s. It shows both the increase in cohort size (the number of people of age 20) due to the increase in population and the steady shift to higher levels of education of these cohorts, particularly after 1944. Most remarkable is the increase in secondary school education in this period, both in terms of the percentage of students, and absolute numbers. The percentage of 20-year-olds who had completed a secondary education rose modestly from 2% to 5% between 1924 and 1944 but subsequently leaped upwards from 5% to 24% in the next two decades from 1944 to 1964. In tandem with the rise in population, this represented a staggering six-fold increase in absolute numbers, or a doubling of class sizes every eight years.

In effect, the educational profile, social formation, and aspirations of a large part of the population underwent a significant change, and did so at such high rates that it effectively created an educational generation gap differentiating those who had been of school-leaving age in the mid-1940s from their younger siblings of just a decade and a half later in the late 1950s. But while the rising tide of free education lifted all boats so to speak, the benefits for a large part of the population were far from spectacular, or appeared at best to be a continuation of the more gradual trend that pre-dated free education. Between 1924 and 1944, the education level of the median student had risen from between 1–2 years of primary education to between 3–4 years. But, by 1964, this had risen to only between 5–6 years. In other words, after two decades of free secondary education, almost half of all children still remained *without* any secondary education to speak of. Indeed, one in six children appeared to have had no school education whatsoever and still entered adulthood as illiterates.

What this suggests is that there were clearly identifiable differences in the ability, and to a lesser extent, the willingness of distinct segments of the population to exploit the expansion in education. One category, amounting to less than one-fifth of the population appears to have been poised to take advantage of the changes to ensure that their children completed a secondary education and at least attempted the requisite examinations. They were in essence the group responsible for the expansion in secondary school completion rates from 6% to 24% over the first two decades 1944–64. For the rest of the population meanwhile, the completion of a secondary education was either an unaffordable step – at least in terms of the opportunity cost of foregone earnings – or an unnecessary one, in the sense that the pressures to use education as a stepping stone out of the status quo were not as compelling. A caveat is required here: despite the provocative use of 'kulaks' in the title of this chapter, there was not as such any sizeable class of rich peasants as such in most of Sri Lanka.[11] There was, nevertheless, a clearly segmented response to the expansion of education in the 1944–64 period, so that a relatively wealthier stratum of rural households was better positioned to take the best advantage of the expansion in education. James Manor's biography of S.W.R.D.Bandaranaike, which contains a careful review of the events of 1956, describes this rural stratum, and the role it played in the rise of Sinhala Buddhist nationalism as a popular political force:

[T]he generation of that excitement and of the MEPs mass vote was largely the work of these five groups – local board members, ayurvedic physicians, Sinhala-medium schoolteachers, educated youths, and bhikkus. Far from being 'the masses', these groups constitute a set of village-level elites. Some are even inclined to call them a rural middle class, although that term overstates their cohesion. But they were not ordinary villagers.

If members of these groups did not constitute a rural middle class, they at least shared middle-class aspirations and grievances which were probably alien to most village dwellers. These aspirations caused them to look beyond the village to supra-local and national arenas, to urban or semi-urban areas. ... When they are considered alongside the westernised, prosperous urbanites in Parliament before the 1956 election or even alongside the UNP's wealthy backers in the hinterland, members of these five groups seem humble figures. But when they are viewed alongside common villagers, they clearly fall within the upper-middle stratum of village society (Manor 1989: 250).

It is important to consider that within this rural middle class, most of these figures described are Gramsci's 'traditional' intellectuals: they were long-standing fixtures in village society. What brought dynamism and political momentum in this milieu were the new 'organic' intellectuals. Beginning in Jaffna at the turn of the century, this social transition from middle peasant to middle bureaucrat spread slowly across the densely populated lowland

---

[11] Large farmers using mostly hired labour have for the most part tended to convert themselves and be categorised as commercial farmers (planters) rather than as rich peasants. The only significant extent of large farm holdings growing traditional non-export crops was in the Eastern province.

Sinhala regions by the 1930s, and accelerated at far more rapid rates after the spread of free education in the 1940s. The multiplying numbers of educated youth, and the widespread aspirations that they gained beyond the scope of rural life and peasant farming triggered a political avalanche that reached critical mass.

Central to the fulfilment of this social transition was the Secondary School Certificate (SSC).[12] With the reforms of the post-1944 period, the distinction between overseas English credentials and inferior Ceylonese vernacular qualifications was at least nominally being done away with (although it took until the end of the 1950s for its formal implementation). The SSC was the basic pre-requisite for employment as a government clerk, and as such became a heavily sought after qualification, particular by those for whom the gates of secondary education had only recently been thrown open. In the early 1940s, around 10,000 students entered for the SSC examinations each year, but this multiplied quickly to 40,000 by 1948, and 100,000 by 1956. The incoming cohorts of the burgeoning 'malaria survivor generation' swelled classroom and exam-hall sizes even further in each subsequent year, such that there were 250,000 candidates for the exam by 1963.[13]

The number of people who actually passed the SSC was of course far smaller, but increased nevertheless from 5,000 a year in the early 1940s to 10,000 in early 1950s to 20,000 in the early 1960s. The percentage of SSCs in the population age group increased from 2% to 5% from 1924 to 1944, although these figures are exaggerated since they combine English and vernacular language school-leaving qualifications (including overseas qualifications such as the London Matric and Senior Cambridge) at a time when there was a substantial difference between their relative status and employment value. The elimination of this difference in the post-war period coincided with a significant change in the employment profile of the population, such that by the early 1960s, as much as 12% of the school-leaving age group held an SSC (with a quarter of these going on to higher education).

---

[12] By the 1960s this was re-named the GCE O Level, such that 6 O Level passes were considered equivalent to the old SSC.

[13] For a sense of the logistical crisis that this created during the 1950s, read the reports of the Commissioner for Examinations. In 1959, the Commissioner, one Mr. Perinpanayagam even reports that the police had uncovered a fake SSC certificate printing racket (AR Examinations 1959: 35–37).

Employment and Communal Tension

By the mid-1950s, the next phase in this social and demographic chain reaction was set in motion. The repercussions of free education had brought about a surge of newly credentialed youth who entered, crowded, and quickly engulfed a relatively small segment of the labour market. The number of qualified applicants looking to become government clerks snowballed each year after the mid-1940s, and had by the early 1950s completely overwhelmed the available supply of such jobs.

This evident mismatch between the supply and demand of white collar jobs was a constant refrain in reviews of the education system from the 1920s onwards. From the 1950s onwards, it became a central theme in the economic analysis of unemployment from the 1953 World Bank report to the 1971 Dudley Seers report (ILO 1971). The World Bank report (citing a 1950 survey of secondary school students) reported a

> glaring disparity between ambitions and opportunities among secondary school pupils in Ceylon. Only a quarter show an interest in such productive activities as farming, handicraft work and skilled labor, whereas nearly two thirds of the gainfully employed are engaged in these fields. On the other hand, over half the pupils questioned aspire to service occupations, while only 15 percent of the population find employment therein (World Bank 1953: 56).

But while such observations made in this and numerous other survey based reports are technically accurate, they actually invert the order of the logic of the underlying phenomenon. It is not quite the case that secondary students had unwarranted aspirations to service occupations as such. Rather the entire purpose of secondary education was to provide the means to enter 'service' occupations, and specifically to *escape* a life as farmer, handicraft worker or skilled labourer. As Bryce Ryan describes it, clerkdom was so sought after that it became a 'hallowed and omnipresent' occupation. He writes:

> An almost pathetic sign of this anointment of the government clerk was observed in our queries made of low status women (largely coolie labour) working in factories. When asked their preference in marriage for self or for daughter between a government clerk making 100 rupees a month and a building contractor making 500 rupees a month two thirds of these women chose the clerk and still others were undecided (Ryan 1961: 464).

Government employment dipped significantly in the early 1930s under the fiscal constraints of the depression, from levels of 70,000 in 1930 to 60,000 by 1934, recovering slowly to around 67,000 by 1930 (AR General Treasury 1939, p.J8). It is during this period that the growing competition for scarce government jobs was first identified as a source of ethnic tension between Tamils and Sinhalese. As Jane Russell describes of the period:

> [R]ank communalism was displayed by both communities in the State Council whenever a discussion of qualifications for, or modes of recruitment of, the public services was mentioned, and immediately the issue of racial proportions would be brought into the discussion. In fact, ... the only matter on which there was a purely Sinhalese versus Tamil conflict was the public services. ... it was not the factual reality that mattered ... but the cognitive fears and suspicions of such discrimination that provided the impetus for communal hostility and recrimination (Russell 1982: 25–26).

Similarly, Governor Caldecott wrote of

> the desire of every parent to see a son get a Government job, and intense jealousy if that job falls to somebody of a different family, caste, or race. The extent to which this obsession obtains may be illustrated by a proposal which was made to me, though not in any official representations, that appointments to Clerkships should be by rotation between the races. I have no doubt whatever that a great deal of the communalism that is so unfortunately rampant derives directly from competition and jealousy about Government appointments.[14]

By independence in 1948, much of this depression-era tension had evaporated, as government employment increased significantly during the war and early post-war years. By 1947, the government employed more than double the numbers that it had in the late 1930s.[15] On an annual basis, the employment of central government clerks (many initially on a temporary basis) rose from depression era lows of around 200 per year to over 1,300 per year in the late 1940s.[16]

But after a decade of strong growth in the 1940s, employment in government ministries remained virtually static for the whole of the 1950s. Once again, Ceylon's economic fortunes were tied closely to global commodity prices, and

---

[14] Quoted in Kearney (1967) p.71. Also see Kearney (1971) chapter 4, for a summary of the dispute over government jobs as it played out in the 1954–56 language campaign.

[15] Author's calculations, based on data from the AR General Treasury, 1939 (p.J8).

[16] Author's calculations based on the length of employee service by employment category (table 5) in the 1951 Census of Government and Local Government Employees.

the slump that followed the end of the Korean War triggered a fiscal crisis and austerity. In response, the UNP government struggled against enormous political opposition to withdraw the rice subsidy and eventually instituted a hiring freeze in late 1953.[17]

The number of government employees (including teachers) increased from 155,000 in 1948 to a peak of 223,000 in 1952. But it subsequently dropped after 1952 and remained at 202,000 in 1959. The renewed expansion of the state, and particularly of the public sector after 1959 brought about another period of strong expansion. Through the opening of new state enterprises and the nationalisation of several sectors, the number of people employed in the government and public sector together doubled during the 1960s to 400,000.[18]

What this effectively meant is that SSC holders were able to find government jobs relatively easily during the 1940s when the supply of educated candidates was still relatively low, and the demand unusually high. But by the 1950s this situation had reversed, as a stagnant and declining supply of jobs was met with a doubling in the annual output of SSCs from 10,000 to 20,000. Government recruitment for posts that required the SSC remained flat at under 2,000 per year during the 1950s, increasing slowly to 3,000 per year by the end of the 1960s. While government employment did grow rapidly in the 1960s, much of it was in segments that required more than an SSC, such as school teachers, who doubled in number from 50,000 to 100,000.

Meanwhile, the growth in the public sector that occurred in this period often did not necessarily involve an increase in employment at all, as much of it was the result of the nationalisation of existing private sector enterprises and the incorporation of their existing staff. Even where new public sector companies were established, employment opportunities were heavily weighted towards manual and skilled workers, and qualified technicians and managers, rather than those with generic SSC qualifications.

The expansion of secondary education in the two decades after Caldecott meant very simply that the supply of educated aspirants hoping to make the well-worn transition from the farm to the clerical office occurred at a much faster rate with no commensurate availability of such jobs. In consequence, joblessness among SSC holders grew so fast during the 1950s that they became the group with the highest and the fastest rising rate of unemployment

---

[17] AR General Treasury 1953 refers to a directive from the prime minister dated 1/10/53 to this effect.

[18] Compiled from various sources, including the AR General Treasury and Statistical Abstracts.

among all educational categories. Concerns about jobs for school-leavers was evident even in the most elite English schools in Colombo such as Royal, St. Thomas and St. Joseph's, who enjoyed the best connections and proximity to networks of influence.[19] But unemployment was in reality a far more serious problem for the group that Jennings identified: the educated young men from the villages.

Table 3.3 | Unemployment Rates by Level of Education, 1963, 1971, and Extent of Long-Term Unemployment in 1971 (>3 Years)

Education level	1963	1971	1971 3 yrs+
None	3%	3%	1%
Primary	4%	3%	1%
Secondary (no SSC)	15%	22%	11%
SSC pass	29%	34%	20%
Higher	2%	10%	5%

Source: 1971 data based on tables in 1971 census vol 2, part 2. 1963 data is a composite of data from 1963 census data vol 1, part 1, table 21, vol 1, part 2, and 1963 CFS.

The growing problem of unemployment among SSC-qualified youth had become a major political issue by the 1954–55 period, with the government of Sir John Kotelawala genuinely confused and overwhelmed by the scale of this problem. Concerned at the political repercussions it may generate, the government scrambled to announce a variety of piecemeal solutions. One minister argued for SSC youth to be given military training.[20] A scheme to provide SSC youth with free land was implemented, but was quickly recognised as a failure by one of its main sponsors.[21]

The restive Sinhala educated youth had begun to organise rallies and island-wide demonstrations under the banner of the opposition Sri Lanka Freedom Party of S.W.R.D. Bandaranaike, who had promised to vernacularise the state and avenues of state employment.[22] Jaffna Tamils had long been over-

---

[19] CDN 20 May 1954 'Old Schools Seek Jobs for Past Pupils'.

[20] CDN 7 February 1955 'Quasi-army service for SSC youths'.

[21] CDN 22 March 1955 'SSC Men will be put onto State Farms', CDN 5 July 1955 '2000 Acres a Year for SSC Farmers' – then CDN 4 January 1956 'SSC Farmers are a Failure'.

[22] CDN 19 August 1954 'Swabhasha Educated to Protest', and CDN 23 August 1954, 'Girl Will Lead "Army" to Temple Trees'. Also see CDN 1 March 1955 'SSC People are Rallied for Struggle Ahead'.

represented in the public services since at least the 1920s, and there is evidence to suggest that it had become the source of Tamil–Sinhala friction since the 1930s. The re-emergence of tight competition for public service jobs in the changed socio-economic conditions of the mid-1950s brought this issue once again into sharp focus. By 1955, in the context of the then raging campaign for 'Sinhala only', there were once again allegations raised in parliament over ethnic discrimination in the recruitment of government clerks.[23]

Many leading Tamil personalities were well aware of this underlying economic dimension to the language campaign, and addressed it directly. A senator declared in parliament:

> It is these men, these middle-class unemployed seeking employment, who are jealous of the fact that a few Tamils occupy seats of office in the Government – these are the people who have gone round the country-side, rousing the masses and creating this problem.[24]

Similarly, N. Sanmugathasan of the CP (Peking) writes:

> Compelled by the pressure of unemployment, the Sinhalese wanted Sinhala only to be the official language ... the battle of the languages was in reality a battle for government jobs for the respective middle classes (Sanmugathasan 1972: 63).

In sum then, the growth of Sinhala nationalism occurred in the context of a rapid multiplication in the numbers of unemployed Sinhala-educated SSC youth in the mid-1950s. These issues came together in the context of the Sinhala only language campaign and formed the subtext within which the elections of 1956 were fought.

This is in many ways, also what Paul Brass describes in the broader context of nationalist mobilisation, and helps to situate Sinhala nationalism in its South Asian context:

> The mass base for nationalism may be created when widespread intra-class competition occurs brought about by the movement of large numbers of people from either a previously overwhelmingly rural group or from a disadvantaged

---

[23] See CDN 9 August 1955, 'Vavuniuya MP Alleges Communal Discrimination at GCS Exam' reporting remarks of C.Suntharalingam, M.P.

[24] Remarks of a leading Tamil senator (un-named) in parliament, quoted in Kearney (1967) p.71.

group into economic sectors occupied predominantly by other ethnic group (Brass 1991: 65).

One of the central demands of Sinhala nationalist ideologues in this period was for the competitive exam for the General Clerical Service to be held in the vernacular, and for government employees to be required to pass a proficiency exam in Sinhala. W. Dahanayake of the Bhasa Peramuna, one of the most outspoken Sinhala nationalists of the time, spoke to a rally of Sinhala-educated SSC youth, exhorting them 'Don't beg for jobs, snatch them!'[25] At another such election rally a few months later, he specifically promised the SSC unemployed that, if elected, his party would provide them with thousands of jobs.[26] Meanwhile, a leading Tamil MP lamented: 'the door to government jobs is now closed to the Tamils and the time is fast approaching when we will be called upon to face a life of austerity and hardhip'.[27] A news report from Jaffna suggested that unemployed SSC youth in the area were possibly turning to toddy-tapping out of desperation.[28]

Structural Unemployment

Despite the fact that SSC-level unemployment was an important factor in the Sinhala language movement and the electoral tide that brought the SLFP into power, the problem of SSC educated unemployment persisted and worsened in subsequent years, becoming a structural fixture of the Sri Lankan labour market. Data from the socio-economic surveys indicate that between 1953 and 1963, unemployment at the SSC level increased from 25% to 39%.[29]

Indeed, the peculiar nature of the social and demographic transition underway in Sri Lanka at the time is illustrated in the inverse-U-shaped relationship between education and unemployment. Unemployment levels were the lowest for the two thirds of the labour force in the most poorly paid occupations requiring minimal levels of education. It subsequently rose steeply

---

[25] CDN, 15 August 1955 'Don't Beg for Jobs but Snatch Them'.

[26] CDN, 21 March 1956 'Dahanayake Promises Jobs for All'.

[27] CDN 14 November 1955, 'Door to Govt Jobs Closed to Tamils', reporting speech by V.Kumaraswamy in Chavakachcheri.

[28] CDN, 8 September 1954 'SSC Students Turn to Toddy Tapping?'.

[29] CFS 1963, table 33. This does however appear to be an over-estimate for the latter period. Based on alternate data sources, this is estimated as an increase from 29% to 34% between 1963 and 1971 (see table 3.3).

for those with a secondary education, and peaked at the SSC pass level before dropping again for those with further education.

Between 1963 and 1971, unemployment increased appreciably for those with a secondary school and higher level, but remained at very low levels and actually declined for those with a primary education or less. By 1971, not only was more than one-third of the total SSC population unemployed (this excludes those not actively searching for employment), but one in five had remained unemployed for over three years. Lacking the social background and connections that they could use to advance themselves in their new environment, many newly minted SSC holders from rural backgrounds suffered the most. Rather than accepting and getting trapped in the plentiful supply of lower-paid, lower-status work, or suffering a humiliating status-downgrade with a return to the family farm, they remained unemployed for years to form an expanding backlog of job applicants hoping to eventually make it to the front of the queue and find an appropriate government job. Jayadeva Uyangoda describes how this situation progressed with an inflation of educational qualifications to poor, rural university graduates:

> Parents of many of these young men and women are from the employment categories of small-holder peasants, day-labourers, fishermen, lower-grade employees in the private sector, small-shop owners, and if one is lucky, government clerks and trained school teachers. Free higher education, backed by the expectations of public sector employment is, in almost all their life experiences, the most powerful social emancipatory force. It has enabled them to symbolically rise above the rest of the family, the neighbourhood, the village and the locality. But the 'system' cannot help them beyond purchasing one-way tickets to higher education. A university degree in social sciences or humanities would not ensure secure life chances for rural young men and women who are essentially monolingual, culturally un-urbane and socially uncomfortable with the world of state bureaucracy or the corporate private sector. The 'system' is then a blind alley (Uyangoda 2003: 49).

Table 3.6 clearly shows that unemployment levels peaked at those categories where the pattern of available employment opportunities was incommensurate with the changing education profile of new job-seekers. The SSC category accounted for 9% of the incoming cohort of 20 year olds, but only 5% of all existing jobs. Between 1963 and 1971, the supply of new jobs at the SSC level (both through the expansion of overall employment levels and natural attrition) amounted to only around 9,000 per year – far lower than the growing annual demand from 16,000–22,000 newly created SSC holders. In 1971, an estimated 22,000 SSC holders entered the job market, most of whom went straight to the back of a long queue formed by an existing army of four times that number of SSC unemployed, still struggling to find a job.

Table 3.4 | Employment, Unemployment and Distribution of Age 20 Year Cohort by Education Level, 1971

Education level	Total Employed	Total Unemployed	Age 20 yr cohort	Unemployment Rate %
None	841,231	28,503	33,000	3%
Primary	1,430,524	46,028	46,000	3%
Secondary (no SSC)	1,104,992	316,234	140,000	22%
SSC pass	174,414	88,993	22,000	34%
Higher	97,714	10,334	8,000	10%

Source: 1971 Census vol. 2, part 2.

The expansion in education after the mid-1940s also had important consequences for the social composition of government employment, which reflected more or less that of the pool of available qualified candidates. Before 1945, the middle and upper ranks of government employment were drawn entirely from the small number of English-language secondary schools, meaning in effect, that they were heavily weighted towards Burghers (Eurasians), Jaffna Tamils, and Sinhalese Christians. It corresponded to the fact that large parts of the country and large segments of the population were both unaffected by the dynamics of rural demographic pressure and/or effectively shut out of the alternatives provided by the education system. Over 60% of the university student population in 1944 was drawn from these three groups, who together accounted for 15% of the population. The exclusion of large segments of the rural population from secondary education and in the 1940s was reflected in the fact that the Sinhala Buddhist majority, comprising 64% of the actual population, actually accounted for only 38% of the university intake.[30]

The available information on the exact composition of the government service in the late-colonial and early post-colonial period is almost entirely devoted to the upper-most ranks of gazetted officers. The literature on this subject is absorbed in describing the 'Ceylonisation' of the elite ranks of the Ceylon Civil Service, as Europeans were slowly replaced by Burghers, Sinhalese

---

[30] Blue Book (various).

Christians, Tamils and finally, Sinhalese Buddhists over the 1930s–50s. Data on the ethnic composition of the far more numerous lower cadres is generally unavailable, except in occasional, almost anecdotal, references. For example, the parliamentary papers of 1928 report that 'In 1928 the strength of the clerical staff of the Customs Department was 120, out of which there were 57 Burghers, 32 Tamils, and 31 Sinhalese. There were only two Kandyan Sinhalese.'[31]

Table 3.5 | Percentage of Population with SSC or Higher Qualification, by Ethnic Group, 1953–73

	1953	1963	1973
Kandyan Sinhalese	1.8%	3.0%	5.2%
LC Sinhalese	2.0%	5.6%	8.4%
SL Tamil	2.6%	6.4%	10.0%
Indian Tamil	0.0%	0.7%	0.8%
Muslim & Malay	1.6%	3.2%	3.9%
Other	4.0%	20.3%	15.5%
Average	1.8%	4.4%	6.7%

Source: Calculations based on Socio-Economic surveys and Census data.

A census of government employees in 1951 reported no data on ethnicity, but data on education by language suggests that the ratio of Sinhalese to Tamils in the clerical and higher ranks of government employment was roughly 68:32.[32] Similarly, data from the 1911 elections (Bastin 1977: 411) show how 36% of the limited franchise of 'Educated Ceylonese' were Ceylon Tamils, who comprised just 13% of the population.[33] It must of course be borne in mind that the 'Sinhalese' and 'Tamil' categories themselves would have included disproportionate numbers of Sinhalese Christians and upper caste Jaffna Tamils, who each amounted to approximately 5 per cent of the total population. But with the advent of free education, and the progressive elimination of employment barriers to those with vernacular qualifications,

---

[31] Report of the Salaries Committee, SP XLVIII of 1928, p.102.

[32] The Census of Government and Local Government Employees, 1951 (table 7) shows that, of the 26,000 English qualified staff, 68% had some level of Sinhalese education while 32% had some level of Tamil education. I have taken this to approximate the ratio of Sinhalese to Tamils. Despite obvious problems (most Muslims would also have been educated in Tamil) the level of error is likely to be small.

[33] Also see Roberts (1977), Introduction for further evidence.

the profile of the SSC qualified and the clerical ranks of the government began to change. By bringing large numbers of previously excluded population segments (both Sinhalese and Tamil) into the education system, the ethnic composition of qualified school leavers increasingly resembled their respective national averages by the late 1960s.

Conclusions

Within the context of an ongoing crisis of peasant agriculture, the expansion of public health and education precipitated complex social changes that played out over several decades. It changed the educational profile of a large percentage of the population and created a flood of newly minted school-leavers who expected that their credentials would grant them access to government employment. These socio-economic and demographic transformations occurred together with the rise of a new electoral politics, so that the state came to encompass and encircle the lives of its citizens in unprecedented ways. The socialisation, livelihoods, and day-to-day experiences of the most distant and hitherto irrelevant citizens were – over the span of two decades – transformed by elections, public education, public health, and state sector employment. The nodes of citizen–state relations multiplied manifold and across different dimensions in a short space of time, and citizens adopted and adapted their frames of reference to this new context.

There is of course an ambitious leap made here in causally connecting these structural social-demographic changes to the transformation of identity and consciousness. Gellner often frames this interface between the inner and outer worlds of nationalism in terms of a straightforward functionalist and instrumentalist logic that has led many to question and even reject his entire model:

> Men do not in general become nationalists from sentiment or sentimentality, atavistic or not, well-based or myth founded: they become nationalists through genuine, objective, practical necessity, however obscurely recognised (Gellner 1964: 160).

But leaving aside these instrumentalist excesses, the circumstances still provide a compelling link between these elements. Large numbers of people embraced and openly affirmed an explicitly Sinhala Buddhist political identity in the 1950s. They did so at a time when their lives were transformed by politics and by the state. Moreover, they did so in ways that legitimised their aspirations to upward mobility and material improvement, embracing a language of morality and entitlement that advanced their claims to accessing state resources as a matter of right. While the connection at stake here between a socio-economic transition and a form of widely shared nationalist consciousness is not to be assumed away, it would be implausible to suggest that there is *no* causal link here, and that these sequences occurred as happenstance or some extraordinary historical coincidence.

With the passionate advocacy and divisions of the 'Sinhala-only' language campaign of 1955–56 in motion, the scene was set for the institutionalisation of the Sinhala–Tamil ethnic conflict as a central and enduring political divide. The demographic aspects of the rise of the conflict in the mid-1950s, and the competition over government employment, goes a long way in explaining two otherwise difficult to explain issues about the rise of Sinhala nationalism in that period (Ryan 1961, Farmer 1965).

Firstly, in terms of timing, the very rapid pace of the social, educational and demographic changes in the 1940s–50s helps explains the otherwise abrupt and puzzling rise of the 'Sinhala only' campaign and the spread of nationalist consciousness in the 1954–56 period, which was largely unforeseen. Secondly, it also helps to explain how the nascent nationalist movement that was otherwise associated primarily with hostility towards the English language, Christianity and the Sinhalese elites took a sharp anti-Tamil direction. The 'Sinhala only' language movement had very definite material underpinnings, in that it urged educated, unemployed rural Sinhalese youth to look towards the disproportionate presence of the Tamils in the public services as the source of their continued marginalisation and unemployment.

4 | The Politics of Market Reform at a Time of Ethnic Conflict

In 1977, the newly elected UNP government of J.R. Jayewardene initiated a landmark change in the direction of Sri Lanka's economic policies. After almost four decades of the steady expansion of state welfare provision, and of the heavy regulation of private sector economic activity, Jayewardene inaugurated a risky and radical programme of market liberalisation. Sri Lanka was one of the first countries in the developing world – after Chile and Indonesia – to embrace market liberalisation, and soon enjoyed the benefits of a wave of foreign aid by western donors who were eager for these to be seen to succeed. In the first two years of the reforms, the UNP deregulated foreign trade, removed import controls, devalued the exchange rate by 43 percent, eliminated subsidies on food and petrol, liberalised internal agricultural markets, reduced export duties, encouraged foreign investment, established export processing zones, modified labour legislation, and deregulated credit markets (Athukorala and Jayasuriya 1994, Jayewardene et al 1987, Stern 1984, White and Wignaraja 1992, Herring 1987).

The economic reform period, and the aftermath of the 1977 elections also witnessed a paradoxical escalation in the island's ethnic conflict. After three decades of pursuing federalism through parliamentary means, the centre of gravity of Tamil political activity was shifting decisively in the direction of separatism in terms of its goals, and militancy in terms of methods. The 1977 elections had led to the ascendancy of the Tamil United Liberation Front (TULF), an umbrella organisation formed largely out of the old Federal Party (FP), which had contested and won a decisive share of the Tamil vote on the basis of an explicitly separatist platform. Over the period 1977–83, the Colombo-based parliamentary leaders of the TULF were overtaken and eclipsed by the Jaffna-based militant youth groups that they had earlier patronised and presumed to control.[1]

---

[1] On Tamil nationalism, see Ponnambalam (1983), Bose (1994), Gunasingam (1999), Wilson (2000), Rasaratnam (2016).

It had long been supposed by the UNP leadership of that time that faster economic growth, and a reduction in youth unemployment would help to address the economic drivers of the ethnic conflict. For a combination of economic and social-cultural factors, the UNP's traditional support base in the business community has been the segment of society least invested in the logic of Sinhala nationalism, and most interested in bringing a quick end to the ethnic conflict. As Jonathan Spencer explains:

> The political and class interests of Sri Lanka's rulers in late 70s and early 80s would have been best served by a speedy settlement of the Tamil problem. That such a settlement was not reached must in part be attributed to the rulers' own reluctance to depart from imperatives of national destiny (Spencer 1990: 246).

Sunil Bastian (1990) similarly describes how the 'rational capitalists' of the UNP had little to gain by provoking a civil war and much to lose. It was in the strong material interests of the business elites to defuse the ethnic conflict lest it grow and burden their ambitious plans for economic transformation. Nevertheless, it was on the UNP's watch that the simmering ethnic conflict erupted into civil war.

In July 1983, an LTTE attack on an army patrol in Jaffna, timed to disrupt a critical TULF convention, sparked a furious orgy of anti-Tamil rioting in the capital Colombo and elsewhere. Some 2,000–3,000 Tamil civilians are presumed to have been killed in the violence, leading to the evacuation of hundreds of thousands, either north to Jaffna, or as refugees abroad.[2] Although the heated military engagements of the civil war did not take shape until around mid-1984, it is common to date its beginning to July 1983, as it marked a distinct point of political and psychological rupture from the past. In the many accounts and analyses of the July 1983 riots and the events that preceded it, culpability is frequently attached to the actions and inactions of state agencies and the ruling UNP. The government was held responsible for establishing a culture of authoritarian intimidation in the months preceding the July 1983 riots, particularly in their conduct of the very violent and probably fraudulent referendum in December 1982 (Samarakone 1984). UNP party activists, and particularly the outspoken minister for industries, Cyril Mathew, were accused of having inspired, if not to have actually organised, anti-Tamil violence. Mathew is widely suspected to have been involved in the

---

[2] On the 1983 riots, see Race & Class 1984b, Kanapathipillai 1990, Tambiah 1986 ch 2–3, Senaratne 1997: chapter 1).

burning of the Jaffna library in June 1981 during his visit there, an incident that inflamed Tamil opinion and that helped to propel it firmly towards the direction of separatism (Race & Class 1984a).

What then is the relationship between the market reforms of 1977, and the outbreak of civil war that occurred in 1983? Why did the UNP, a party identified primarily with the interests of Sri Lanka's social elite and capitalist class, and with the pursuit of the market reform programme, become a key participant in the escalation of a brutal civil war that was counter-productive to its material interests? This chapter reviews some of the existing approaches to the relationship between reforms and conflict in Sri Lanka, and in doing so, advances an alternative proposition. In brief, the argument is that the outbreak of the conflict was the unintended consequence of the primary policy agenda, the market reforms. More specifically, it was in strategising the politics of market reforms – the process by which the government sought to find legitimacy and win public consent for their policies – that the circumstances of the exacerbation of the civil war occurred.

As a corollary to this, there is a more general proposition to be advanced: that market-reforming governments in Sri Lanka are in a weak position to implement a peaceful resolution to the ethnic conflict, because they lack the political capital, legitimacy and authority needed to do so; and because the actual economic impact of the reforms is likely to catalyse a joint, double-barrelled opposition to both the reforms and the peace process. The basis for this proposition lies in the alignment of the Sri Lankan party system with respect to both these issues, and also in the fact that market reform and the resolution of the ethnic conflict are both complementary and overlapping counter-populist projects for reforming the Sinhala-dominated social democratic state. Market reforms thus bear the latent potential of inviting opposition of a Sinhala nationalist colouring – an outcome that can have strong negative consequences for the government's capacity to promote a settlement to the ethnic conflict.

The politics of market reform at the time of the first two UNP governments of 1977–93 revolved around three types of mechanisms – institutional, ideological, and material. This explanation and emphasis is of course a departure from most conventional descriptions of the UNP governments of 1977–93, which concentrate on the issue of authoritarian domination. In institutional terms, it involved the creation of the new presidential system to strengthen executive authority and insulate it from populist pressure (chapter 9). In ideological terms, the market reforming UNP affected an exaggerated performance of Sinhala Buddhist authenticity to compensate for the latent moral deficit inherent in the reforms. In material terms, it compensated for the withdrawal of the state in some spheres by the expansion of the state in other spheres. Chapter 5 explores one way in which the civil war played a functional role in providing material and, to some extent, ideological support for the reform agenda through the multiplier effects of military fiscalism. By the 1990s, the army had become the single largest employer in the country, offsetting the reduction in civilian state employment under the reforms, and mitigating the growing inequalities of this period. This had the largely unintended and unforeseen consequence of facilitating the market reform agenda by helping to win passive quiescence, if not active consent, for a policy regime that was broadly opposed by large segments of the population.

Causal, Functional or Accidental?

Did Sri Lanka's market reforming elites promote Sinhala nationalism and engineer the civil war in order to mask their economic agenda under a veil of false consciousness? Or did the economic consequences of the reforms, in terms of greater poverty and inequality, spur Tamil grievances or Sinhalese mob violence? These and related arguments are recurrent themes in an influential stream of literature that has sought to establish that there is actually a causal relationship between market reforms and civil war.

In a series of thought-provoking articles written shortly after the July 1983 riots, the late Newton Gunasinghe described the differential impact of the reforms on the Sinhalese versus Tamil business strata. Gunasinghe focused on the role of small import-substituting Sinhalese industrialists, who had previously benefited from state intervention and the high tariffs to consumer imports (Gunasinghe, 1984). The removal of import restrictions in 1977 was to the detriment of this group as they could no longer compete with cheaper imports or capitalise on their preferential access to state power. In contrast, Colombo's Tamil merchants, whose lack of access to the state had for long restricted them to commerce rather than industry, appeared to have benefited greatly from the removal of trade barriers and the consequent boom in imported goods and foreign trade. This, he argued was the context within which anti-Tamil sentiment escalated in the period of the 1983 riots.

Dunham and Jayasuriya (2001), in contrast, argue that the liberalisation process, midwifed by unprecedented levels of aid flows did not actually disrupt ethnicised state patronage networks, but expanded them, drawing in new groups that benefited from the climate of heightened tension and authoritarianism. Politicians, bureaucrats, police and military, for example, found 'fertile ground for large-scale self-enrichment through the control of state power....A mutually reinforcing process of economic 'reforms' and socio-political decay was thus set in motion.' (Dunham and Jayasuriya 2001:2).

Obeyesekere (1984) and Tambiah (1986), among others, suggest that the sudden, unequal economic impact of the reforms caused abrupt and disorienting social repercussions, and was subsequently accompanied by the institutionalisation of political violence and greater government authoritarianism. Along similar lines, Dunham and Jayasuriya (2000) contend that Sri Lanka's generous welfare subsidies had important positive externalities in terms of buying social peace, and that their dismantling unleashed a social unravelling that has been manifest in terms of worsening problems of social order and violent conflict. As such, the growth of Tamil militancy is explained as just one manifestation of an all-encompassing violence that gripped Sri Lankan society and politics since the late 1970s. It emerged from the social upheavals, poverty, lumpenisation and socio-political decay engendered by the reforms as well as from the increasingly violent and undemocratic measures used by the government to suppress opposition to the reforms.

Moore (1985) describes the differential impact of agricultural trade liberalisation based on the regionalised distribution of tradable versus non-tradable crops. Due to agro-climatic and historical reasons, the island's export agriculture sector – in tea, rubber, and coconuts – was concentrated largely in the south, while agriculture in the Jaffna peninsula was restricted to minor food crops – such as bananas, onions, and chillies – for domestic consumption. While trade liberalisation benefited the export sector in the south, it hurt domestic food crop prices in the north.

There are, as such, a variety of fairly disparate hypotheses all of which seek to connect liberalisation to conflict. These include (i) the unequal impact of the reforms between rich and poor; (ii) the unequal impact of the reforms upon different elements of the ethnically-segmented business strata; (iii) the unequal regional impact of the reforms upon the north versus south; (iv) the heightened opportunities for ethnicised patronage engendered by the massive aid boom that accompanied the reforms; (v) the increase in political violence and state authoritarianism which arose partly in response to suppressing these manifestations of social disorder, both spontaneous and organised, which emerged from the reform process.

These different explanations share a common understanding that in a society where gradations of occupation and class often intersect with regional and ethnic identities, the frustrations that resulted from the abrupt and unequal distribution of costs and benefits from the reforms either resulted or were engineered in the direction of Sinhala–Tamil hostility.[3] But ultimately, that is about all that they have in common. Some of them are complementary, some are mutually contradictory, while yet others bear no relation whatsoever to one another. For example, was the conflict caused by the misdirected rage of the Sinhalese urban poor at their absolute or relative impoverishment? Or was it the negative effect of trade liberalisation on import-substituting Jaffna farmers that fuelled Tamil separatist sentiment? Or did liberalisation anger Sinhalese import-substituting industrialists who were put out of business by Tamil merchants in the import-export trade?

Even more confusing are the cases where the arguments are mutually contradictory or where the effects of liberalisation operate in different directions for different segments of Tamil society. For example, liberalisation is said to have hurt Tamil farmers on the one hand and this is viewed as having aggravated the conflict. But other accounts of the conflict find causality in the way it disproportionately benefited Tamil merchants and aroused Sinhalese envy. It is certainly plausible that both of these occurred, but how is one supposed to aggregate these offsetting mechanisms to understand what, if at all, was the composite causal impact of liberalisation on Tamil separatism and the conflict?

Similarly, import-substituting Sinhalese entrepreneurs are supposed to have been hurt by trade liberalisation. But others have advanced a liberalisation-conflict link from the exact opposite supposition, i.e. that Sinhalese entrepreneurs gained handsomely and disproportionately from the new opportunities for state patronage that emerged in the reform period.

Unfortunately, the proliferation of theory and conjecture on this issue has not been matched or resolved in any measure by empirical substantiation. The evidence that does exist is sparse, sketchy, fragmented, and even anecdotal. Or else, as Moore (1990) argues convincingly, it is incomplete in the sense that it does not adequately track the complete chain of events from liberalisation to conflict; from economics to politics. In general, there is a need for greater explanation and contextualisation in the circumstances and constraints posed.

---

[3] See for example, Akram-Lodhi (1987) for a very classic Marxist interpretation of the Tamil–Sinhala conflict as 'class struggles cloaked in the guise of communal contradiction'.

Any attempt to formulate a plausible hypothesis linking reforms to the conflict has to contend with the great fluidity and indeterminacy in defining most of the critical variables. There are a large numbers of possible actors and actions captured within the broad categories of 'reform' and 'conflict', and these are aggravated by the peculiarities of the Sri Lankan case. The actual process of economic reforms was no simple, radical shift from state to market. State expenditures and public sector employment actually increased sharply during the reform period under a mammoth wave of aid-funded public sector investment projects (Herring 1994). Furthermore, most of the causal variables and measurable outcomes of the ethnic conflict – such as Tamil separatism, Sinhala nationalism, militancy, anti-Tamil riots, and state authoritarianism – did not suddenly spring into being in the post-reform period, but already existed well before the first set of market reforms were proposed in the budget speech of November 1977. There is, as such, no simple, reductive, testable cause-effect sequence between reforms and war.

The Politics of Market Reform

The problematic of the politics of market reform in Sri Lanka can, for most purposes, be reduced to the simple question of how democratically elected governments set about implementing unpopular economic policies that are certain to damage their electoral prospects. Sri Lanka's market reform agenda suffers from an inherent lack of popular legitimacy, and is an electoral handicap for any party that wishes to implement it. Yet, the prerogatives of a perpetually insolvent treasury, combined with pressure from foreign donors, and the powerful lobbying of domestic and foreign business groups has forced every government from 1977 to 2004 to pursue this unpopular agenda. How, one must ask, did they win the consent of the electorate to undertake this difficult task?

Sri Lanka's expansive social welfare state has grown since the 1930s in close connection to incentives provided by the system of popular democracy. Under the cut-throat electoral pressures of universal franchise, political parties competed with one another by promising to expand the role of the state. They responded to, and in turn, helped create, popular conceptions of the legitimate role of the state and its relationship to the people, which became articulated in terms of a new moral vocabulary of rights and entitlements. The establishment of public services such as free education and health, the provision of public employment, the protection of peasant agriculture and rural life against the pressures of internal capitalist expansion and international price pressures, the alleviation of poverty and social inequalities, together with the promotion of the Sinhala language and patronage of the Buddhist religion, had over this period come to comprise the moral parameters within which the very legitimacy and stability of not just any single government, but of the state itself and the political system, was hinged.

That is, the social democratic/welfare state as a political, economic, and ideological project emerged in close connection, and in a self-reinforcing logic with, the advancement of Sinhala nationalism and electoral politics. The illegitimacy of the market reform agenda thus stemmed from the fact it was a project intended primarily to dismantle and bypass the social democratic state – it thus transgressed the moral basis upon which state-society relations were balanced. For the several million people tenuously straddling the social class continuum from peasant agriculture to the semi-urban lower middle class, the state remained a critical vehicle for economic stability, basic welfare provision, and upward social mobility in an economy characterised by widespread insecurity and deprivation. By increasing the space of the capitalist economy and diminishing that of the state, the market reform agenda has clear economic repercussions that retain the latent potential to be viewed, interpreted, evaluated, and rejected on the basis of a system of thought and a moral universe constructed out of the elements of Sinhala nationalism.

It is within this universe of political morality, hinged on the role of the state in promoting social justice and articulated through the vocabulary of nationalism, that one needs to situate the paradox of the politics of market reform. How would the government and the institutions of electoral politics survive such a direct assault upon the system of legitimacy which had sustained it thus far? There is, and has been, in Sri Lanka and in other countries, the perpetual anxiety that the contradictions of this process would become untenable – that either democracy or reforms would give way, leading to free-market dictatorships or dirigiste democracies. And indeed, a review of the comparative literature of the politics of market reform features numerous cases where this contradiction led to great stress, and spurred the innovation of creative new political strategies.

Jeff Herbst describes how Ghana's surprising success in implementing reforms lay in 'a particularly effective combination of coercion and legitimacy to deter outright opposition' (Herbst 1993: 45). Jerry Rawlings was not just a military dictator who dealt firmly with political opponents, but had also cultivated an image as a revolutionary champion of the poor. As a result, he was able to secure the acceptance even of those who were driven deeper into poverty by his reforms. It also meant that any potential opponents to his reforms were actually his political protégés, and were thus compromised and neutralised from the outset.

As with much of the mainstream politics of adjustment literature, this study operates within an implicit neo-Machiavellian ethical framework whereby the ends (successful market reforms) ultimately always justify the means, however unpalatable they may be. And indeed, there are some often stunningly frank policy conclusions that emerge of how reforms can be pushed through in the teeth of popular opposition and democratic norms. The success of reforms, one study plainly stated, requires centralised, extraordinary executive powers by which its opponents can be overcome:

> [T]he insulation of central decision makers from distributive claims will enhance the state's capacity to launch new initiatives. ... Change teams are relatively autonomous, even free floating, technocratic actors who are protected from the pressures of interest groups and bureaucratic rivals by strong backing from the chief executive. Though such groups must eventually forge coalitions of social supporters, *the centralisation and concentration of executive authority outside of normal institutional channels is essential for breaking antireform networks* (Haggard and Kaufman 1992: 23, emphasis added).

At a broader level, the new policy prescriptions that focused on technocrats and their insulation from electoral pressures were indicative of a significant shift in the international development policy agenda by the early 1990s. While earlier researchers asked only how the reforms could be most expediently forced through unwilling polities, later studies were modified to ask how the same results could be obtained without disturbing the often nascent liberal democratic institutions and the legitimacy they would provide to the reforms. Would democratisation and the pressures of populist politics force backtracking on market reforms leading to dirigiste democracies? Or, contrarily, would the imperatives of market reform bring about authoritarian politics leading to free market dictatorships? In one of the early texts on the issue, Adam Przeworski elaborated on the nature of the problem facing Eastern Europe: 'Under democratic conditions, where the discontent can find political expression at the polls, even the most promising reform strategies may be abandoned' (Przeworski 1991: 136–7).

Without digressing into an expansive review, what emerges clearly from the comparative literature is that where democratic political structures were preserved through periods of aggressive market reform, they did so only in form, but not in content. Case studies systematically describe how successful reformers manipulated and misled electorates, disoriented their opponents, and adroitly exploited loopholes in the political structure to neutralise, divert, and insulate themselves from anti-reform pressure. Reforms were also frequently introduced as post-election surprises: reformist leaders were able to exploit sources of legitimacy and popularity entirely unrelated to their economic agenda, for example, as erstwhile pro-democracy activists. This enabled them to win power and to subsequently unveil a comprehensive package of unpalatable economic policies that were little discussed in their election campaign. Przeworski concludes that reforms are always introduced by surprise, and uses formal mathematical reasoning to explain why economic shock therapy upon an unsuspecting population is the more difficult but ultimately, the preferred option: 'the success of the bitter-pill strategy depends on its initial brutality' (Przeworski 1991: 183).

Rob Jenkins' study on the politics of reform in India is an unorthodox and refreshing break from this genre, if only because it exposes the pious hypocrisy of the mainstream literature on the issue of democracy (1999). He contends that India's complicated political structure facilitates the implementation of a complex and contentious market reform agenda – but it does so not because of its democratic content as such, but quite the reverse. The existence of mature liberal democratic institutions does not lead to a more inclusive reform process, but rather one that provides pro-reform leaders a variety of strategies and levers by which to subvert, diffuse, corrupt, divide, and divert sources of opposition. As he describes, 'Pushing through reform measures requires a broad range of underhanded tactics', and India's democratic, federalist structure is more amenable to such tactics than a more monolithic state or dictatorship (Jenkins 1999: 206). He concludes that, 'the federal ordering of political power helps to reduce the political pressures facing reformers at the apex of the political system' (Jenkins 1999: 119).

In summary, a selective review of the comparative experience of adjustment demonstrates that the onerous task of winning consent for market reform policies has spurred the innovation of various methods. These include the establishment of authoritarianism – either in terms of political dictatorships and the sheer absence of democratic mechanisms, or more often through the domination of extant democratic mechanisms by a pro-reform party or coalition, and the insulation of the reform agenda from the pressures of electoral politics. In other cases, reforms involved the containment of sources of opposition through coercion, co-option or corruption, but more often through legislative, political or administrative measures, such as restrictions on trade unions. Yet another set of strategies involved the promotion of alternative sources of legitimacy and political division to neutralise the illegitimacy and centrality of the reforms, and thus to win public consent.

Ideological and Economic Compensatory Mechanisms

Market reforms were first introduced in Sri Lanka under the 'open economy' agenda of the UNP government of J.R. Jayewardene after its election in July 1977 – and in situating their political strategies for implementing the reforms, one first has to go back to their recent history. The UNP was the party to which power had been transferred at independence in 1948, but had from 1956 suffered a serious problem of electability – indeed, they were out of power for 16 of the next 21 years after 1956. As President J.R. Jayewardene later described 'the thinking in the country was that the UNP was a spent force which had outlived its purpose' (Jayewardene 1992: ix).

Figure 4.1 | Sri Lanka Parliamentary General Election Vote Percentages, 1952–77, UNP Versus Left + SLFP[†]

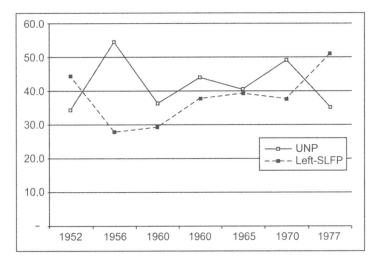

[†] 'Left parties' here refers to the CP and LSSP

This problem of un-electability had much to do with the social and economic character of the UNP, a party historically composed of and for the island's westernised bourgeois elite, a party of 'cosmopolitan capitalists' as it were, largely dominated by merchants, professionals, and planters from low-country Sinhalese origins, but in reality quite broad-based in terms of the caste, religious and ethno-linguistic basis of its supporters, financiers, and core constituency (Shastri 2004b). With the UNP as the transparent organisational vehicle of their political interests, they were identifiably a class in itself and for itself.

The source of the UNP's defeat and near-banishment from electoral politics after 1956 was largely to do with the joint ascendancy of these factors, and to the way in which they fashioned the language and moral parameters of electoral politics. As the party of cosmopolitan capitalists, the UNP was on the losing end of the two dominant issues that were animating electoral populism: economic and ethnic. Indeed, in terms of electoral arithmetic, the UNP has been defeated on every subsequent occasion when the Marxist left and the Sinhala nationalist right coalesced – which happened in 1956, 1970, and 2004.

The historical role played by J.R. Jayewardene in Sri Lankan politics is that he effectively resolved the problem of the UNP's electability, which as he himself described, was a task to 'correct the image of the UNP which was considered a conservative, capitalist party' (Jayewardene 1992: ix). After assuming leadership of the party in 1973, what Jayewardene did, together with his lieutenant Ranasinghe Premadasa, was not dissimilar to the 'popular Toryism', of Benjamin Disraeli and Randolph Churchill in 19th century Britain.[4] That is, they found a way to render the narrow economic interests of a party of traditional elites electorally viable by fusing it with populist electoral appeal on issues such as imperial fervour or religious bigotry.[5] In the Sri Lankan case, the UNP's task was complicated by the fact that the available raw materials for electoral populism were by definition anti-UNP, so that the party had to completely transform itself in order to preserve itself. It was a process guided by the rationale that Giuseppe Lampedusa's fictional character, Tancredi Falconeri, put so succinctly in describing the pragmatic compromises

---

[4] Whether by coincidence or otherwise, Jayewardene's biographers specifically mention that he was an admirer of Disraeli; see De Silva and Wriggins (1994: 327).

[5] See De Silva and Wriggins (1994), particularly chapter 14–16 for a fairly sympathetic account of Jayewardene's reforms within the UNP in the 1973–77 period.

and cosmetic reforms endured by the Sicilian aristocracy in order to maintain their privilege and wealth through the Risorgimento: 'if we want everything to stay as it is, everything will have to change' (Di Lampedusa 2008, 50). Between 1973 and 1977, Jayewardene transformed the UNP by cultivating entirely new sources of support in the rural hinterland from lower classes and lower castes; by inducting an entirely new set of youthful rural populists as their election candidates; by elevating a 'man of the masses' from a low caste and distinctly non-elite background, Ranasinghe Premadasa, to the position of deputy leader of the party, then prime minister, placing him in the position to become the next president; by infusing the party and the new government they formed with the symbols and rituals of Buddhist religiosity. And in the election campaign that brought the most dramatic switch from state to market in Sri Lankan history, the UNP were careful to never ever spell out the radical economic reforms that were their core policy agenda. Instead, they sought to appropriate the very language of morality that had been used against them by claiming that they were actually a socialist party, and that they would once in power, usher in the 'real socialism' that Mrs Bandaranaike and her leftist partners had failed to do.

In a process that began grudgingly in the aftermath of the 1956 elections, and more seriously after Jayewardene's rise to the leadership in 1973, the party that was associated in the public mind with wealthy, urban, westernised businessmen at its helm tried to convince the public that it was now a party of the rural Sinhala Buddhist poor. Typical of the UNP's pre-market reform election rhetoric was the speech from the head of a newly opened UNP branch in Trincomalee in 1977: 'The UNP was confined to the capitalist class once but it has now been transformed into a party of the common man.'[6] The UNP's 1977 election manifesto similarly stressed that:

> The UNP is not only a democratic party: it is also a socialist party ... Our policy is to ... terminate the exploitation of man by man.

Once in power, the UNP's strategy in implementing market reforms had three components: authoritarian reversal, nationalist performance, and off-setting developmental programmes. The most direct such strategy was authoritarian reversal: to weaken populist nationalism by restricting the oxygen of electoral democracy that it lived on. This was the project of the executive presidency introduced in the 1978 constitutions: a powerful, centralised,

---

[6] CDN 27 May 1977, 'UNP No More a Capitalist Party'.

political structure to pursue a counter-populist agenda insulated from electoral pressure (chapter 9, Wilson 1980, Welikala 2015).

Secondly, the UNP sought to counter and compensate its perceived deficit of native authenticity by affecting an exaggerated display of Buddhist religiosity. Just as it had successfully appropriated and neutralised the language of socialism and equality during the election campaign, Jayewardene also consciously sought to appropriate the vernacular and religious idiom of Sinhala nationalism and to disguise his economic agenda within its structure of signification, in order to pre-emptively neutralise the possibility that this potent language of political legitimacy be turned against him.

In the 1930s, the expansion of electoral democracy with universal franchise gave rise to a political stereotype known as the 'Donoughmore Buddhist': the Christian-born elite Sinhalese politician who converted to Buddhism out of expediency to improve his electoral appeal. The two best known Donoughmore Buddhists were of course S.W.R.D. Bandaranaike, and J.R. Jayewardene, both of whom were born into Anglican families and who converted to Buddhism as adults to further their political careers (Manor 1989, De Silva and Wriggins 1994). Later in life, the same Jayewardene, first as UNP leader, and later as president, executed a far grander version of Donoughmore Buddhism. That is, in order to gain the authenticity and credentials needed to win power, the UNP demonstratively sought to display its Sinhala Buddhist credentials. It did so by co-opting large numbers of the *Sangha* and embarking on grandiose religio-cultural projects (Kemper 1990, Abeysekara 2002). Sarath Amunugama describes what the UNP did to overcome the legacy of their defeat by Sinhala nationalists in 1956:

> The UNP, emulating the SLFP, proclaimed that they would create a 'Dharmista' (Righteous) society, a phrase resonant with Buddhist hopes. Bhikku organisations were established by the UNP in every Sinhala electorate, thereby neutralising the SLFP's advantage (Amunugama 1991: 125).

The UNP governments of the market reform period consequently became known for their extravagant patronage of the Buddhist religion, for commissioning numerous high profile public works and development projects that had a specifically Sinhala nationalist appeal, for patronising (and thus to some extent compromising) numerous senior Buddhist monks, and through their highly visible sponsorship of religious rituals of state that recalled the glories of the Sinhala past. Jayewardene sought to co-opt core rhetorical and symbolic elements of Sinhala nationalism and its language of moral righteousness in order to mask and compensate for the public illegitimacy of his pro-business economic programme.

Thirdly, Jayewardene's approach to market reforms involved an offsetting strategy of public expenditure – that is, compensating for the dismantling of some parts of the social democratic state by preserving and expanding other parts of it. In effect, the UNP bought support for the market reform programme by implementing massive rural development schemes along highly compressed deadlines, expanding the scale, depth and sheer concentration of state patronage down into the village as never before, much of it funded by a massive foreign aid extravaganza. Indeed, all the talk of socialism, and of empowering the common man, was not as absurd or outrageous a deception as it appeared. Alongside the deregulation of the private sector and liberalisation of trade, the government expanded the size of the government budget and the public sector to an extent never seen before.

Consequently, many who study economic reforms in Sri Lanka are struck (in some cases appalled) by the fact that the size of the state actually increased significantly under reforms. In Sri Lanka, the size of the public sector increased by 20% in the first five years of market reforms, as the budget deficit reached 18% of GDP. Stern (1984) finds that half of the increase in employment during the post-liberalisation period was due to this massive expansion in aid-funded public sector investment projects.

Table 4.1 | Sri Lanka, Public Sector Employment, 1977–83

Year	Total PS
1977	1,039,500
1978	1,127,119
1979	1,219,222
1980	1,245,208
1981	1,259,674
1982	1,268,046
1983	1,275,189

Source: CBSL Annual Report (various years).

One of the most high-profile of these offsetting schemes was a massive public housing project called the Hundred Thousand Houses Project (HTHP), sponsored by the prime minister and minister of housing, Ranasinghe Premadasa. Upon completion, the success of the HTHP led to a ten-fold follow-up project in 1985 called the Million Houses Project (Sirivardana 1986,

Robson 1983). James Brow describes the opening of one of these housing projects in Anuradhapura district:

> Celebration of the national past, and recital of the exemplary lessons it contained, were prominent features of the ceremony. The official speeches recalled that the splendid civilisation of the Anuradhapura kingdom was sustained by devotion to Buddhism, and emphasised that prosperity could again be achieved if the people, assisted by government projects like the village Awakening programme, were to acquire the habits of self-reliance, mutual co-operation and virtuous living that their ancestors had displayed. In this connection much was made of the discovery within the village of a rock inscription, dating from the first century A.D., that recorded the dedication of a local tank to the upkeep of Buddhist monks (Brow 1990a: 131).

Premadasa wove the housing project within a new and innovative scheme for rural development called *Gam Udawa* or Village-Awakening. Each year, one site in the country would be picked – typically an impoverished, lower-caste village – for a concentrated plan of accelerated development, including housing, infrastructure, construction of new schools and public buildings, and employment generation, which would then be ceremonially unveiled, after a massive week-long exhibition, on 23rd June, Premadasa's birthday.

Figure 4.2 | Map of Gam Udawa Sites, 1979–93

Year	Location
1979	Yapahuwa
1980	Ampara
1981	Tissamaharama
1982	Dambulla
1983	Nikaweratiya
1984	Anuradhapura
1985	Hingurakgoda
1986	Embilipitiya
1987	Kataragama
1988	Anamaduwa
1989	Mahiyangana
1990	Pallekele
1991	Kamburupitiya
1992	Buttala
1993	Mihintale

Source: Compiled from CDN (various years). Thanks to Nigel James of the Bodleian Library for help with map design.

The 1990 *Gam Udawa*, for example, was held in a village near Kandy. According to the official tally, it involved 425 million rupees in expenditure including new houses to 10,899 families, 21 're-awakened' villages, water supply schemes, 150 tube wells, electricity schemes, new rural roads, bridges, improvements of local bridges, temples, churches and mosques, administration buildings, urban market construction, direct employment for 10,000 people, and youth skills training. An exhibition site of 85 acres was prepared for the opening in June 1990, with a model village, and a massive fair-ground with mini models of important monuments in Colombo such as Town Hall, Independence Square, and the residences of the president and prime minister. There was a Gallery of Past Kings, an amusement park, an exhibit of the Mahaweli project, and a mini-science park.[7]

One of the most emblematic ways in which the UNP's new market reform strategy was formulated was in the Accelerated Mahaweli Development Programme (AMDP), a massive $2 billion irrigation and hydro-electric power scheme which was Sri Lanka's biggest ever development project. Originally conceived in the 1960s as a grand project covering 39% of the total island, and phased over 30 years, the project was radically compressed by the new UNP government down to an incredible six years. The revised AMDP project involved the construction of six reservoirs, five hydro-electric power plants, and the irrigation of about 112,000 hectares of land.

Despite the fact that the narrow time-frame had adverse repercussions for the economic and environmental feasibility of the project, donors such as the World Bank and Britain nevertheless came forward to fund it. This became a controversial issue within the World Bank where reports noted that it occurred 'before the full engineering and economic studies usually required were available,' (World Bank 1986:28) and also because the project was subsequently evaluated as a failure. A 2004 review of one of the largest of the World Bank's six Mahaweli loans downgraded the project outcome rating from 'unsatisfactory' to 'highly unsatisfactory', describing how the development effectiveness of the scheme was 'extremely limited', and how the incomes of resettled farmers have declined over time, with mean incomes now below the poverty level (World Bank 2004: 19).

Nevertheless, the AMDP did generate important economic and non-economic returns for the government at the time. In political terms, the unprecedented extent of the project created vast new opportunities for

---

[7] CDN, various issues 20 June 1990 – 28 June 1990.

patronage distribution and electoral consolidation at a variety of different levels. It also served the UNP's ideological agenda, as it had immense cultural significance for the Sinhala Buddhist imagination as a project to revitalise and repopulate this ancient territory of Sinhalese civilisation. In his speeches and writings, the ambitious young minister in charge of the project, Gamini Dissanayake infused the Mahaweli project with the geographic, historical, and religious imagery of Sinhala nationalism; such that it was never just a development project, but a vast enterprise in the accumulation of symbolic capital for the government. The pioneering ethnographic work of Serena Tennekoon describes how the government ceremonially inaugurated each of the AMDP's dams and resettlement colonies with elaborate *jala pujas*, high profile Buddhist ceremonial rituals, and water prayers: events in which the nation's traditional past and its developed future were symbolically brought together (Tennekoon 1988).

Indeed, even the World Bank's review of the AMDP in the mid-1980s recognised that, while this mammoth development project – which they had financed heavily – was a failure on its own account, its real value lay elsewhere:

> A more important argument was the importance of Mahaweli to the fundamental shift in strategy which the Government was planning. We have already referred to the need seen by the Government, and recognised by the Bank, for an alternative vision of the future of the Sri Lankan economy. If there were to be some tampering with a central aspect of the welfare state (subsidised rice), there had to be an alternative program which caught the imagination of the people. The accelerated Mahaweli was the centrepiece of that alternative vision. In the Government's political judgment, if the Bank wanted to provide effective support to the radical policy change, it needed to support the Mahaweli (World Bank 1986: 29).

A decade later, Jayewardene's successor Premadasa would inaugurate a new second generation of market reforms in 1989–93 period, under a similarly dizzying panoply of high-profile and in this case, quite innovative rural development and poverty alleviation schemes. It was a period in which the garment industry expanded vigorously, and indeed, entrepreneurs and the private sector view the Premadasa period as the golden age in terms of the government responsiveness to their needs; and it was a period of strong economic growth (Dunham and Kelegama 1997). Dunham and Jayasuriya (2001: 8–9) characterise the Premadasa period as similar to Indonesia under Suharto: 'corrupt and dictatorial, but efficient and good for economic growth'

(Stokke 1997). At the same time, Premadasa raised the level of public displays of Buddhist religiosity, and the extravagance of state patronage of religion to unprecedented, 'frantic' heights (Van der Horst 1995: 131). As Janaka Biyanwila describes it, 'In promoting the interests of capital, the Premadasa regime merged ethno-nationalism with a popular religiosity, while enhancing the religiosity of the state' (Biyanwila 2003: 256).

In summary, the strategic politics of market reform in Sri Lanka emerged in the course of the historically path-dependent process by which the traditional party of cosmopolitan business elites struggled to find ways to become re-electable and to win consent for its policies from an electorate that had become hostile to it on economic and cultural grounds. The 17 years of UNP rule from 1977 to 1994 is remembered by posterity for the institutional decay it presided over: for its authoritarian excess, the creation of a powerful executive presidency, the brutality with which it treated its opponents, the questionable referendum result of 1982, its role in the 1983 anti-Tamil pogrom, the extraordinarily violent suppression of the JVP rebellion, and the civilian atrocities that marked the early years of the civil war. But, all of this notwithstanding, the UNP did not rule by domination and violence alone.

The key element, and innovation of its governing strategy was to win consent for its market reform policies by cultivating religious patronage, promoting rural development, and funding a lavish patronage machine, all on an unprecedented scale. To the extent that consent was sought, and that nationalist ideology was involved in doing so, it is this period of Sri Lankan political history that comes closest to a Gramscian model of hegemony, although there are still important ways in which this fails to adequately frame the relationships at work. Through this complex of mechanisms, the UNP was, briefly, able to break out of the electoral confines that had kept it out of power, and that had forced it to depend on the ethnic and religious minority vote (Muslims, Catholics and Tamils). For a brief while in the late 1970s and 1980s, the UNP succeeded in winning a substantial part of the rural Sinhala Buddhist vote.

All this is not to say that the reform agenda sailed through smoothly under a shower of patronage spending and prayer mongering.[8] Even outside the north and east, where anti-government sentiment was palpable, the market reform programme and the government's authoritarianism was widely resented.

---

[8] Some of the discussion of the UNP's relationship to the Buddhist orders in the post-liberalisation period draws upon three very original studies that explore this issue in great detail – see Abeysekara (2002), Van der Horst (1995), and Kemper (1990).

Leading Sinhalese literary and cultural personalities such as Ediriweera Sarachchandra and Gunadasa Amarasekera challenged the 'open economy' society as immoral, inhumane, and contrary to the Sinhala Buddhist ideals of righteousness that they were purportedly based on. The rise of an influential new Sinhala nationalist intellectual current in the early 1980s known as *Jathika Chinthanaya*, or 'national consciousness' are also critical in understanding the way in which opposition to market reforms and the preservation of the social-democratic state became articulated through the ethical and moral idiom of Sinhala nationalism. As Gunadasa Amarasekera, one of the founders of the *Jathika Chinthanaya* school explained:

> Buddhism has a socialist ethic. It condemns the two extremes of self-mortification ... and is against capitalist ethics and against sensual excess (hedonism) ...When JR [Jayewardene] tried to introduce a capitalist ethic, we were against it culturally. [9]

Indeed, the government's attempts to press Buddhism in the service of the 'open economy' began to falter by the early 1980s, as ideologically oriented Buddhist monks struck back, finding justification for their opposition to the 'open economy' within the Buddhist canon. Ananda Abeysekera describes how the relationship between J.R. Jayewardene and the Buddhist clergy deteriorated steadily through the 1977–87 period, as he sought to restrict their political influence and activism (Abeysekara 2002). Tambiah describes how a number of influential Buddhist monks such as Maduluwawe Sobitha, Palipane Chandananda, and Murutettuwe Ananda, who had been co-opted into supporting the UNP in the 1970s had, by the 1980s, become its most vigorous public critics (Tambiah 1992: 83–108). As such, a powerful moral source of opposition to the reform agenda was being articulated through the very Sinhala nationalist framework that the UNP had sought to appropriate and dominate. The elevated presence of Sinhala nationalism, both in their own rhetoric, and in that of their growing number of opponents had, by the 1983–84 period, effectively trapped the government within a defensive battle to preserve its moral standing, so that they increasingly struggled to time the launching of new initiatives such that they would be least problematic.

The role of the ethnic conflict, and later, the civil war can be situated within this desperate, defensive compulsion of the UNP to retain control of the mantle of Sinhala nationalism, and to starve its opponents of this potent

---

[9] Interview, Gunadasa Amarasekera, Colombo, 7 April 2007.

source of political oxygen. A government vigorously pursuing the war, rather than negotiations, became unassailable as the champion of Sinhalese interests, and was able to shield its economic agenda, however unpopular, under the umbrella of patriotism. Opposition to a war-time government, especially economic opposition by trade unions, was easily dismissed at such a time as unpatriotic, and brushed aside with the heavy hand of authoritarian violence and emergency regulations.

One important corollary of the prerogative of preserving legitimacy and remaining more Sinhalese than the opposition, is that it constrained market-reforming governments from taking any meaningful steps to resolve the conflict by compromising with Tamil nationalist demands. Having already risked substantial political capital on the reforms, such governments have already placed themselves on the defensive and have been reluctant to further jeopardise their stability by opening themselves up to attack as complicit in the division of the nation. Besides, having positioned themselves as authentic Sinhala nationalists, and having unleashed and encouraged chauvinism among their rank and file, it was becoming impossible to push the Sinhala nationalist genie, which they had unleashed, back into its bottle. Having, for tactical reasons, inducted and promoted Tamil-baiters such as Cyril Mathew, the UNP found that consequent alienation and radicalisation of Tamil opinion was a factor in destabilising the country. That is, it became counterproductive to their own material interests.

Conscious of the party's vulnerability to an economically-inspired political backlash articulated through the vocabulary of nationalism, Jayewardene was, throughout the 1981–86 period, forced to be hesitant and reluctant in offering any concessions on the ethnic conflict to the moderate parliamentary Tamil leadership of the TULF. Any hint of granting concessions to the TULF was sure to energise nationalist opinion, not just in the narrow sense, but because it would also ignite the latent anti-reform, anti-capitalist, anti-elite, sentiment contained within Sinhala nationalism, and would revive the economic opposition, which the government had hitherto successfully dispersed, beaten, and bribed into submission.

As a result, Jayewardene refused to take the relatively modest steps required at that early stage in the conflict to resolve the ethnic crisis, even though such a solution would have been in the interests of the UNP and their economic programme. Instead, the festering ethnic conflict became incorporated at a tactical level into the everyday politics of survival for a government that was deeply defensive of its ethnic authenticity, and that had demonstrated political commitment and spent serious political capital only on the issue of economic reform.

When, in July 1984, Indira Gandhi urged Jayewardene to consider a more meaningful political response to the TULF (ironically perhaps, considering that it was three weeks after she had ordered Operation Bluestar), he confessed that it would be impossible to sell such a package to the Sinhalese people: 'We will lose our entire base. We will lose everybody,' he told her grimly.[10] Indeed, the UNP government, and their economic agenda remained internally stable and domestically viable as long as they prosecuted the war in military terms and maintained an unbending obstinacy against concessions to the Tamils. Having slid into civil war partly as a result of a re-orientation towards Sinhala nationalism, the UNP found that any backtracking on this agenda would imperil the stability of its government and all it had achieved.

To this end, Jayewardene's strategy, as manifest through the tortuous All Parties Conference (APC) exercise that he dragged out from January to December 1984, was in fact not to negotiate with the TULF at all, for this could force him to make concessions that would be politically damaging. Instead, he schemed to discredit the TULF, and postpone a political settlement to the extent possible. This, in turn, elevated the Tamil militant groups (a counterpart who he could legitimately refuse to deal with), to a position of leadership in Tamil politics. When the APC eventually produced a series of modest devolution proposals in December 1984, they were immediately condemned and opposed by the Buddhist prelates. Within a week, Jayewardene himself hastily backtracked and abandoned his own proposals, which he had nurtured and developed over a full year.

Indeed, when Jayewardene was eventually, under extreme external pressure, forced to sign up to the political solution contained in the Indo-Sri Lanka Accord of July 1987, it did what he had feared all along: it triggered an almost fatal destabilisation of the Sri Lankan state. The controversial provisions of the Accord allowed for the creation of devolved units of power at the provincial level (within a united Sri Lanka), and the temporary merger of the northern and eastern provinces (Bose 2002). In addition, the implementation of the Accord in the north and east was to be supervised by the induction of thousands of Indian soldiers. Predictably, this united Sinhala nationalists in furious, massive opposition, and in doing so, it also gave expression to the deep hostility to

---

[10] T.Sabaratnam (2003), *Prabhakaran*, chapter 19, http://www.sangam.org/Sabaratnam/index.htm.

the economic reforms which had thus far remained submerged, suppressed, and scattered.

In anticipation of the Accord, a powerful umbrella organisation of monks, nationalist opposition parties (SLFP, MEP and JVP) and lay Buddhist associations sprang up in mid-1986 called the *Maubeema Surakeema Vyaparaya* (MSV), the Movement for Safeguarding the Motherland (Matthews 1988). The MSV's growing campaign of opposition to the Accord had by the end of 1987 become overshadowed by the increasingly radical and violent methods of one of its most extreme constituents, the Janatha Vimukthi Peramuna (JVP). Fuelled by a hybrid Sinhala nationalist – Marxist ideology, and with a social base among educated, under-privileged youth in university campuses and schools, the JVP's opposition to the Accord escalated to an underground guerrilla-style insurrection that paralysed the government for more than two years.

As Sarath Amunugama describes:

> What was more significant for the monks however were the consequences of the UNP's 'free market' economy. Though the state sector continued to be the dominant component of the economy, the UNP managed to liberalise the manufacturing and trade sectors leading to an influx of foreign goods and the creation of wealth and employment. This also meant, however, an increase in inequality in the distribution of income. Traditional positions were downgraded while the 'mudalali' (trader) ethos was on the ascendant. It also meant that monks, intellectuals, artists, etc. who as custodians of traditional culture depended on state patronage, would be challenged by creators of new, more market oriented cultural products. Consumerism was a challenge to the 'modest life style' (alpecca) that Buddhism prescribed (Amunugama 1991: 125-126).

In relative terms then, the situation that the UNP faced in 1987, as a market-reforming government that sought to implement the Accord and offer substantial concessions to resolve the ethnic conflict, proved to be untenable. It placed the party back in the cross-hairs of unpopularity along both the main axes that have animated Sri Lankan electoral politics since 1956. As happened in 1956, and would happen later again in the 2002–2004 period, the UNP had once again occupied the position of being a party that was vulnerable both for promoting a counter-egalitarian, pro-capitalist economic agenda, and also on grounds of having betrayed the interests of the Sinhala Buddhist majority.

The extremely violent insurgency of the JVP between 1987–89, which at its peak threatened to consume the state, emerged from a massive pent-up outpouring of popular opposition to the UNP government (Chandraprema 1991, Gunasekara 1998, Gunaratna 1990). It was an opposition that was triggered, articulated, and animated by widely held nationalist concerns. But within it was also embedded a deep-seated economic opposition to the decade-long reform programme, which had long been overwhelmed and smothered into silence by the UNP's electoral manipulation, violent suppression, and religious demagoguery.

Conclusions

This chapter has revisited the historical experience of the 1977–93 period to advance a more generalised proposition on the relationship between economic reform and conflict: that a government intent on pursuing market reforms is in an inherently weak position to implement a political settlement on the ethnic conflict. In trying to advance these two equally controversial agendas in parallel, the underlying unpopularity and illegitimacy of the reform programme compounded and magnified the growing public suspicion in the south of the peace process. In the Sri Lankan context, it had, in 1987, recreated political competition along the same axes of polarity that had caused the dramatic defeat of the UNP in 1956. At that date, the UNP's defeat was blamed largely on the personality of the then prime minister, Sir John Kotelawala, and on his poor grasp of political timing, public comportment, and popular sensibility. But the fact that such a debacle was repeated three decades later, when the UNP was under the command of an exceptionally shrewd and Machiavellian political leader suggests that there are issues of structural significance beyond personality, style and tactics which need to be given greater consideration.

The proposition on the incompatibility of market reforms with ethnic settlement advanced here is of course, subject to limitations and exceptions which should be readily conceded. The possibilities for implementing an ethnic settlement and placating the TULF were arguably far greater in the early years of the Jayewardene period, when the District Development Council system was established (Matthews 1982). The immediate post-JVP insurgency period of 1990–91 was also arguably such a window of opportunity due to the totalising political, military, and ideological authority that Premadasa commanded. Similarly, the Chandrika Kumaratunga government, which incorporated elements on all sides of the spectrum on virtually every contentious issue – held the possibility that extreme elements might be marginalised or neutralise each other. The government of Mahinda Rajapaksa in the 2009–14 period had strong Sinhala nationalist credentials and has suspended most market reforms – and was thus extraordinarily well-placed to implement significant concessions to resolve the ethnic conflict, which it plainly refused to.

In the course of developing this argument, this chapter has examined the issue of how the strategic politics of Sri Lanka's market-reform agenda came to be connected to the escalation of the ethnic conflict during the 1980s. This involved the establishment of a more authoritarian political structure, an exaggerated performance of Sinhala nationalism, and off-setting government programmes to compensate for the compression of the state. That is, market reforms were viable only if they were accompanied by massive development projects such the Mahaweli, high-profile poverty alleviation schemes such as *Janasaviya*, or other ways in which the negative economic consequences of the reforms could (at least in image if not reality) be compensated by other schemes that would mitigate its effects. As a result, market reforms in practice survived because they resulted in an expansion, rather than a reduction in the size of the state; an expansion rather than a reduction in the Sinhalisation of the state.

5 | Military Fiscalism

'We live because of our son who is in the army' (cited in Lindberg 2012: 69)

In the early 1970s, a controversial study by the economist Emile Benoit made the unusual and counter-intuitive finding that there was a positive, causal correlation between military expenditures and economic growth in poorer countries.[1] Military spending, Benoit concluded, had a Keynesian fiscal effect on aggregate demand, generating positive multiplier effects. It created beneficial externalities for the civilian economy by

> feeding, clothing, and housing a number of people who would otherwise have to be fed, housed, and clothed by the civilian economy-and sometimes doing so, especially in LDCs, in ways that involve sharply raising their nutritional and other consumption standards and expectations (Benoit 1978: 277).

Benoit's findings provoked a series of critical rejoinders in the coming years, in which the empirical validity of the results and their theoretical foundations were subject to vigorous challenge (Ball 1983, Faini et al 1984, Deger 1986). At about the same time, Paul Sweezy and Paul Baran's classic work on monopoly capital also saw a positive correlation between military spending and economic growth, although this argument primarily applied to mature capitalist economies. One of the key links posited by Sweezy and Baran is that millions of jobs are generated by military expenditure, and this, in turn, absorbs the reserve army of labour:

> Some six or seven million workers, more than 9 per cent of the labor force, are now dependent for jobs on the arms budget. If military spending were reduced once again to pre-Second World War proportions, the nation's economy would

---

[1] See Benoit (1973, 1978). Benoit's work has been contextualised and connected to the larger conclusions of cold-war era modernisation theory (Lucian Pye 1962), that view third world militaries as modernising institutions that promote stability.

return to a state of profound depression, characterised by unemployment rates of 15 per cent and up, such as prevailed during the 1930s (Baran and Sweezy 1966: 531).

This chapter deploys a modified version of what can be termed the 'military fiscalism' explanation used by Benoit, and Baran and Sweezy to the context of the relationship between economic development, political stability, and the civil war in Sri Lanka. In brief, it sets out an argument that the high levels of military expenditure associated with a prolonged civil war had a positive impact in addressing youth unemployment and rural poverty in some parts of the country. With growing inequalities and social tensions generated during the market reform period, military employment created the stabilising socio-political conditions within which the market reform-driven economic growth of the 1990s could unfold. The growing importance of military employment to the rural economy of the Sinhalese hinterland also helps explain why high levels of military expenditures and military employment were sustained well after the end of the war in 2009. In the post-war period, the now largely under-employed military forces became available for deployment in civilian tasks of governance, development projects, and policing. In the north and east, the military embarked on commercial enterprises including farming, construction, security, and tourism. This occurred not just in the formerly war-affected areas of the north and east, but also in the south, where urban renewal, and even sports were briefly placed under the purview of the defence ministry.

The term 'military fiscalism' features widely in the historical literature on state formation in early modern Europe, relating the growth of formal state institutions and domestic capital accumulation to the compulsion of funding increasingly expensive militaries (Tilly 1975). Military fiscalism also features in the history of state formation in South Asia, for example in the works of Chris Bayly (1988), Burton Stein (1985), David Washbrook (1988), and Douglas Peers (2007). As with the European experience, they describe how military imperatives forged the innovation of centralised bureaucracies dedicated to systematised revenue collection. In this chapter, 'military fiscalism' is used to describe a very different sequence of relationships, but one that nevertheless involves military expenditure and political stability as its basic building units.

Growth Amidst War

By the late 1990s, almost two decades of civil war in Sri Lanka had wrought a heavy economic cost: the physical destruction of economic infrastructure, lost production, foregone investment, the flight of human capital, and the diversion of vast resources to military purposes. Arunatilake et al (2001) quantified this as over a full year's worth of lost GDP. Another study quantified the cost of the war as a loss of between 2 and 3 percent of economic growth per year, implying that *ceteris paribus*, Sri Lanka's 2002 GDP of $900 per capita was half of what it would have been if there had been no war.[2] The northern and eastern parts of the island, in particular, suffered to a very disproportionate extent during these years, and came to have the lowest income levels, the highest poverty levels, and the worst provision of health and education in the island (Sarvananthan 2008). Indeed, due to the exclusion of the north and east from national accounts and most census statistics during long periods of the war, much of the cost of the war is not incorporated into and captured within national aggregate statistical data.

Nevertheless, despite the extent of economic destruction and missed opportunities, what is striking about Sri Lanka, particularly in comparison to other such countries, is the extent to which economic *normality* prevailed through the war years in most of the country. A comparative study of the economic and social consequences of civil war in seven countries finds that Sri Lanka is unique not just in having experienced economic growth amid war, but in economic growth rates that exceeded the pre-war period (Fitzgerald, Stewart and Wang 2001, O'Sullivan 2001). Compared to other conflict-ridden countries where war has caused the substantial destruction of the formal economy and resulted in negative growth rates, Sri Lanka stands out as a curious exception (Stewart and Fitzgerald 2001).

Indeed, the war years, and particularly the decade of the 1990s, were paradoxically a time of strong economic growth, continuing market reforms, and substantial structural transformation of the economy. During the first 15 years of war, between 1983 and 1998, real GDP growth averaged 4.6% annually while exports multiplied almost three-fold in real terms.[3] Throughout the war period, governments from different political parties continued to implement market reforms while promoting a successful export-driven industrialisation strategy. During the 1980s and 1990s, Sri Lanka developed a two billion dollar garment export industry virtually from scratch, ending a century of reliance on the tea crop.[4] Considering that this growth was partially offset

---

[2] CBSL (1998), *Annual Report* 1998, quoted in World Bank (2004), p.10.
[3] World Bank *World Development Indicators* 2001 CD ROM.
[4] UNCTAD *Handbook of Statistics 2000* CD ROM.

by war-related destruction (estimated at 2%–3% each year), it would appear that the underlying momentum of economic growth during the war period was actually quite spectacular. Similarly, the market reforms which began in 1977, also continued to unfold and expand through the war, proving resilient and even gaining in momentum through periods of economic, political and military crisis.

What accounts for this curious paradox of economic growth and policy reform amidst the destruction of civil war? Compared to other countries, where the disruptions of war caused major delays, reversals, and even the complete abandonment of the market reform process, Sri Lanka appears unique – even exceptional. Indeed, within mainstream development economics, where the quest for the sources of economic growth remains paramount, the Sri Lankan experience might even be seen as a triumph – as a useful example from which policy experiences of relevance to other conflict-ridden countries might be extracted on how economic growth and reform can be achieved despite war. Instead, in this and subsequent chapters, the paradox of growth/ reform amidst war forms the point of departure to formulate a different set of research questions on the relationship between development and conflict. Importantly, this does not start off with the casual assumption that growth and reform took place *despite* war, but suggests that to some level, it occurred *because* of the war.

The simplest and most intuitive explanation for this paradox of economic growth amidst war in Sri Lanka is in terms of the physical separation of the dynamics of the two processes. In geographical terms, the locus of destruction in the north and east was clearly segregated from that of economic growth in the south. Although the south has been quite seriously affected by the war through suicide bomb explosions, the constant stream of casualties from the front, and the militarisation of daily life (De Mel 2007), it bears little comparison to the scale, intensity and duration of human suffering and economic dislocation in the north and east. The war compounded the pre-existing economic marginality and backwardness of this area, which had long before been neglected, remote, and impoverished, characterised by an arid, austere, agricultural economy. Indeed, the difference between the two parts had for long been so stark that a journey from the rest of 'normal' Sri Lanka, past Anuradhapura, to the north or Polonnaruwa to the east during these years, not only gave one the appearance of entering an entirely different space with a different language, culture, and topography, but of travelling a few decades back in time to an age of innocence without cars, telephones, paved roads or electrical appliances.

As a result of the fact that the war was confined within the bounds of the economically peripheral north and east at a time of rapid economic growth in the south, it became not just more impoverished in absolute and relative terms, but ever more economically disconnected and irrelevant to the island's economic development as a whole. Consequently, the pre-existing differences between the two parts were magnified by a growing economic rift. The simple answer to the paradox then, is that Sri Lanka experienced economic growth amidst war because the war was confined to the economically peripheral north and east, while the more prosperous south, centre, and west, with the tea plantations, export-processing zones and tourist resorts remained insulated from its direct effects, and enjoyed a large measure of political and economic normality.

There is, however, much that remains unexplained and under-explained by viewing this problem in terms of the segregation of these two processes. In reality, development and destruction were never entirely separated as such, but have developed forms of interaction and inter-dependence. The much-vaunted economic prosperity of the south was in reality, very geographically imbalanced, such that large parts of the rural hinterland, further away from Colombo, had little to show for it, and many areas were only marginally better off than the war-torn districts of the north or east that they border. For the most part, it was the Western province that enjoyed the benefits of growth, expanding its share of national GDP from 40.2% to 49.4%, between 1990 and 2000.[5] The very skewed and unequal nature of the prosperity generated in the 1990s is also evident in terms of the negligible impact it had on the poverty headcount in that period. Partly as a consequence of this imbalance, large parts of the south were not insulated from the war at all, but instead found themselves drawn into it and even became dependent upon it in a variety of ways.

The 'separate spheres' paradigm explains the sources of Sri Lanka's war-time growth by viewing the north and the south as disconnected spaces, and by categorising growth and conflict as analytically discrete, distinct phenomena belonging to separate, self-contained domains of policy formulation and implementation. Instead, there are grounds to consider that the civil war in the north and market-reform-driven economic growth in the south have actually co-evolved, finding sustenance in each other. Economic development and ethnic conflict became connected in a variety of unexpected ways that went beyond the received wisdom that conflict retards development, and that under-development causes conflict.

---

[5] CBSL Annual Report (various).

The previous chapter advanced one such unusual pathway in the course of arguing against a deterministic understanding of the role of economic reforms in fuelling ethnic conflict. In brief, the argument was that the prerogative of winning consent for the market-reform agenda contributed towards the catalysis of the civil war. In seeking to compensate for the sources of their electoral failures in the past, the UNP governments of the post-1977 period sought to pre-empt the opposition by seizing the mantle of Sinhala nationalism and social justice. As a result, the prosecution of the reform agenda effectively created the conditions that shrivelled the political possibilities for compromise on the ethnic conflict. The underlying factor that this pointed towards was that market reform and the resolution of the ethnic conflict were both controversial and, to some extent, mutually complementary projects of state reform.

Many of the underlying problems of the ethnic conflict were caused in terms of the way in which the social democratic state had been constructed under the development enterprise of the 1940s–70s in response to the pressures of Sinhala nationalism, demographic change, and the prerogatives of preserving the peasantry. As a consequence, the politics of market reform revolved around two mechanisms – ideological and material. In ideological terms, the market reforming UNP affected an exaggerated performance of Sinhala Buddhist authenticity. In material terms, they compensated for the withdrawal of the state in some spheres by its expansion in others. This chapter extends the analysis of the war-time expansion of the state by looking at the effects of the escalating military budget and the vast expansion in military employment during the war.

By the second decade of war in the mid-1990s, the expansion of the military campaign against the LTTE had led to steady increases in the size of the military, so that the army had become the single largest employer in the country. Growing military employment offset the reduction in employment in the civilian wings of the state, mitigated the growing inequalities of this period, and served as an important poverty alleviation mechanism in a weak rural economy – although this relates overwhelmingly to the Sinhalese rural poor. Military employment helped to significantly bridge the structural unemployment gap for school-educated rural youth that had been an endemic feature of the Sri Lankan economy since the 1950s, and that remained a fertile source of political discontent and radical political campaigns. It helps to explain the continuing high levels of military expenditure in the post-war period. Evidence for the nature and effects of military fiscalism are provided in terms of statistics on the size of the military, fiscal data on military expenditures, and household level data on employment.

Before proceeding, there are several important qualifications and issues of relevance to note. Firstly, the relationship between political stability, economic growth and war outlined here is a functional, not a causal relationship. Although instability in the north helped to sustain stability in the south, this relationship holds only in the sense of a static equilibrium, and it does not explain the evolution of the conflict, or how this paradox came into being. The spirit of the functional relationship between conflict and stability outlined here draws upon the similar way that James Ferguson's ethnography of foreign aid in Lesotho frames the impact of development on the bureaucratisation of state power (Ferguson 1994). Ferguson searches for instrumentality behind the veil of disorder and dysfunction to ask what agendas are served and upheld by the persistent condition of failure (Foucault 1979).

In much the same spirit, the argument developed in this chapter seeks to go beyond the rhetoric of failure and dysfunctionality that pervades the literature on the development implications of the conflict in Sri Lanka. In contrast to the idea that it was a source of development failure, one should instead ask what functions did the war serve? What interests does it serve to uphold? What kinds of less visible transformations has it given rise to? [6]

In framing the relationship in this manner, there is an important qualification to bear in mind: by looking for instrumentality within disorder, there is no suggestion here that disorder is the handiwork of those that benefit from it. As Ferguson describes:

> If unintended effects of a project end up having political uses, even seeming to be 'instruments' of some larger political deployment, this is not any kind of conspiracy; it really does just happen to be the way things work out (Ferguson 1994: 255–256).

Similarly, the functional role that the conflict played in promoting the reform agenda was not the result of a conscious conspiracy hatched by far-sighted manipulative elites. Sri Lanka's capitalist class and pro-reform elites did not invent and instigate the ethnic conflict in order to smuggle in their class agenda under a cloud of false consciousness. Indeed, as explained in Chapter 4, market reformist elites were arguably the segment of southern society who were least invested in the project of Sinhala nationalism, and least interested in the continuation of the civil war.

---

[6] This framing draws on the way David Keen (2006, 2008) has productively questioned the motivations behind violence.

Military Employment

Before proceeding to examine exactly what this signified, it is important to recapitulate the historical role of the public sector and welfare spending in its period of expansion (see chapter 3). The opening of free secondary education in 1944 and the expansion and vernacularisation of the social democratic state in the 1950s and 1960s had in this period, made it possible for tens of thousands of relatively poor families to escape rural adversity through free education. It was a time of unprecedented upward social mobility, although it is probable that the new opportunities for social advancement and inter-generational class mobility were disproportionately exploited by relatively more advantaged segments of rural society.

As the state grew rapidly in size from the mid-1950s onwards, the composition of white collar segments of the government service, down to and including clerks and typists, were gradually transformed from being disproportionately dominated by upper-caste Jaffna Tamils, Sinhalese Christians, and Burghers of urban, middle class, English-educated backgrounds, to vernacular-educated Sinhala Buddhists of rural backgrounds, in many cases, straight from the village. Between the late-1940s to the mid-1980s, it provided a significant portion of the rural population with a viable and realistic opportunity for upward mobility.

This dynamic had however, begun to change quite significantly by the 1990s, when the possibilities of escaping rural poverty through education and state employment became far more restricted than they had been for the previous two generations (Hettige 2000). As table 5.1 shows, the 1990s were a decade when the public sector share of total employment dropped from 21.5% to 13.4%. It reflected a growth in private sector jobs and stagnant numbers of absolute public sector employment. This latter, in turn, included an increasing military component.

The diminished opportunities for upward mobility that accompanied the shift from public to private employment are reflected in a number of different indicators, such as income inequality. As Osmani describes, 'there is clear evidence to suggest that post-reform growth has been of an exceedingly unequalising kind' (Osmani 1994: 294). Figure 5.1 shows how the income shares of the top 10% versus the bottom 50% declined steadily under welfarism from the 1950s to the mid-1970s. But following the introduction of the reforms in the late 1970s, inequality levels increased very sharply, undoing in one decade what had been achieved under welfarism over the previous three decades.[7]

Table 5.1 | Currently Employed Persons 1990–2001 by Employment Status (Percentage of Total Employed)

Year	Total Employed	% Public Sector	% Private Sector	% Employer	% Own Account	% Unpaid/ Family
1990	5.0 m	21.5%	33.7%	1.8%	29.2%	13.8%
1995	5.4 m	15.6%	44.3%	2.5%	28.3%	9.4%
2000	6.3 m	13.4%	42.9%	2.3%	28.4%	13.0%
2006	7.1 m	13.4%	42.1%	3.1%	30.8%	10.5%
2010	7.7 m	14.3%	41.2%	2.6%	31.5%	10.4%
2015	7.8 m	15.1%	41.0%	3.1%	32.3%	8.4%

Source: Labour Force Survey Annual reports (various).

Subsequent studies have shown that inequality continued to grow in the 1990s, fuelled by high rates of economic growth that were matched by very low rates in poverty reduction. The World Bank's 2004 development policy review of SL describes the following situation:

> Of particular concern is the fact that poverty reduction has been slow while income inequality has risen in recent years. At 22.7 percent, the national poverty headcount ratio remains high for a country with US$ 900 per capita GDP. Furthermore, the rate of decline in this ratio has been modest despite sustained per capita annual GDP growth of over 3 percent per year over the last two decades (World Bank 2004: i).

Similarly, the Government of Sri Lanka's Poverty Reduction Strategy Paper (PRSP) describes:

> ... a modest growth rate has been accompanied by little or no income redistribution. In other words, the benefits of economic growth have not automatically trickled down to the poor (GOSL 2003: part 2: 28).

---

[7] This pattern of a historic reduction in inequality during the post-war years, followed by a sudden increase in inequality from 1980 corresponds with similar findings over long-term inequality data in the US, UK, Canada and India. In particular, see the work of Ed Wolff on historical measures of inequality for the US, and Thomas Piketty who examines the income shares of the top 1% or 0.1%.

Figure 5.1 | Percentage of Total Income by Ranked Spending Unit

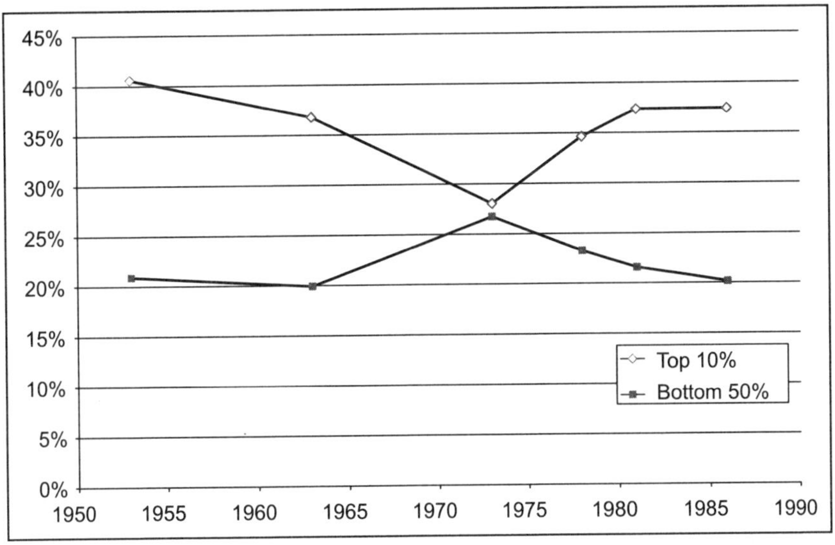

Source: Data drawn from World Bank (1995), table 1.1. (Percentage of total one month pre-tax income received by each decile of ranked spending units.)

Gunatilaka and Chotikapanich (2006) find that there was a steady increase in inequality between 1980 and 2002, but with a particularly sharp increase during the 1990–2002 period. Narayan and Yoshida (2005: Table 6) similarly find that, in these years, the mean real per capita consumption of the top quintile of the population increased by 50.4%, while that of the bottom quintile increased by just 2.2%. Per capita income increased in this period by a total of 45%, but it had a marginal impact on the poverty headcount, which went down just 3.4 points from 26.1% to 22.7%. This, too, was overwhelmingly concentrated in urban districts such that the poverty headcount was either the same or had increased in 9 of 17 districts during the 1990s (excluding the north and east).

The increase in economic inequality manifest in these data can be disaggregated further into regional and sectoral dynamics. For example, a very disproportionate share of the growth in this period was regionally concentrated in the Western province. There was also a significant sectoral imbalance in the growth, which came largely from the industrial and service sectors such as finance. In contrast, there is evidence of an unusually rapid decline in the agricultural economy, both in relative and absolute terms. In just the decade 1990–2001, the percentage of the workforce employed in agriculture had declined from 47% to 33%, while the contribution of agriculture to national GDP dropped from 26% to 20%.[8] This extent of decline in the agricultural economy was, in many ways, a return to the burgeoning crisis of the peasant sector that was first observed in the 1930s, and which the active developmentalist and welfarist policies of the 1940s–80s had partially reversed and delayed.

With the global decline in agricultural commodity prices over the 1980s and 1990s, peasant agriculture and particularly paddy farming had, according to the cost of cultivation statistics, been producing negative returns, even on a pure cash basis.[9] That is, many farmers, especially paddy farmers, were barely recouping their cash costs of production in terms of seed, fertiliser, insecticide, and hired labour, even without incorporating the imputed value and opportunity cost of unpaid family labour.

The economic growth of the 1980s and 1990s created a significant expansion in private sector employment, particularly in areas such as construction, garment factories, and tourism – and there was a historic reduction in the unemployment rate during the 1990s. But upon further scrutiny, the actual kinds of private sector employment created fall mostly into three categories. Firstly, there is the overwhelmingly female employment in garment factories (Lynch 2007, Hewamanne 2008). Secondly, there is the casual labour available in small, service-sector enterprises, which are the lowest paid, lowest status, most manually demanding jobs with the least security. Thirdly, there are white collar sales and clerical jobs in the formal private sector, which are typically dominated by people from urban, middle class origins. What stands out about these categories of private sector employment is that they offer very little for rural male Sinhalese youth; a segment of society that has historically depended on free public education and state employment for social mobility. This is also the segment of society that has formed the social base of two episodes of armed insurgency against the state in the 1970s and 1980s.

It is within these circumstances of greater economic inequality, an expanding rural-urban gap, and a serious decline of peasant agriculture that military employment came to occupy an important role in the Sinhalese village. Sri Lanka's military grew more than ten-fold, from 15,000 in 1982 (the year before the war started), to over 200,000 at the time of its conclusion in 2009.

---

[8] CBSL Annual Report, (various).
[9] Department of Agriculture (various).

Figure 5.2 | Sri Lanka, Numerical Strength of Security Forces, 1983–2013

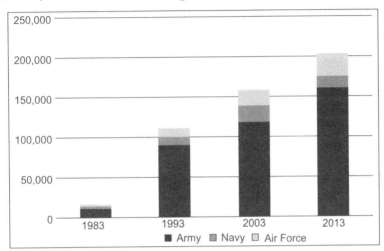

Source: IISS, The Military Balance (various). These figures do not include various the police or paramilitary organisations such as the Special Task Force or the Civil Security Force (formerly the Home Guards). Their combined strength at the end of the war is estimated to be 45,000.

Given that civilian public sector employment had shrunk in this period as a result of privatisation, the security sector had, by 1997, come to comprise one in five of all government jobs. In fiscal terms, the salaries of the armed forces had, as a proportion of the government's total wage-bill increased from 3% before the war, to 47% at its end.

Table 5.2 | Military Salaries as Percentage of Total Government Salaries

1979–82	1987–90	1995–98	2001–2005	2006–09	2010–14
3%	14%	39%	38%	41%	45%

Source: Calculations based on data from CBSL Annual Report (various).

Despite the burgeoning role of military employment in Sri Lanka, and the widespread anecdotal evidence of its increasing significance in the Sinhalese rural economy, there is little data published on the extent of military employment, and consequently very little analytical or policy discussion of its repercussions. For example, the Census of Public Sector and Semi Government Sector Employment excludes uniformed staff of the military altogether from their data; the Labour Force data captures only a fraction of the military. The available information on the significance of military employment in rural livelihoods emerges from a series of village-level studies (Korf 2004, Nigel 2009, Kulatunga and Lakshman 2013) of marginal Sinhalese villages. This chapter effectively expands the insights from those micro-level studies to a macro-context, using a large, nationally representative household survey data set of 7,500 households to examine if these same inferences can be made at a larger scale.

Sri Lanka Integrated Survey (SLIS) 1999/2000

The Sri Lanka Integrated Survey (SLIS), commissioned by the World Bank in 1999–2000 and executed by the Sri Lanka Business Development Centre contains data on 7,500 households surveyed in 500 distinct communities. These are geographically representative across Sri Lanka, with the exception of what were then described as 'uncleared areas', or LTTE-controlled parts of the north and east – largely in the districts of Killinochi, Mullaitivu, Mannar and Vavuniya, as well as pockets of Trincomalee and Batticaloa. The data obtained is, as a result, biased due to these omissions, although this is in reality not entirely relevant because these are overwhelmingly Tamil areas, and this chapter is primarily interested in employment patterns and alternatives among young Sinhalese. It can be reasonably assumed that there was negligible military employment from the omitted LTTE-occupied areas.

The SLIS data demonstrates that the structure of employment in 1999–2000 varied significantly by age, ethnicity, region, and education. Indeed, the data reveals rather unsurprisingly that military employment was concentrated amongst young Sinhala Buddhist males aged 18–30. Furthermore, it was very disproportionately drawn from the overwhelmingly rural areas of the outer periphery distant from the capital Colombo. That is, military employment is heaviest in areas such as Polonnaruwa, Anuradhapura, Kurunegala, Trincomalee, and Ampara. In terms of educational background, military employment is concentrated heavily on those who have completed secondary school, with 10–11 years of education, a category that accounts for almost half the total 18–25 age group.

There is also data to suggest that military recruitment is higher in predominantly agricultural districts, as there is a close correlation between districts with a high degree of military employment among males in the 18–30 age group, and those where the older male generation, aged 45–65, include a high proportion of farmers.

Table 5.3 | Ethnic Composition of Individual Occupational Categories for Males, 18–30

	Public Sector	*Military*	*Private Salaried*	*Casual Labour*	*Business*	*Farming*	*Total Employed*	*Count*
Sinhalese	63.2%	97.1%	61.2%	60.5%	63.9%	75.5%	65.5%	1,796
SL Tamil	20.3%	1.4%	23.0%	25.6%	13.0%	21.3%	21.6%	593
Ind Tamil	0.5%	0.0%	2.8%	3.0%	1.4%	1.6%	2.2%	59
Muslim	15.6%	1.4%	12.4%	10.1%	18.5%	2.1%	9.9%	270
Others	0.5%	0.0%	0.7%	0.8%	3.2%	0.0%	0.9%	26
Total	100%	100%	100%	100%	100%	100%	100%	2,744
Count	212	210	575	1,020	216	440	2,744	

Source: SLIS 1999/2000

On a national basis, the military only accounted for around 3% of all employment, but as table 5.4 shows, this figure increases substantially for younger Sinhala Buddhist males. For this group, military employment varied from a low of 7% of employment in the Western province (even here it was concentrated in the more rural Gampaha district and was negligible in urban Colombo) to a high of 23% in the Eastern province, where most of the Sinhalese population are second or third generation settlers in irrigation-based colonies such as Gal Oya or Kantale – and where as Korf (2004) and Nigel (2009) describe, they are likely to include a substantial number of Home Guards. In terms of education, military employment is concentrated among those that have completed secondary school, but have no further education – a large category that comprises almost 50% of the total 18–25 age group. Among young Sinhalese males of this group, which has high rates of unemployment, the military accounts for 17% of all employment, compared to only 5% in the civilian public sector.

Indeed, the contrast between employment in the military versus the civilian public sector is very stark for this demographic sub-category. In absolute terms, civilian public sector jobs far outnumber the military: there were by the late 1990s, about 900,000 civilians in the public sector, and about 100,000 in the security forces. But the data suggests that there is a very strong age barrier to civilian public sector jobs; for the 18–25 age group, the extent of civilian public service employment is marginal, and accounts for between 4% and 6% of occupations. Excluding self-employment (including self-employed farmers), the real employment alternatives to a life in the army are in casual labour, or for those living nearer the urban areas, private salaried jobs.

Table 5.4 | Occupational Breakdown for Employed Sinhala Buddhist Men, 18–30 by Province

	Public Sector	Military	Private Sector	Casual Labour	Business	Farming	(Count)
Western	9%	7%	39%	33%	9%	2%	356
Central	6%	11%	21%	40%	6%	15%	191
Southern	6%	6%	18%	47%	8%	14%	312
Eastern	19%	23%	3%	6%	4%	45%	112
North-West	7%	16%	14%	39%	10%	14%	184
North-Central	6%	19%	3%	26%	3%	40%	205
Uva	4%	13%	11%	19%	8%	46%	141
Sabaragamuva	<u>7%</u>	<u>12%</u>	<u>21%</u>	<u>35%</u>	<u>13%</u>	<u>12%</u>	<u>179</u>
Total	8%	12%	19%	34%	8%	19%	1,680
(Count)	128	200	326	562	133	324	1680

Source: SLIS 1999/2000

Thus, within the multiple dimensions of segmentation in Sri Lanka's labour market, the military had, by the late 1990s, come to dominate employment in a particular demographic category defined by age (18–30), gender (male), ethnicity (Sinhalese), region (the rural periphery) and education (secondary school). For this segment of the population (taking the districts of Ampara, Trincomalee, Polonnaruwa, Anuradhapura, and Moneragala), military employment became a necessity due to the absence of civilian alternatives in the private or public sector. Some 31% of the young men in this demographic category were unemployed, a figure that would have amounted to almost 43% if not for the abundant presence of military employment due to the war. For those that are in employment in these districts, it is extraordinary to note that the military accounted for just over half of all paid occupations (figure 5.3).

The only alternative to unemployment or the armed forces is the life of a casual labourer, a fate which most would seek to avoid to the extent possible, as it almost certainly implies a life of continued poverty. As Alex Argenti-Pillen describes in her research among families of Sinhalese soldiers, 'Most young soldiers in the national armed forces come from extremely poor backgrounds. Their parents and siblings survive by means of casual labour in the tea plantations or rice paddies' (Argenti-Pillen 2003: 2).

Figure 5.3 | Sources of Cash Employment for Sinhala Buddhist Men in the Outer Peripheral Districts, 18–30 with 10–11 Years Education, (Ampara, Trincomalee, Polonnaruwa, Anuradhapura and Moneragala, 114 obs.)

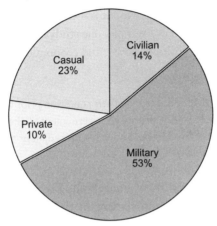

Source: SLIS 1999/2000.

Indeed, salary levels for military employment[10] are of a magnitude more than double what casual labourers would get, and almost double what salaried private sector jobs pay. The only category of employment with earnings that approximate the military are civilian government jobs, which account for a very small fraction of the available employment for this group. It is also important to bear in mind that private sector employment is concentrated in urban areas and the south-west, but it is quite absent in the rural periphery.

Table 5.5 | Average Salaries for Sinhalese Males, 18–26 (SL Rupees/Month)

	Public	*Military*	*Private*	*Casual*
Mean	4,656	6,761	4,275	2,998
Median	4,000	6,550	3,800	2,750
Count	38	118	183	313

Source: SLIS 1999/2000

Finally, and as a corollary to this, the data shows that overall household incomes for military families (which of course includes all other sources of

---

[10] The salary levels presented here are averages, and do not normalise for differences in the composition of educational qualification or rural/urban differentials.

income) are significantly higher than those of non-military families. This is corroborated by qualitative studies which suggest firstly that families with military personnel are drawn from very impoverished backgrounds, and secondly that military employment has enabled these households to lift themselves out of poverty. For example, one study describes how: 'a soldier in the family can bring recognition, power and economic security to people who have no social status':

> 'Poor' is how they generally describe their condition prior to their enlistment in the army. Most have not possessed a permanent shelter prior to joining the military, but have lived in mud houses with cadjan or tin roofs (Liyanage 2004: 28).

Indeed, 72% of the military households surveyed in this study had experienced a substantial improvement in their living standards, having either built or bought permanent houses. Unlike others in the village, military households had television sets, refrigerators, proper furnishings, access to clean water and electricity, and ate better food. One young farmer described the mobility effects of the military very clearly:

> Small scale agriculture is an income source which hardly allows us to manage with the bare necessities. This source of income can never foster a significant change in living patterns, or assist us to achieve our long-term objectives. … Significantly, families which have members enlisted in the military have achieved very prominent economic development (Liyanage 2004:29).

Kulatunga and Lakshman's study of livelihoods in Medawachchiya similarly describes 'higher levels of wealth and prosperity' among military households, and goes on to explain a number of economic and non-economic advantages beyond the higher salary (Kulatunga and Lakshman 2013: 614). Korf's research in a village in Trincomalee describes how 'state and military support provides about one third of the households with new income sources' (Korf 2014: 283).

These findings resonate closely with those of other qualitative surveys, such as Michele Gamburd's study of military employment in Naeaegama in the south-western coastal strip, and the Asian Development Bank 'Voices of the Poor' report (ADB 2001) from Moneragala and Hambantota – both of which find that the main reason cited for joining the army were the lack of other job opportunities and poverty (Gamburd 2004).

Conclusions

The macro- and micro-level statistical data summarised above demonstrate the extent to which military employment had come to occupy a very particular niche in the labour market in terms of education, ethnicity and regional background. The results in themselves are not remarkable, for they are in conformity with, and corroborate widely held perceptions and a considerable body of anecdotal evidence on the social characteristics of the Sri Lankan military forces. They help to substantiate the argument laid out earlier, that the civil war perversely became an important source of livelihood diversification, asset accumulation, and poverty alleviation for the rural Sinhalese population.

Under circumstances of a worsening agricultural economy, increasing rural-urban disparities, and the diminishing role of civilian state employment as a viable route for upward social mobility, military employment had, by the 1990s, come to occupy an important position in the economy of the Sinhalese village. Jonas Lindberg's study of rural livelihoods in Hambantota in 2007 describes this well:

> In the case of one poor household in the old village where the son had decided to join the army without the consent of his parents, the father admitted towards the end of the interview that his son's income was fundamental for the household economy: 'We live because of our son who is in the army. We made the bricks to build this house but the son in the army took care of the other expenses' (Lindberg 2012: 69–70).

With over 200,000 formal sector jobs, the military had by the end of the war become the country's single largest employer. More importantly, it was the most important source of employment among poor rural Sinhala Buddhist youth. By signing up a sizeable proportion of this demographic segment, the military also played a unique and largely unrecognised role in absorbing this reserve army of labour, and redirecting what has traditionally been a potent social constituency of rebellion and political unrest in the direction of a hierarchical, nationalistic, conservative form of socialisation.

As discussed earlier, the instrumentality and functional benefits of military employment for the market reform agenda does not equate to a conscious conspiracy designed by self-interested political or economic elites. As James Ferguson describes:

Whatever interests may be at work, and whatever they may think they are doing, they can only operate through a complex set of social and cultural structures so deeply embedded and so ill-perceived that the outcome may only be a baroque and unrecognisable transformation of the original intention (Ferguson 1990: 17).

In discussing the possible reasons why military expenditure might benefit economic growth, Emile Benoit speculated that militarisation had important positive spillover effects:

Military training may be peculiarly effective in promoting certain modernising attitudes and ways of life: in part because it has available the instruments of compulsion; in part because the value which justifies its activity national security-exercises a strong influence on most individual consciences and appears to justify imposing difficult and often painful adjustments on the individual. This process is facilitated by the fact that the military conscript is isolated from his family and community and living in an artificial community where he is under continuous government control (Benoit 1978: 278).

Indeed, the 'painful adjustment' he refers to describes not just to the transformation of the individual military recruit, but is an apt metaphor for what happened to Sri Lankan society and the economy as a whole, in an equally painful adjustment to the market under the shadow of civil war (De Mel 2007). Military employment, which escalated significantly in the 1990s, helped to cushion the impact of the market reform programme, in much the same way that the Mahaweli project did in the early 1980s; that is, by an offsetting logic through which the dismantling of the social democratic state, state employment, state patronage on the one hand, particularly through the vigorous privatisation programme of the Premadasa and Kumaratunga years, was balanced, offset, minimised and mitigated, through an expansion of the state, state employment, state patronage on the other. As figure 5.4 shows, the steady growth in the numbers of the security forces over 1983–2013 substantially compensated for the reduction in civilian public sector employment over these years.

There are, of course, as I have discussed at the beginning of this chapter, important limitations to be noted. The absence, and indeed, the impossibility of obtaining and testing valid counter-factuals to this proposition means that the functional relationship between war and market reforms remains tentative. Yet it bears scrutiny, and has explanatory power. For example, the idea of calibrating an analysis of the conflict against the politics of market reform can be fruitful in explaining the failure of the 2002 peace process (see chapters 6–8). Similarly, there are important grounds to cast doubt on the idea that the parallel processes of development/destruction, war/reform are not distinct spheres of analysis and policy formulation, but are in reality closely linked.

Figure 5.4 | Civilian and Military Components of Public Sector Employment, 1983–2013

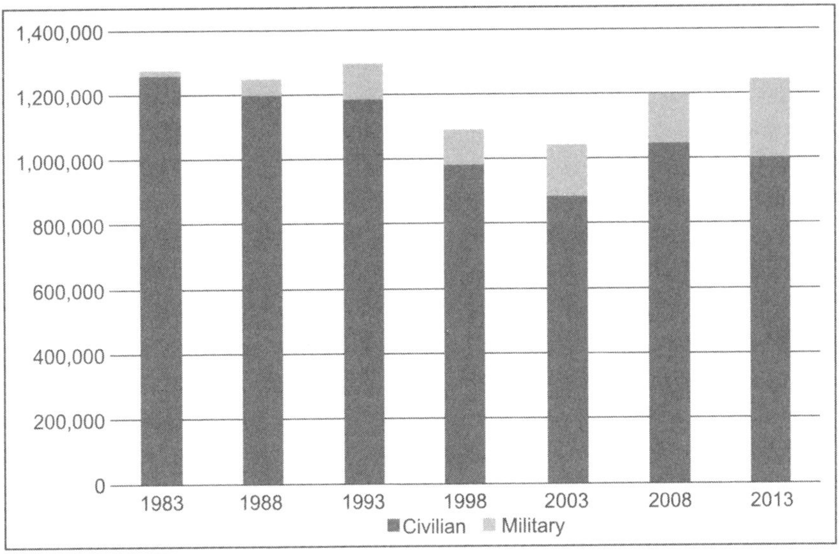

Source: CBSL Annual Report (various), and IISS Military Balance (various).

Militarisation remains an important phenomenon in post-war Sri Lanka, and there is a growing literature on the subject, much of which relates to the military presence in the north and east, the securitisation of development, and the militarisation of the state (International Crisis Group 2012, Anonymous 2013, Kadirgamar 2013, Satkunanathan 2015). Without necessarily contradicting any of those elements, the analysis presented in this book contributes a different kind of explanation that emerges from the socio-political role it plays in the Sinhalese south. This perspective provides a different way of understanding why the government has continued to maintain war-time levels of military recruitment and defence spending well past the end of the civil war, expanding its functions into tourism, farming, commercial ventures, and urban development. Charles Tilly famously described how 'war made the state, and the state made war' (Tilly 1975: 42). In much the same way, the Sri Lankan state came to have a symbiotic relationship with the war that it became embroiled in for so long. As the state made war, the war deeply insinuated itself into the fibre of the state, and into the way that state-society relations were structured. This holds true not just for the way that the state relates to minorities in the north and east, but also to the way it generates support, neutralises opposition, and preserves legitimacy with the majority community.

6 | The 'Best and Last' Chance for Peace

The Context

The Cease-Fire Agreement (CFA) of February 2002, and the peace process that followed, gave rise to unprecedented optimism that the long-standing civil war had finally come to an end (Saravanamuttu 2003, Balasingham 2004, Uyangoda and Perera 2002, Uyangoda 2002, Goodhand et al 2005). With strong public support, and with the strong diplomatic and financial support of the international community, the government of Sri Lanka and the Liberation Tigers of Tamil Eelam (LTTE) engaged in six rounds of direct negotiations, and had reached substantial agreement on critical conceptual issues. By late 2002, a final settlement of the conflict came clearly within sight as the Norwegian mediators announced that both parties had reached a 'paradigm shift' in their respective positions, and had agreed on the broad outlines of a future settlement:

> [T]he parties have agreed to explore a political solution founded on the principle of internal self-determination in areas of historical habitation of the Tamil-speaking peoples, based on a federal structure within a united Sri Lanka.[1]

The LTTE's chief negotiator, Anton Balasingham, announced that 'both the parties have made an unprecedented historic decision to work out a political formula for the solution of the protracted ethnic conflict.'[2] Chief government negotiatior, Professor G.L.Peiris, was equally optimistic, announcing: 'I think an interim solution can certainly be arrived at in a matter of months rather

---

[1] Statement issued by the Royal Norwegian Government at the conclusion of the third session of peace talks between the Government and the LTTE in Oslo, 5 December 2002.

[2] Tamilnet, 5 December 2002, 'LTTE–GOSL reach historic agreement'.

than years.'[3] By then, the cease-fire had already held for an entire year, the longest cessation of hostilities since 1983. There remained numerous irritants on the ground level, as well as some clear provocations, but nothing of a scale that could disturb the clear momentum of the peace process. The benefits of peace were so overwhelming and self-evident that it seemed irrational that either side would ever want to return to war. There was a warm relationship and considerable goodwill between the LTTE and government, epitomised by the reported bonhomie that developed between the two chief negotiators. On the ground level, the return to normality was characterised by widespread reconstruction, the return of refugees, the removal of military checkpoints, the de-mining of roads and farmlands, and a general atmosphere of optimism.

But within three years of the euphoric 'Oslo Declaration', the peace process had unravelled to the point of complete collapse, and both sides were clearly preparing for a renewed phase of war. It is not possible to pinpoint any one precise moment in time when the peace process came to a halt, or when the war started, for both actually co-existed with each other amidst much uncertainty for a considerable period of time over mid-2004 to mid-2006. With the benefit of hindsight, the elections of April 2004 appear to be the key turning point in this process, when the UNP-led government that had signed the CFA and negotiated with the LTTE lost power. Even though the war as such did not start until August 2006, there was in fact no further progress on the peace process from April 2004 onwards. Instead, there was a steady expansion in the number and scale of cease-fire violations.

What happened? Why, given the extent of its public support, the rational benefits of peace, and the unprecedented progress in the negotiations, did this 'best and last' chance for peace fail?[4] Among pessimists, ill-wishers, and partisan ideologues of all stripes, the collapse of the peace process was an occasion to enjoy the satisfaction of successful naysaying. The collapse of such a monumental and extended effort at peace resulted in a commensurate extent of recrimination within which the analysis of the causes of failure frequently took the form of the apportioning of blame. The prevailing climate of disappointment and exhaustion served to reinforce the prejudices and preconceptions of all parties: on the one side, that the LTTE was an unreformable fascistic terrorist group wedded to a cult of violence and incapable of embracing peaceful democratic political competition; or on the other, that

---

[3] CNN 'Insight' interview, 16 September, 2002.
[4] For a rigorous and exhaustive account of Norway's role, see Sørbø et al, 2011.

the Sri Lankan state remained in the iron grip of the 'Mahawamsa mindset'; of a deep and pervasive Sinhala Buddhist supremacist outlook, intrinsically incapable of offering even the most minor concessions to the Tamils.

For many on both sides, the failure of the heavily internationalised peace process reflected the failure of an abstract, composite 'international community' at various levels, and was occasion to find this amorphous entity culpable of a variety of crimes of commission and omission. Among Sinhala nationalist ideologues, the internationalisation of the process was strongly criticised as it constrained military action, and provided the LTTE with undeserved external legitimacy and recognition. Furthermore, they considered Norway's role as a mediator to be deeply flawed and entirely prejudiced in favour of the Tigers.[5] The LTTE's ideologues and supporters, on the other hand, viewed the international community's involvement in the conflict with suspicion as part of a strategy of containment and entrapment.[6] They further charged the failure of the peace process as at least partly the result of the failure of the international community to take a balanced approach to the two sides; unjustly punishing the LTTE with proscription as a terrorist group while failing to hold the Sri Lankan government to task for its transgressions. Most retrospective accounts of the failure of the peace process ultimately base their arguments on these key elements: that is, on the intrinsically unreformable or duplicitous nature of the two main participants, or on some institutional element of the organisation of the peace process itself: its internationalisation, the unbridgeable distance between the two sides, the sequencing of issues, the failure to build interim institutions, or the inadequacy of the confidence-building measures. There were also numerous explanations based entirely on idiosyncratic, happenstance or highly individualised factors: the long-standing personality clash behind the cohabitation crisis; the failure of the Mano–Malik talks; the mysterious death of Ven. Gangodawila Soma Thera, Ranil's naiveté, Chandrika's impetuosity, or Karuna's guile.

The literature on comparative conflict resolution similarly offers process-driven explanations based largely on the nature of the interactions and

---

[5] For example, in the pre-election agreement between the JVP and Mahinda Rajapaksa in November 2005, article 5 begins 'As it is axiomatic that Norway has shown unprecedented bias and partiality towards the LTTE....'.

[6] See for example, the 'Maaveerar Day' speeches of LTTE leader V. Prabhakaran, the writings of the late D. Sivaram 'Taraki', and the editorials of the Tamil Guardian, through the 2003–2006 period.

negotiations between the two parties. William Zartman, for example, asks 'why internal conflict is so obdurately resistant to negotiations,' and seeks 'to find ways to bring about successful negotiations' (Zartman 1995: 3). At times, this conflict-resolution model gets expanded to a three-player process, where the third is an independent mediator, typically the international community. Much of the conflict resolution literature is, in fact, authored with outside interveners very much in mind as protagonist, benefactor, and benevolent *deus ex machina*. For example, an authoritative study published in 2002 titled *Ending Civil Wars* starts with a classic statement of purpose:

> When antagonists in civil war sign a peace agreement, what can international actors do to prevent a recurrence of that war? This is a life or death question for millions of people (Stedman et al 2002:1).

Without digressing too far, the fundamental shortcoming of the mainstream conflict resolution approach in this case is that the rise and fall of the peace process cannot be understood solely with reference to the peace process itself. That is, it first needs to be situated within the broader historical ideo-political and socio-economic milieu into which it was born, and where it co-exists with a variety of other contending issues. Thus, an analysis of the peace process cannot be restricted to the actions and inactions of the two sides as stereotyped monoliths, but must explore the dynamics and compulsions that drove their internal decision-making process. Secondly, the international community cannot be viewed as an exogenous party, for in coming forward to offer what they viewed as critical support to the peace process, they consequently became drawn deeply into it, and became deeply complicit in its failure.

Taking the UNP-led coalition government's election defeat in April 2004 as the turning point in the peace process, the next three chapters address the question of why it happened. Why was the government that was voted in on an explicitly pro-peace mandate in December 2001, voted out of power just 27 months later? In addressing this issue, and in making sense of its surprising electoral verdict, there is also a need to unpack the nature of the peace process as envisaged and implemented. Where and how did the peace agenda originate? Does an understanding of its social and ideo-political parentage and its mode of delivery provide explanations for its quick failure?

The answer to this question begins by examining and contrasting the main political formations on either side of the peace process. On the one side, the United National Party (UNP) gave rise to the peace process upon its election in December 2001. On the other hand, the *Janatha Vimukthi Peramuna* (People's Liberation Front, or JVP), spearheaded the opposition to the peace process. The parallel paths of the UNP and JVP in this period take place not just with respect to the peace process, but also with respect to economic policy and market reform, on which they similarly stood on opposite ends of the spectrum. Both parties developed their respective positions on the peace process in the late 1990s, and came into frontal confrontation with one another during the 2002–06 period.

It should, of course, be clear at the outset that this cannot be a comprehensive or complete theory of the failure of the peace process, for it only looks at the internal dynamics of one of the two main parties, and its contribution to the overall failure. The war could conceivably have resumed even if the UNP government had survived the elections and remained in power after April 2004. For example, one of the most complex challenges in the peace process was the paradox of the LTTE's civilian transition. The LTTE was primarily a military organisation, and remained acutely aware of the fact that, as a non-state actor, its standing in the peace process was entirely predicated on its military accomplishments and on maintaining a credible offensive military threat. Yet, the ultimate success of the peace process required the LTTE to undertake a complex and comprehensive internal transformation from a military to political direction, entailing numerous attendant risks and highly unpredictable side-effects. Such a transformation might affect their hard-fought military strength, undermine their position at the peace talks, threaten the integrity of their organisation, and hence, unleash unpredictable consequences of serious detriment to the peace process.

One such entirely unpredicted dynamic which emerged during the peace process was an internal split within the LTTE along northern Tamil versus eastern Tamil lines. In March 2004, Karuna, one of the LTTE's most accomplished senior commanders, decamped with an estimated 2,000–4,000 cadres, amounting to around one-fifth of the total strength of the LTTE. By disturbing the military balance of power that the cease-fire was based upon, the Karuna revolt became a significant factor in hastening the return to war. Karuna himself was given protection by the Sri Lankan military, who subsequently armed and funded him to raise an anti-LTTE paramilitary force in the Eastern province.

The ultimate failure of the peace process was thus the result of several factors that emerged in parallel in early 2004, of which the UNP's election defeat was just one. There are in addition, some difficulties in counter-posing the UNP against the JVP, particularly because the latter is a far smaller party that has never (as of the time of writing) been in power. But they do form a useful contrast to one another insofar as they constitute polar elements within the political spectrum in terms of their social, cultural and economic origins, the socio-economic and geographic location of their support base, the social origins of their leadership, their culture of organisation, and their political positions on virtually every issue of significance. Hostility between the two parties has vivid and violent origins in the 1987–90 *beeshanaya* (terror) period when the then UNP government, and the state machinery at its command, was responsible for crushing a violent JVP insurgency. Almost the entire leadership of the JVP during the peace process period had been its activists and foot-soldiers in that period, and were among those that managed to survive it, while many in the UNP leadership were either the targets of assassination by the JVP in the late 1980s, or were complicit in organising its repression.

The parallel paths of the UNP and JVP during the peace process were defined in the course of the preceding People's Alliance (PA) government of Chandrika Kumaratunga, when both parties were in opposition. In the slow political decline of the PA over these years, various forces began to capitalise and congregate in the political space created in its wake. The UNP, under new leadership and a substantially reformed image, capitalised on the frustration of its traditional support base in the business community, who increasingly viewed the war as an unsupportable economic burden that had to be settled quickly one way or another. They consequently developed a synthesised programme of 'peace with market reforms', emphasising the economic benefits and the synergistic rationality of the two issues in combination.

At the same time, opposition to the PA's devolution proposals, and frustration with the their programme of privatisation, were captured and conflated by a renascent JVP. Building upon their unique political history, substantial support networks from the past, and the vacant political space on these two issues ceded by the two mainstream parties in the post-1994 period, they successfully bounced back as the third force in electoral politics during the late 1990s. In doing so, they re-articulated a hybrid Marxist–nationalist political ideology that linked a traditionally Sinhala nationalist opposition to political compromise on the ethnic conflict, with a distinctly leftist economic opposition to market reforms and globalisation.

The peace process thus came into being in the context of a revitalised ideo-political polarity that pitted the UNP's 'cosmopolitan capitalists' on the one side, against the JVP's 'sectarian socialists' on the other, to capture the fallout from the disintegration of the PA government and its agenda. The peace process promoted by the UNP in 2001–2004 cannot be understood as peace in the abstract, for it was a strategic component of the distinctly economistic logic that it was embedded and developed within. The peace agenda was transparently sponsored by Sri Lanka's wealthiest business groups, was packaged together with donor-funded market reforms that were advocated by and that would directly benefit those very groups, was shepherded through under extensive foreign prodding and funding, and was wrapped within the globalised liberal discourse of peace, human rights, and good governance.

The opposition that emerged to challenge the peace process was similarly multi-faceted, and cannot be caricatured as one of reflexive ethnic supremacism or militarist revanchism. Instead, it drew upon a broad-based mobilisation that appealed not just to ethnic sentiments, but also to those who felt deeply threatened by the market reforms, and the heightened influence of global powers and international agencies that came with it. Nationalist ideologues were able to convincingly present the peace process as a neo-colonial, neoliberal enterprise to divide, conquer and privatise the country, launched by foreign powers with vested interests, and aided by the UNP, the traditional party of the westernised comprador bourgeoisie.

As a result, the circumstances of the political confrontation that emerged in the aftermath of the peace process effectively recreated the party-policy configuration of 1956 and 1987. It reassembled the circumstances of the left–right cross-polarisation described in previous chapters, where the parliamentary party furthest to the right on economic policy was furthest to the (liberal) left on issues of minority rights, the civil war, and the ethnic conflict. In contrast, the party furthest to the populist left on economic policy was also the furthest to the right of the spectrum on issues of minority rights. In the next two chapters, I examine the making of this left–right cross-polarisation in terms of the globalised liberal peace agenda, and its antithesis, a reactive nationalist-leftist opposition.

In exploring the political economy of the peace process, this section is deliberately focused only on the south. It does not explore the extent, impact, or repercussions of the economic agenda in the north and east, which was largely concerned with rehabilitation and reconstruction. Instead, it is aimed at explaining the electoral verdict of the Sinhala Buddhist majority community in the April 2004 elections.

The remainder of this chapter provides a recapitulation of the election mandate for war and peace, and a discussion of the parallel evolution of the political agendas of the UNP and JVP in the prior government. It serves as the introduction to two subsequent chapters that lay out the argument in greater detail. Chapter 7 examines the rise of the UNP peace agenda, and suggests sources for its collapse. Chapter 8 examines the JVP in its latest phase, and looks at the way it came into prominence in this period by becoming the standard-bearer of the anti-peace process forces.

The Electoral Mandate

The peace process came into being with the election of the UNP-led government in December 2001, which explicitly promised to end the war by arranging a cease-fire, holding talks with the LTTE, and negotiating an interim power-sharing arrangement in the north and east. The collapse of the peace process began when this government was defeated in a mid-term election in April 2004. Are there grounds to argue that there was as such, a voter mandate for peace in 2001? And subsequently, a mandate for war in 2004? In arriving at the answers to these questions, it is first necessary to wade through a number of complicating factors.

Table 6.1 | Parliamentary Election Results: 2000–04

	October 2000			December 2001			April 2004		
	Votes	*Share*	*Seats*	*Votes*	*Share*	*Seats*	*Votes*	*Share*	*Seats*
UNP/UNF	3,477,770	40.2%	89	4,086,026	45.6%	109	3,504,200	37.8%	82
PA/UPFA	3,900,901	45.1%	107	3,330,815	37.2%	77	4,223,970	45.6%	105
JVP	518,770	6.0%	10	815,353	9.1%	16			
JHU/SU	127,863	1.5%	1	50,665	0.6%	0	552,724	6.0%	9
Others	622,364	7.2%	18	673,010	7.5%	23	981,838	10.6%	29
	8,647,668	100.0%	225	8,955,869	100.0%	225	9,262,732	100.0%	225

Source: Sri Lanka Department of Elections

Firstly, the making and unmaking of parliamentary majorities and even presidential elections depend not just on the relatively small vote-swings either way, but on the heavily negotiated pre-election seat-adjustment pacts between parties, post-election coalition-building, and attrition through defections. In addition, the structure of representation is affected by the interplay between the electoral rules and the geographical dispersion of party supporters, as well as voter turnout. Under the 1978 constitution, elections to Sri Lanka's unicameral legislature were conducted through a complicated system often described as 'modified proportional representation' . Of the total 225 seats, 196 were elected on a multi-member district basis. The remaining 29 seats were allocated based on the party share of the overall national vote.

One of the most important differences between the 2001 and 2004 elections is the relationship between the SLFP and JVP. Both parties drew upon a very similar core voter-profile of rural and peri-urban poor and lower-middle class Sinhala Buddhists, such that the resurgence of the JVP as an electoral party since the mid 1990s came at the direct expense of the SLFP. When they competed head to head against each other, such as in the 2000 and 2001 parliamentary elections, the two parties inevitably split their common vote bank, and reduced their overall legislative representation. In 2001, their combined vote share of 46.3% won them 93 seats. But when they reached a pre-election agreement in 2004, and cooperated with each other under the banner of the United People's Freedom Alliance (UPFA), their marginally lower combined vote-share of 45.6% returned 105 seats.

Secondly, the 2004 election results were affected by a very idiosyncratic factor in the form of the *Jathika Hela Urumaya* (JHU), an explicitly sectarian Sinhala Buddhist party which fielded a slew of Buddhist monks as their candidates. The JHU gained an unusually large number of votes in the greater-Colombo area, capitalising heavily on the public outpouring of grief over the recent death of their founder, a Buddhist monk and well known public figure, Ven. Gangodawila Soma Thera. An analysis of the 2004 elections suggest that the JHU's vote surge came at the direct expense of the UNP and, to a lesser extent, the SLFP–JVP, although it is impossible to disentangle what is in reality, the highly transitory, conditional, and contingent nature of voter affiliation.

In other words, the election results of 2001 and 2004 which are commonly interpreted as referenda on the peace process, were in reality heavily influenced by some quite idiosyncratic factors, and by negotiations within the apex of the political structure rather than changing sympathies at the base. Indeed, in an interview conducted two years after the elections of April 2004, former UNF prime minister Ranil Wickremasinghe refused to accept that his defeat amounted to voter dissatisfaction with the peace process or his government.

He asserted instead that it was a result of the unbeatable electoral arithmetic of an SLFP–JVP coalition, combined with the sudden rise of the JHU.[7]

But in reality, institutional and idiosyncratic explanations do not provide the whole picture. The election data shows quite clearly that voters did change their allegiance in the three elections of 2000, 2001 and 2004, and that this shift did indeed have a decisive impact in the rise and fall of governments.

Table 6.2 | Voter Swing, 2000, 2001 and 2004 Parliamentary Elections

	Change 2001 vs 2000			*Change 2004 vs 2001*		
	Votes	*Share*	*Seats*	*Votes*	*Share*	*Seats*
UNP/UNF	+608,256	+5.4%	+20	-581,826	-7.8%	-27
Anti-UNP	-350,701	-5.7%	-25	+579,861	+4.7%	+21
All Others	+50,646	+0.3%	+5	+308,828	+3.1%	+6
Net change	+308,201	0.0%	0	+306,863	0.0%	0

Source: Sri Lanka Department of Elections

If the parties in parliament can be divided for the purposes of the peace process into those that directly supported it, and those that were hostile to it, then the extent of the vote swing becomes very clear (see table 6.2). In 2001, the UNP share of the vote went up 5.4% from the prior elections, from 40.2% to 45.6%, and they won an additional 20 parliamentary seats.

Despite the fact that the UNP itself did not win an outright majority of seats in parliament, they nevertheless had the strong support of several minority parties (in the 'all others' category), and, for the 27 months of their government, enjoyed an unusual degree of internal stability. But by April 2004, in the first subsequent public opportunity to vote on the peace process, their vote share dropped sharply by 7.8% to 37.8%, significantly worse than their situation in the October 2000 elections. In effect, the election data shows that there was a strong swing towards the UNP in December 2001, and an even stronger swing away from them in April 2004.

Who then were these shifting voters? And what explains their motivations? Pre-election opinion polls taken over February–April 2004 suggest that there was a sharp divide in the political priorities and perceptions of Tamils and Sinhalese at a variety of levels; although this is not to say that ethnic relations and the peace process was the single most important issue. On a national basis,

---

[7] Interview, Ranil Wickremasinghe, Colombo, 22 September 2006.

two separate opinion polls found that the single most important election issue was inflation.[8] The large majority of voters who live in the south typically prioritised economic issues ahead of the peace process. Only Tamils or voters in the north and east identified the peace process as the single most important issue at stake.[9] This is, of course, not surprising given the fact that the north and east had suffered from the war to a very disproportionate extent, and also because peace was very much an issue of economic consequence in those areas.

In other words, despite the fact that the north and east remained considerably poorer in absolute terms, those areas nevertheless benefited in relative terms from the cease-fire as there was a significant amelioration in economic conditions simply through the absence of violence and the return to civilian normality. Except for the relatively sparsely populated areas bordering the north and east, the south had, in contrast, not experienced that kind of economic dislocation due to the war. There was as a consequence, no immediate commensurate improvement as a result of the cease-fire. One poll revealed that a clear majority of Tamils found the economic situation of their community to have improved significantly post-ceasefire. At the same time, 70% of Sinhalese respondents believed that their community had suffered an economic worsening in this period.[10]

Ethnicity was thus being reinforced and reproduced as a factor of political salience during the course of the peace process in three ways. Firstly, Sinhalese and Tamil voters differed markedly in their evaluation of the peace process. Secondly, they had a different matrix of priorities upon which their voting decisions were based. Thirdly, they had strikingly different perceptions of their economic satisfaction during the peace process. All of these factors suggest that the voting patterns of 2001 and 2004 need to be decomposed along ethnic lines to understand their significance.

To what extent can it be said the Sinhala Buddhist majority participated in bringing the peace process into being? Since the minorities (Muslims, Tamils, and Sinhalese Christians) comprise one-third of the population, and are traditionally pre-disposed towards the UNP or pro-UNP minority parties, the rise and fall of the UNP government could conceivably have been due to

---

[8] See poll results by A.C. Nielsen (Org-Mart Smart) and by the Centre for Policy Alternatives (CPA).

[9] ORG-MART SMART poll wave 2, reported in the Sunday Times, March 21 2004, 'Opinion Polls: Issues Facing a Split Nation'.

[10] CPA 'The Sri Lankan Voter and the April 2004 elections', wave 1. http://www.cpalanka. org/research_papers/SI_Election_Poll.pdf.

something as trivial as the voter turnout among minorities rather than to any serious change of heart by the majority. One way to decompose the election outcome into ethnic categories is to demographically segregate the election data (to the most disaggregated extent possible) to identify areas where minorities have a negligible presence.

Election data can be thus narrowed down to just those 43 polling divisions across the island which were, at the time of their creation, identified demographically as over 90% Buddhist.[11] The votes cast in these polling divisions amount to about one-third of the total number of votes cast nationally. In geographical terms, they cover most of the districts of Galle, Matara, Hambantota, Kurunegala, Anuradhapura, Polonnaruwa, and Moneragala, and a number of pockets in Colombo, Kalutara, Gampaha, Kandy, Badulla, Kegalle, and Ratnapura.

As table 6.3 shows, the vote swing in these overwhelmingly Sinhala Buddhist districts was very similar and in the same direction as the overall swing in both directions. In 2001, there was a distinct swing towards the UNP of +3.9%, and a heavier swing away from them of -7.3% in 2004. This suggests that the rise and fall of the UNF government, and the subsequent rise and fall of the peace process, could not entirely have been due to the nature of the voting system, or the theatre of high politics. It reflected a broad shift in voter preferences in both instances. Indeed, since the minorities are widely supposed to have voted for the UNP or the UNP coalition allies in both elections, it is possible to reasonably infer that the national level voter swing that generated the anti-incumbent election results in 2001 and 2004 came largely from the majority Sinhala Buddhist voters. What then explains the significant swing in their votes between these two elections?

Table 6.3	Comparing Voter Swing in the 2001 and 2004 Parliamentary Elections: National Results Versus 43 Polling Divisions with Over 90% Buddhist Majority

	2001 vs 2000		*2004 vs 2001*	
	National	*SB >90%*	*National*	*SB >90%*
UNP/UNF	+5.4%	+3.9%	-7.8%	-7.3%
PA/UPFA	-7.9%	-6.5%	-0.7%	+1.6%
JVP	+3.1%	+4.1%		

Source: Sri Lanka Department of Elections

---

[11] Report of the Delimitation Commission, 1976.

The Production of Ideo-Political Polarities

In developing an explanation for the making of the election mandates of the peace process period, it is first important to look at the extraordinary national transformation effected in 1994 with the rise of the People's Alliance (PA) government under Chandrika Kumaratunga. When Kumaratunga's PA won the parliamentary elections in August 1994 and later the presidential elections in November 1994, the UNP had been in power continuously for 17 years. The 1977 parliament that brought the UNP to power with an overwhelming majority should have ended its life with fresh elections in early 1983. But, by means of a questionable referendum held in December 1982 (Samarakone 1984), the government of J.R. Jayewardene artificially extended this parliament a further six years through 1989. When parliamentary elections were eventually held after 12 years in February 1989, Sri Lanka was in the midst of a chaotic and exceptionally violent anti-government insurgency by the JVP, which called for a poll boycott. In these traumatic circumstances, where the violence and intimidation by the JVP was matched and compounded by the government's brutal anti-insurgency campaign, the elections recorded the lowest voter turnout in Sri Lankan history.

The SLFP itself had been in the political wilderness for 17 years between 1977 and 1994, when they were paralysed by weak leadership, infighting, desertion, and repression. In addition, they suffered such a violent compression of their ideo-political space from the UNP, and later the JVP, and had such bleak prospects of coming into power that they developed no coherent policies on the economic or ethnic front. The August 1994 parliamentary elections were as such, the first reasonably transparent, meaningfully contested elections that had taken place since 1977. The UNP suffered not only from a backlog of anti-incumbency sentiment, but had gained a well-founded reputation for violence, corruption, criminality, chauvinism, and authoritarianism. The new SLFP-led PA alliance, on the other hand, benefited considerably from the leadership of a new, charismatic, youthful personality. Chandrika Kumaratunga had the strong support of civil society organisations, trade unions, and a broad assembly of quite disparate and hitherto opposing social forces who were strongly united by the desire to remove the UNP from power. But the formidable strength that such a diverse coalition displayed in winning an election soon turned into a handicap once in power. The PA comprised opposing elements across the political spectrum on every issue of consequence: it contained unreconstructed Sinhala nationalists together with campaigners for multi-ethnic peace; rural parochialists and urban sophisticates; Marxist trade union leaders and free-market privatisers; former Tamil militants and former army officers. The UNP caricatured this in their November 1994 election manifesto as follows:

> Within its ranks are free marketers, Sinhala racists, Communists, Muslim Fundamentalists, Trotskyites, Liberals, those who claim to be followers of Lalith Athulathmudali and followers of Vijaya Kumaratunga, and those who are fighting for the right of self-determination of the Tamils.[12]

This diversity was partly a result of electoral necessity: these were the only existing building blocks available to mount an effective challenge to the UNP. In the course of their 17-year rule, the UNP had alienated such a wide number of constituencies, that opposition to them was understandably very diverse. The UNP's new constitution of 1978 had instituted an electoral system with proportional representation, rendering small parties not just electorally viable for the first time, but wielding unprecedented and disproportionate political influence as makers and breakers of coalition governments. But beyond the realm of electoral tactics, the PA did in reality reflect a conscious effort at national reconciliation from the divisive political extremism and vast extent of civilian violence that had brutalised the island under the UNP since the early 1980s. Having been out of power for almost two decades, and having assembled a consortium that contained entirely new political entities such as the Sri Lanka Muslim Congress (SLMC), key individuals in the PA government were, in many respects, political novices. Many were first time ministers, without prior experience of government, administration, and positions of power; but they were as yet uncorrupted by the taint of prior association.

The PA thus climbed to power in parliament and later the presidency with a great degree of internal ideo-political pluralism, and was subject to opposing pressures and constant brinkmanship from within cabinet. One of the repercussions was that the policy formulation process was often interminably long; not because of opposition from the outside, but because virtually every issue had strong supporters on either side of the fence within the cabinet. At an impassioned speech to party colleagues during the dying days of the PA government, Kumaratunga complained bitterly that, 'the PA has had to get the support of minority parties that demand heaven and earth for stability in government'.[13]

---

[12] UNP Manifesto of presidential candidate Gamini Dissanayake, November 1994.

[13] 'Chandrika asks Ranil what he has done for the country'. Island, 18 November 2001.

In terms of the ethnic conflict, the PA's policy after April 1995 was 'war for peace', a parallel policy of prosecuting a war to resist and politically pressurise the LTTE, while simultaneously promoting a unilateral solution of regional devolution and constitutional reforms. In one sense, 'war for peace' was a way of mobilising as wide a political spectrum as possible, and marginalising the extremists on both sides. But by the end of its term in December 2001, the PA government ended up failing in both respects – effectively losing the war with the LTTE, and failing to accomplish its grand project of constitutional reforms and power devolution.

Similarly, in economic policy, the PA stood for 'reforms with a human face', meaning in essence that the political and policy process was bifurcated between different sections of cabinet. Key economic positions such as the head of the Board of Investment (BOI), or the Public Enterprise Reform Commission (PERC) – the agencies in charge of foreign direct investment and privatisation, respectively – were in the hands of market-reformist technocrats, while the PA simultaneously incorporated elements of the Marxist left and contained important trade union leaders within its ranks (Moore 1997). But as with the war for peace agenda, the PA's attempt to be all things to all people created frustrations at all ends of the spectrum, leading to a thinning out of its support base from both sides of the ideo-political divide.

In its attempt to undertake both war and peace, it succeeded in neither, but helped to create a distinct constituency of peace on the one hand, out of the frustrations at the endless war, and a parallel constituency of anti-devolution Sinhala nationalists. Likewise, in its attempt at maintaining both market reforms and its human face, it frustrated the reform constituency, and created a strong business lobby for faster and deeper reforms. But it also created a distinctly new articulation of workers interests, and of political formulations that capitalised on substantial discontent with globalisation and market reform policies.

Table 6.4 | General Election Results, 1994–2001

	Dec–94	*Dec–99*	*Oct–00*	*Dec–01*
PA	62.3%	51.1%	45.1%	37.2%
JVP	0.3%	4.1%	6.0%	9.1%
UNP/UNF	35.9%	42.7%	40.2%	45.6%
all others	1.5%	2.1%	8.7%	8.1%
	100%	100%	100%	100%

Source: Sri Lanka Department of Elections. (N.B. The elections of 1994 and 1999 were presidential elections, while 2000 and 2001 were parliamentary)

The divergent ideo-political trends that emerged from the PA government's internal contradictions subsequently became the major structural pillars along which the politics of the peace process came to be played out in 2001–2005, in the form of the UNP on one side and the JVP on the other. Election statistics from the 1994–2001 period demonstrate the steady decline of the PA, and its loss of support on opposite ends of the spectrum to the UNP and the JVP (see table 6.4). Between the high-tide-mark of the presidential elections of December 1994 and the nadir of the parliamentary elections of December 2001, the PA lost a total of 25% of its vote share. Of this, 8.8% was picked up by the JVP, 9.7% by the UNP, and 6.7% by other smaller parties.

As the PA slowly crumbled in the face of numerous assaults over 1999–2001, these constituencies of discontent became animated and articulated in certain combinations. On the one hand, corporate lobby groups who were frustrated at the slow pace of reform and the cost of the war campaigned openly for a joint programme of peace with economic reforms. This agenda was picked up and emulated by the corporate lobby's traditional political representative, the UNP, which was itself undergoing a period of reform under new leadership. At the same time, the PA's devolution proposals and the programme of ongoing market reforms led to the rebirth of the JVP, and to the re-shaping of this (re)nascent electoral organisation in very distinct directions. After repression and near-extermination in 1989, the JVP slowly re-emerged in the 1994–95 period in the aftermath of Premadasa's assassination.

By late 1995, the JVP was mobilising on economic issues from a largely traditional Marxist basis, but was, at the same time, increasingly taking strong exception to the government's devolution proposals. They mobilised on economic issues with all the symbolic and rhetorical accoutrement of a Leninist party, but drifted into strategic alliances with a new brood of Sinhala extremist forces that were mobilised into action in opposing devolution. The JVP also gained considerably from popular dissatisfaction with the PA's economic policies, privatisations, corruption scandals, and the increasing disparities in wealth during this period. Since the UNP (as the party of the rich) was, by definition, the enemy, and since the 'old' left parties were so shrivelled, compromised by their membership in the PA, and lacking in populist fervour, the JVP was well placed to capitalise on the increasing economic anxieties of this period. Thus, emerging out of the PA period was a corporate-led peace lobby, and simultaneously, its antithesis, in a populist Sinhala nationalist inflected left-wing movement.

The December 2001 elections that brought the peace process into being emerged within very specific ideo-political circumstances through which it was yoked to a controversial corporate-friendly agenda of market reforms. This is not to say that it was an opportunistic marriage of convenience that lumped together two disparate and contradictory policy trajectories – the two were organically interwoven in terms of their rationale and inspiration, and in terms of the identities of their primary sponsors. The peace agenda emerged directly from the articulation of the material interests of the corporate sector in the late 1990s, and was bound together in a coherent and compelling manner with the rest of the corporate agenda. Peace was one element, albeit a critical enabling element, of a sweeping economic programme that included regional integration, labour market reforms, privatisation, and infrastructure development (Bastian 2005).

Leading elements of the corporate sector, chambers of commerce, and the employers' organisations, who were transparently associated with the making of the UNP agenda became, from 1997 onwards, increasingly vocal in demanding an end to the war and in accelerating the market reform programme. The economic crisis that was catalysed and exacerbated by the failing war effort in 2000–2001 pushed the corporate sector to an even more explicit and energetic level of activism. After the Katunayake airport attack in July 2001, the heads of some of the largest corporates, comprising among the wealthiest individuals in the country took the unusual step of forming peace NGOs, and launched a high profile media campaign against the war that within a few months quickly turned into a thinly veiled election campaign in favour of the UNP.

The Elitist Peace and the Populist War

The new UNP-led coalition government that came into power in December 2001 quickly began work on a two-point programme of peace and economic reform. Indeed, given the way in which the two were rationalised as contingent upon one another, it could be argued that there was, in reality, a one-point programme of rapid private-sector led economic growth, of which peace in the north and market reform in the south were simply inter-dependent components. Many of the leading cabinet ministers in charge of the peace process, such as G.L. Peiris and Milinda Moragoda, actually headed ministries in charge of economic reform. The government's energetic prosecution of this programme in their first 18 months in power earned it the strong support and approval of the international community, who in a landmark donor conference in June 2003, pledged a record $4.5 billion in aid.

But given the nature of the government's agenda, and the identities of their domestic and international partners, it was the JVP that was able to emerge as the most coherent and articulate force in opposition. With its hybrid Marxist–nationalist ideology, the JVP stood poised to spearhead the attack on both the peace process and the reforms. It stood to gain as the perfect counter-foil to the UNP, with the exact combination of polar opposite ideo-political positions to the government's entire programme. Despite being a relatively small party, they provided the clear ideo-political articulation and the organisational energy that dominated the campaign to oppose the peace process, and became critical in engineering its downfall.

At the same time, the JVP's rapidly growing trade union strength in the public and private sectors provided it with a critical new base of support that could be strategically deployed to leverage what had previously been a largely university student-led presence. As a highly visible and vocal political force, it harvested the growing opposition to privatisation, market reform, and even the pro-US orientation of the UNP government at the time of the second Iraq war. The JVP mobilised support from the many social, economic, political, and cultural constituencies that sought the safety and security of the social democratic state, in opposition to the internationally supported liberal peace. Opposition to the UNP was certainly aroused by concern about the peace process at many different levels. But it also came from other directions, primarily from the insecurities generated by the market reform process, the headlong embrace of economic and cultural globalisation, and the heavily internationalised nature of the new dispensation. In effect, the UNP's controversial pursuit of peace negotiations was rendered more vulnerable by its simultaneous pursuit of an equally controversial programme of market reforms, and its close collaboration with the international community.

For example, the trade union movement, which has historically been influenced and owes allegiance to the 'old left', and which instinctively supported the peace process nevertheless found it impossible to support the UNP government because of the economic agenda. Others did so because of pressure from their union membership, which the JVP was aggressively luring away. Indeed, the Sri Lankan parliamentary left has been forced to contend with this very same dilemma ever since the mid-1950s. The realities of electoral politics and the peculiar ordering of the Sri Lankan political spectrum have constantly forced the Marxist left to prioritise and choose between two critical elements of their platform: advocacy of an economic left-wing agenda, and opposition to Sinhala nationalism.

The two subsequent chapters expand upon this brief outline of the peace process, and dwell at greater length on many of the arguments presented here.

7 | Cosmopolitan Capitalism

Today, Sri Lanka has a great window of opportunity. The United National Front (UNF) Government that came to power in December 2001 with a mandate to secure peace and accelerate economic growth has already embarked on a bold program of peace/reconciliation and a comprehensive set of economic policy/institutional reforms to promote private sector-led growth (World Bank 2003b: 1).

Introduction

This chapter is concerned with the United National Party (UNP) before and during their period in power as the leading partner in the United National Front (UNF) coalition government between December 2001 and April 2004. It broadly describes the circumstances under which their agenda for a ceasefire and negotiations with the LTTE came into being in the late 1990s, and develops an analytical narrative for its subsequent failure in terms of its economic agenda. The material presented in this chapter is not stand-alone, and is integrally connected to a historical contextual discussion, literature review, and issues of theoretical relevance discussed in preceding chapters, as well as to the subsequent chapter that discusses the JVP. Following from the questions raised in the previous chapter, this chapter explores the collapse of the 2001–2004 peace process, and in particular, why the Sinhala Buddhist majority turned against it in 2004.

The matter presented here is based largely upon primary material gathered during 2002–07, including personal interviews with a large number of people in the UNP-led government and party structure, including the prime minister, cabinet secretary, UNP chairman, and the treasury secretary. In addition, it draws on interviews and documents from members of leading corporate associations and aid donors, such as the Employers Federation, the Ceylon Chamber of Commerce, 'business for peace' NGO organisations, the World Bank and IMF. This material was combined and contrasted with a review of the available English language news media sources of that period, translated compilations of the vernacular media, financial statistics, secondary literature, and interviews with a number of trade unionists, opposition political parties, journalists, and civil society activists.

A Party in Reform

The UNP that came to power in December 2001, with an audacious agenda of ceasefire and negotiations with the LTTE, was a substantially different party from the one that had lost power seven years earlier in August 1994. Indeed, whilst in power during 1977–94, the UNP had initiated, accelerated, and prosecuted the civil war. Leading elements of former President J.R. Jayewardene's government and the UNP party machine were implicated in inciting and organising the July 1983 anti-Tamil pogroms that triggered the escalation to war. By the end of its 17 years in power, the UNP had earned a widespread and well-deserved reputation for chauvinism, militarism, the abuse of human rights, and the subversion of democratic norms. Surprisingly then, the UNP that returned to power in 2001 managed to present itself as the antithesis of all this – as peaceful, democratic, and genuinely interested in bringing a negotiated end to the conflict and winning back the confidence of the minorities.

The remodelling of the UNP's image was greatly assisted by the economic, political, and military crisis that slowly engulfed the PA government of Chandrika Kumaratunga during 1994–2001. The UNP in opposition thus stood to gain by default from the many failings and the dissatisfaction aroused by the PA government that occluded the memory of its own not dissimilar past record. Secondly, many of the key personalities of the previous UNP government and potential successors to the leadership had all either retired or had been assassinated. The retirement of Presidents J.R. Jayewardene (in 1988) and D.B. Wijetunge (in 1994), and the assassinations of four senior leaders – Deputy Defence Minister Ranjan Wijeratne (in 1991), former defence minister Lalith Athulathmudali (in 1993), President Ranasinghe Premadasa (in 1993), and presidential candidate Gamini Dissanayake (in 1994) – removed some of the most prominent UNP leaders associated with that period from the political scene altogether. It cleared the way for a concerted effort by the party in opposition to rehabilitate its image with a generational change in leadership composed for the first time from the post-independence generation that had come to political maturity in the era of liberalisation and market reforms.

The new leader to emerge in the 1993–94 period was the minister for industries, Ranil Wickremasinghe, an urbane, youthful patrician who formed a distinct contrast in age, style, substance, and social background to the assassinated President Ranasinghe Premadasa. Wickremasinghe was born into the wealth and privilege of Sri Lanka's westernised ruling oligarchy, and is part of the extended clan structure that has produced many of Sri Lanka's post-independence political leaders. He is a nephew of former President J.R. Jayewardene, and his father, Esmond Wickremasinghe, was a powerful pro-UNP press baron who ran the Lake House newspaper group. As such, Wickremasinghe's rise to power in 1993–94 is often characterised as a recapture of the party by the oligarchs from the populists. He also reflected a generational change from his own older relatives as a result of the changing material basis of the island's economic elite in the post-1977 liberalisation era.

Having been first elected to parliament in 1977, Wickremasinghe's political career related to the 'new economy' of foreign investment, Export Processing Zones (EPZs), the tourism industry, and garment factories. It was a period of unprecedented opportunity and rapid uneven prosperity that brought forth a new breed of energetic entrepreneurship – all of which had little resemblance to the sedate and sedentary culture of plantation exports and state capitalism that marked the formative years and political careers of his predecessors. As his cabinet secretary, Bradman Weerakoon described:

> To him, real development and the future of Sri Lanka lay essentially in the services sector – in banking, finance, IT, 'call centres' and so on. ... While the earlier Sri Lankan leaders would have thought of employment generation in rural development, Ranil Wickremasinghe saw it in urban development in the growing towns and cities (Weerakoon 2004: 343).

During the 1950s–1970s, the UNP struggled to shed its elitist, pro-business image and expand its electoral base to accommodate the tide of majoritarian nationalism. But despite its most strenuous attempts to erect a façade of Sinhala Buddhist authenticity, the UNP never abandoned its core identity as a party of the westernised, urban comprador elite. The rise to power of Ranil Wickremasinghe in 1993–94 similarly involved a considerable make-over of the party's socio-cultural image, implying, as he frequently described, a 'break with the past'.[1] Nevertheless, despite his constant reassurances to the

---

[1] *Sunday Times* 8 June 1997 'Ranil Ready to Ride Storm'.

public that 'The party under my leadership has changed a lot',[2] the negative hangover from the Jayewardene and Premadasa periods remained an issue of concern.

Much of the UNP's internal transformation during the late 1990s was synchronous, and occurred in close coordination, with a parallel transformation in the attitudes of the corporate sector. The rise of Chandrika Kumaratunga as a popular political leader in the 1993–94 period had, at first, caused some concerns among the captains of industry, who feared a lurch to the populist left in economic policy and a reversal of the 'open economy' that J.R. Jayawardena had introduced. But Kumaratunga was able to reassure the corporate sector that she would continue the market reform programme, and remained personally committed to private-sector led economic growth, albeit in a more moderate and calibrated manner. She appointed a number of market-friendly technocrats in positions of key economic responsibility such as the head of the Board of Investment (BOI) and the Public Enterprise Reform Commission (PERC),[3] and, contrary to earlier fears, persisted with economic reforms and even accelerated the controversial privatisation programme (Moore 1997, Shastri 2004a, Dunham and Kelegama 1997).

Nevertheless, business elites clearly missed the intimate influence, authoritarian efficiency, and managerial competence that characterised previous UNP governments (Dunham and Kelegama 1997). As the then chairman of Ceylon Chamber of Commerce (CCC) described, 'The private sector held back during the Chandrika period. Things did not happen, or happened slowly'.[4] The rise to power of the SLFP's left wing after 17 years in opposition also meant that there were, now, after a very long time, a number of powerful union-friendly coalition members and even ministers in positions of power. The election of the PA government was followed by a massive wave of strikes in 1995–97, which was at least partly the result of the pent-up frustrations of the unions who had suffered years of authoritarianism and repression by the UNP (Teitelbaum 2007). Business organisations were also exasperated by the new 'Workers Charter' being developed by the union-friendly labour minister Mahinda Rajapaksa, which threatened to run counter to the labour market reforms and flexibility that the influential chambers of commerce were lobbying for.

---

[2] Sunday Times 16 March 1997, 'Don't be Provoked – Ranil', (Interview with M. Ismeth).
[3] Respectively, the agencies in charge of foreign direct investment and privatisation.
[4] Interview, Chandra Jeyaratne, Colombo, 7 August 2006.

By Kumaratunga's third year in power, corporate actors had become evidently frustrated and more vocal about her government. The government was increasingly criticised for its lack of vision and direction, partisan bickering, and in general, the lethargic pace of reform and the routine difficulties that the private sector encountered in 'getting things done'.[5] A series of crippling power shortages also helped to focus the anger and discontent within the business community, and became emblematic of what they believed to be the incoherence of vision and lack of direction on economic leadership. Moreover, despite the vast sums being spent on the war, funded largely from taxing the formal private sector, it was clearly escalating beyond control. Firstly, the government's peace initiative with the LTTE had failed: the LTTE unilaterally broke the ceasefire and plunged the country into a new and more expansive phase of the civil war that would last more than five years. Secondly, the new phase of the war was proving to be intractable and unwinnable. After a period of early successes when the army gained in momentum and recaptured LTTE controlled territory, including Jaffna, the tide soon turned. The LTTE struck back with a series of devastating attacks which were restricted not only to military targets in the north and east, but also economic targets in Colombo. What this meant was that Sri Lanka's business elites were directly and intentionally targeted and exposed to the horrors of war.

In January 1996, the LTTE attacked the Central Bank building in Colombo, killing 91 people, injuring over 1,000, and destroying a large part of the financial district. In July 1996, the government suffered its worst ever military defeat when the LTTE overran an entire army base in Mullaitivu, killing over 1,000 soldiers and capturing a vast stockpile of heavy armaments and ammunition. In October 1997, the LTTE launched another powerful bomb blast in the Galadari Hotel that again targeted the financial district in central Colombo. By 1999, the LTTE was clearly gaining the upper hand even in the conventional war in the north, and were quickly regaining large tracts of territory that the army had won at great expense over the prior three years.

The corporate sector increasingly found the war to be an expensive indulgence, fought over a remote and economically irrelevant region for reasons that were receding in importance if not entirely redundant. As this synergistic overlap of peace and unrealised economic opportunity became compelling and urgent, it was also being adopted by the reformed UNP in opposition,

---

[5] See for example, Sunday Times 17 March 1996 Business Section, 'Private sector seeks Economic vision above petty party politics'.

who continued to maintain very close links with corporate elites at a variety of different levels.[6] Between 1998 and 2000, the business lobby's stance on the war evolved significantly from one of supporting bipartisan cooperation over devolution proposals in 1998, to one of direct talks with the LTTE. Not un-coincidentally, Ranil Wickremasinghe had by December 1998 also begun to advocate direct talks with the LTTE.[7] In the December 1999 presidential elections, his position on the ethnic conflict was the most generous ever by a mainstream southern leader: an immediate cease-fire with the LTTE, followed by direct negotiations and the establishment of an interim power-sharing institution in the north and east.

The period December 1999 – December 2001 was characterised by a mounting and pervasive economic, political, and military crisis, capped by the July 2001 LTTE attack on the Katunayake air force base, which is adjacent to, and shares facilities with, Colombo international airport. The airport attack resulted in the imposition of crippling war-related insurance surcharges on air and sea freight, and sharply affected tourism and sectors dependent on external trade. Sri Lanka consequently suffered its first ever period of negative economic growth of -1.4% in 2001,[8] and in the weeks that followed, also suffered the suspension of much-needed IMF funding due to failed performance targets. Overall, between early 1997 and late 2001, the Colombo stock exchange had steadily lost over half its total value.

In the face of such a sudden and visible economic loss, the logic of resuscitating the failing economy by ending the failing war suddenly became far more compelling and urgent. Business elites quickly swung to a much greater and more open campaign for an urgent negotiated end to the war with the LTTE. In the aftermath of the airport attack, the Ceylon Chamber of Commerce explained its priorities: 'The immediate need is only one that the peace process should start as early as possible; … Thereafter, a second focus should be in law and security, labour and educational reforms, infrastructure, good democratic governance'.[9]

Within weeks of the airport attack, two high profile public relations campaigns were launched by the business community that advocated an

---

[6] See for example, the description of the UNP-business community meeting, *Sunday Times*, 21 July 1996, The Political Column – 'UNP means business'.

[7] 'Ranil tells govt. to accept Prabhakaran's peace offer.' *Island*, 1 December 1998.

[8] CBSL 2002

[9] LMD magazine v8 no.2. (September 2001) Benchmark Q&A interviews reprinted in LMD, v8, no.2.

immediate end to the war. On 2nd September 2001, Lalith Kotelawala of the Ceylinco Group launched an organisation called the Society for Love and Understanding (SOLO-U), dedicated to 'bringing peace and economic prosperity to Sri Lanka'. He called for an end to the war, a negotiated end to the conflict, and at the same time, asked the government to provide relief to Sri Lanka's struggling industries, which had been hit by rising costs and cheaper imports. In his inaugural press conference, Kotelawala explained 'We can no longer watch helplessly while our political leaders stumble'.[10] At the same time, the Ceylon Chamber of Commerce launched a 'business for peace' campaign organisation called Sri Lanka First. Sri Lanka First was supported by some of Sri Lanka's most high profile corporate brands, including diversified conglomerates such as John Keels and Hemas, and leading apparel exporters such as MAS, and Brandix.

As its literature describes:

> The airport attack in July of 2001 by the LTTE virtually brought Sri Lanka to its knees. It was a definite wake up call to the entire county and demonstrated to the business community how vulnerable Sri Lanka was as a nation. Tourism was virtually dead with exports and imports severely affected. With Sri Lanka suddenly being classified a 'High Risk Country' the repercussions were devastating. The then government had to underwrite guarantees to the insurers amounting to billions of rupees which the country could ill afford.

> The business community recognised that one more attack like the one at the airport could be even more devastating and business would just not be able to survive, as thousands would lose their jobs resulting in a far worse uprising than 1989 apart from pushing the cost of living up even further. It was with this in mind that the business community took the initiative to put Sri Lanka First by jointly working together for peace.[11]

Although it claimed no direct inspiration, Sri Lanka First had clear resonance with putatively non-partisan civic activism of business leaders elsewhere, such as 'London First' and 'Bombay First'. It also came in the wake of two very successful 'Business for Peace' initiatives in the prior decade, of the Consultative Business Movement (CBM) in South Africa and the Confederation of British Industry (CBI) in Northern Ireland. The chairperson

---

[10] 'SOLO-U aims to find peace and economic prosperity in Sri Lanka.' Sunday Times, 2 September 2001. Business Section.
[11] Sri Lanka First brochure.

of Sri Lanka First, Neela Marikkar, herself the head of a large advertising agency, explained, 'My largest client, Sri Lankan Airlines, lost half their fleet with the Katunayake attack of July 2001. We had a large amount of staff working directly on that account, and we lost heavily'.[12]

On 19 September 2001, some eight weeks after the Katunayake attack, Sri Lanka First, together with SOLO-U and others organised a landmark public hand-holding exercise called 'A Million Hands for Peace'. Office workers around Colombo's central business district and elsewhere assembled on the streets at midday in a massive public demonstration for peace. In the mid-term parliamentary election of December 2001, Sri Lanka First (SLF) launched a massive campaign asking people to 'vote for political parties and candidates who are sincere towards peace'. Kotelawala's SOLO-U similarly took out a number of huge half page advertisements in the leading newspapers similarly calling for peace; in effect, a thinly veiled appeal to vote for the UNP-led coalition.

Cosmopolitanism

This is of course not in any way to suggest that those members of the business world involved in peace activism were not individually motivated by well-meaning, humanitarian concerns, or that they would, in the absence of pressing financial stress, have preferred war to peace. Many of the corporate activists who came forward did so at considerable personal risk. Most, if not all, were urbane social cosmopolitans, and were personally committed to multi-ethnic co-existence. A large number of the leaders of the business for peace campaign were in fact themselves members of linguistic and religious minority communities, and were as such instinctively uncomfortable with the Sinhala nationalism and jingoism that underpinned the conflict and the war effort. The diverse ethnic origins, urban cosmopolitanism, and global economic connections behind the peace campaign are course, characteristic of the traditional support base and leadership profile of the UNP. While the SLFP and JVP traditionally draw support from poorer, more rural and semi-urban Sinhala Buddhist majority, the UNP's core base lies in its converse: the ethnic and religious minorities, and the commercially oriented, wealthier, urban population.

---

[12] Interview, Neela Marikkar, Colombo, 2 August 2006.

The social origins of the UNP lie in the westernised and often Christianised low-country Sinhalese planters, merchants, and professional notables who formed its precursor organisation, the Ceylon National Congress (CNC), and despite almost six decades of concerted effort to broaden its electoral appeal among the Sinhala Buddhist rural masses, the party retains this core character. It also enjoys the support of a large majority of the religious and linguistic minorities (primarily Sinhalese Christians, Tamils, and Muslims) who account for one third of the total population, and who are themselves disproportionately represented among the business community. Indeed, the UNP gets as little as 35% of the Sinhala Buddhist vote, and has only won power because they win as much as 80% or more of the minority vote, which, across much of the heavily populated south-west, accounts for between 20% and 50% of the electorate. James Jupp described in the mid-1970s:

> While the few UNP safe seats are predominantly urban and four out of ten of them are dominated by Christians and Muslims, all the SLFPs twenty two safe seats were rural and Sinhalese Buddhist (Jupp 1978: 198).

Jonathan Spencer's ethnography of a village in Sabaragamuwa captures a fairly typical picture of the kinds of social background and economic identities of the people identified with the UNP and SLFP at the local level. The key village activists of the SLFP are the local school-teacher and Buddhist monk – the traditional rural intelligentsia. The UNP's chief activists on the contrary, are a wealthy Muslim gem dealer, and a group of unscrupulous Sinhalese businessmen, led by a man who is 'better known for his partying than his piety' (Spencer 1990 : 47).

The sociological basis for the UNP as a pro-business and pro-minority party has thus always rested upon the fact that there was a considerable overlap between the two constituencies. Commerce, commercial agriculture, and the capitalist economy in general its various layers has traditionally been dominated by members of communities other than Sinhala Buddhists, and this remains the case despite the emergence of a sizeable number of Sinhala Buddhist entrepreneurs under the wing of state patronage in the 1960s and 1970s (Moore 1998). In addition, the assertive presence of a Sinhala Buddhist nationalist politics under the SLFP since the mid-1950s has caused even poorer segments of minority communities, threatened by this phenomenon, to strengthen their identification and allegiance with the UNP. In summary, it is important to qualify the visibly instrumental and opportunist association of Sri Lanka's corporate sector with the peace process, and to bear in mind that this association has broader roots.

Policy Formulation and Donor Processes

The victory of the UNP-led United National Front (UNF) in the December 2001 elections was widely celebrated by the business for peace lobby. Lalith Kotelawala said he was 'delighted' at the election result as it showed that 'all the racial sentiments expressed before the election that spread hatred and misunderstanding had been rejected by voters'. Ranjith Fernando, one of the leading promoters of the Sri Lanka First campaign declared 'From the point of view of the business community, here and overseas, we certainly rejoice at the result.'[13] He subsequently joined the new government as secretary of the Ministry of Enterprise Development and Industrial Policy.

Beyond the improved atmospherics and economic outlook created by the new ceasefire agreement with the LTTE, many of the leading individuals the new dispensation began articulating a more sophisticated, medium to long-term rationale that linked the mutual benefits of peace and economic reforms. As one of the government's leading economic advisors explained, 'Ranil [Wickremasinghe] always saw reforms as central to the peace process'.[14] The first step of this conceptualisation of a virtuous cycle between peace and reforms was the idea that war was constraining economic growth in key sectors, and peace was the key to economic stability, foreign aid, growth, and prosperity. Sustainable economic growth was possible only with an end to the war. The second step was that the benefits of the peace dividend and economic growth would create prosperity in the north and south, increase living standards and creating rational economic reasons to remain peaceful and prevent a return to war.

There was in addition, a related, but more cynical rationale for the cease-fire that circulated at the time, as follows. Signing a cease-fire and granting the LTTE an interim administration in the economically devastated north and east would cost very little, but would lift the economic burden of war and end the threat of terrorist destruction in the south. It would contain the LTTE, and redirect their destructive energies into the tedium of petty politics, embroiling them in the local administration of a remote and impoverished province. Lured out of the jungles to taste the spoils of office and resume normal family life, the Tiger would become domesticated, sedentarised, and corrupted to the point where the organisation would either slowly disintegrate, or else remain

---

[13] 'Business leaders hail UNP's victory march.' Business Section, *Sunday Times*, 9 December 2001.

[14] Interview, Jim Robertson 28 August 2006.

united, but seek in time to peacefully continue in legitimate power in their peripheral domains.[15]

Yet another elaboration of the UNP's rationale for peace and economic growth was promoted by Milinda Moragoda, the new minister in charge of privatisation, who was at the time viewed as a potential future leader. In his October 2001 Sinhala book *Peravadanak*, and in several subsequent newspaper articles and interviews, Moragoda argued that Sri Lanka's economic future was as the gateway to India; as an entrepôt metropolis that would do for the fast growing southern Indian economy what Hong Kong did for southern China.[16] This role, he warned, was being usurped by Dubai, and Sri Lanka needed to act fast to reclaim it. He went on to elaborate that for Sri Lanka to play this role, a land link to India would be essential. The logical route for such a link would be through Mannar in the war-torn north, and that required an end to the war.[17] Peace was thus being strategised within influential circles as a critical component of an economic strategy in the broad context of positioning Sri Lanka to reap the benefits of globalisation and regional economic integration.

The key players in the peace process that kicked off in December 2001 were not just the UNP and its corporate backers, but included the increasingly ubiquitous 'international community'. Most prominent among them was Norway, which had served as intermediary and neutral facilitator between the two sides, and which organised a ceasefire monitoring mission on the ground, staffed and funded by the Nordic countries. There were also global and regional powers – the US, EU, India, Japan, and China who viewed the evolving peace process in Sri Lanka in terms of their own strategic and commercial concerns. There were international donors and international organisations of various sizes and types – the World Bank, ADB, UN agencies, and the bilateral donors who had a diverse set of interests in infrastructure, agriculture, poverty, refugee relief, capacity building and market reforms. Finally, there were a growing number of international NGOs and relief agencies who sought to establish programmes for a range of activities including land mine clearance, psycho-social support, peace education, and child combatant rehabilitation.

---

[15] This is a composite version distilled from numerous interviews, articles, seminar comments and private correspondence.

[16] 'Peravadanak stimulates discussions by the voting public on wider issues.' Daily News, 5 January 2002.

[17] See Moragoda interview: 'Finding the right economic mix.' Sunday Times, 6 January 2002.

In the late 1990s, the aid donor community, and particularly the World Bank, was undergoing a transformation in its attitude and practices towards conflict-ridden countries. As with the Sri Lankan corporate community, many donors felt that they could no longer work around the conflict and pretend it did not exist, (Goodhand 2001, Bush 1999), but would have to address it more directly through their programmes, through policy dialogue with the government, and perhaps even through conditionality (Ofstad 2002). By 2001, international development workers increasingly talked of the need for 'mainstreaming conflict sensitivity' into their practice. The World Bank's 2001 internal evaluation audit on Sri Lanka remarked self-critically that the bank's activities needed to be far more directly conflict-sensitive.

But leaving aside the rhetoric of conflict sensitivity, the substantial policy agenda that was advocated by aid donors was little different to the new consensus within the corporate community and the new UNP-led government: a two point agenda of structural economic reforms and a negotiated end to the conflict:

> Completion of the structural reform agenda and a resolution of the conflict in the North and the East are the key missing elements for Sri Lanka to accelerate growth and achieve further poverty reduction. Bank assistance should help overcome both these constraints' (World Bank 2001: 14).

One World Bank document suggested that the fragile situation in the immediate aftermath of Sri Lanka's February 2002 cease-fire provided an ideal 'window of opportunity' to implement 'difficult market reforms' which had proved politically problematic in the past (World Bank 2003a:13). The election of the UNP government and the ceasefire of February 2002 was hailed as an extraordinary moment of visionary thinking and new possibilities. As the World Bank South Asia region chief, Mieko Nishimuzu, declaimed in the donor forum of June 2002:

> In my years at the World Bank, I have been blessed to witness a few such moments. This, ladies and gentlemen, is such a moment, for the sovereign people of Sri Lanka. It is also such a moment for us, Sri Lanka's development partners.[18]

---

[18] 'Action needed to realise expectations.' The Sunday Times Economic Analysis. The Sunday Times. 16 June 2002. Accessed 23 Nov 2017. http://www.sundaytimes.lk/020616/columns/econ.html

Crisis Overhang

Within three months of taking power, the new UNP-led government had negotiated a detailed cease-fire agreement (CFA) with the LTTE, opening the door for further normalisation and direct negotiations. At the same time, they also began drafting a comprehensive medium term economic growth strategy to be presented to the aid donors. The new government's first task was to resuscitate a standby funding agreement (SBA) with the IMF that had been suspended under the previous government (IMF 2002). They also inherited an economic crisis from the 2000–2001 period, and had to contend with the fiscal hangover from the previous government's pre-election splurge in late 2001.

As a result, the government's economic policy agenda, which remained at a largely conceptual level, took shape and emerged in the course of tackling the pressing economic problems that it inherited, and in negotiating the donor funding that it desperately needed. The immediate target was not only to revive the SBA, but to secure quick approval of the IMF's highly concessional Poverty Reduction and Growth Facility (PRGF). The PRGF also acts as a gatekeeper to further official aid and private capital flows: as the governor of the Central Bank of Sri Lanka explained, it was 'like a "character certificate" indicating that the country's economic policies were sound and would give confidence to investors.'[19]

The pursuit of the SBA and the PRGF dominated the course of the government's economic policy agenda during its first year in government. The immediate compulsion of restoring macroeconomic stability and implementing the conditionalities required by the IMF to revive the SBA tranche made the government focus heavily on fiscal austerity measures and expenditure control. Austerity was compounded by the fact that the cease-fire delivered very little reduction in defence expenditures, of which around 85% consisted of recurrent expenditures, and 71% consisted of wages and salaries alone. Furthermore, the capital expenditure component also remained high from the deferred payments due on military hardware orders made during the war.

Since defence expenditure reduction was minimal, the fiscal compression required by the IMF had to come from cutting other areas such as infrastructure and subsidies. As Kelegama notes,

---

[19] 'Prayers Answered.' Financial Section, *Sunday Times*, 27 April 2003.

Fiscal tightening through expenditure restraint therefore occurred at precisely the time when the public finances should have been orientated to building peace. ... Over-obsession with fiscal targets therefore proved to be counter-productive in terms of delivering the immediate economic dividend that could have helped the peace progress (Kelegama 2005: 434).

Furthermore, while there was much aid promised, there was actually very little disbursed during these early months. The uncertainty of the political situation and the peace process restrained large investments by the private sector. As a result of the implementation of the IMF's conditionalities during the government's first year in power, the initiation of the peace process coincided with the unveiling of urgent fiscal austerity measures. These included the 'rationalisation' of *Samurdhi*, the government's main poverty-relief programme, cutting down its recipient base by 250,000 in order to achieve better targeting. It also included the fertiliser subsidy, a perpetual drain on the treasury, but one that many marginal farmers had come to depend on.

One of the most critical and consequential of the IMF-required fiscal measures, taken in 2002, was a hiring freeze ordered by the Treasury, which cancelled all existing vacancies in the public service, provincial public service, local authorities, public corporations, and statutory bodies.[20] It immediately affected not only the thousands of aspirants for whom government employment was the traditional route out of rural poverty, but the government's own patronage distribution system. Ministers protested vigorously (but to no avail) that they were no longer able to reward loyalists and constituents.[21] As UNP chairman Malick Samarawickrame explained, 'We had very strict policies, even people associated with the party were not given jobs'.[22] During the UNF government's brief period in power, the public sector workforce shrank by 10.5% – partly because of the vigorous implementation of the hiring freeze, but also because of a voluntary retirement scheme, and the removal of thousands of temporary workers hired in the public sector as a pre-election giveaway by the previous government.[23]

---

[20] Ministry of Finance and Planning, Management Service Circular no. 16, 1st October 2002.

[21] Interviews with Charitha Ratwatte, Colombo, 8 August 2006, Jim Robertson, Colombo, 28 August 2006.

[22] Interview, Malick Samarawickrema, Rajagiriya, 26 August 2006.

[23] CBSL Annual Report 2005, statistical appendix, table 60.

Table 7.1 | Government Employment, 2001–03

	2001	2002	2003
Permanent	981,414	957,147	945,691
Temporary	183,576	104,252	97,518
Total	1,164,990	1,061,399	1,043,208

Source: CBSL Annual Report (various).

In anticipation of the final review of the SBA, which required that the government achieve set targets and demonstrate a certain 'pace of reform' ahead of the PRGF discussions in October, the government had by July 2002 decided that it would fast-track 36 items of legislation through parliament in the month of August.[24] As the subsequent IMF review noted with satisfaction:

> VAT was introduced on August 1, the privatisation and banking reform benchmarks were completed by mid August, the Welfare Benefit Law was submitted to parliament and approved on August 26; Cabinet approved the draft Electricity Reform Act which was gazetted on August 16, Cabinet approved amendments and special provisions bills on the Industrial Disputes and the Termination of Employment of Workmens Acts on August 28. Although the electricity and labour market bills have not been presented to parliament, the PM has instructed that they be tabled in Parliament by September 6. [25]

In sum, the first year of the cease-fire agreement was a period of fiscal compression, unpopular economic measures, and economic reform legislation. This was problematic at a number of levels, because as Saman Kelegama describes:

> Under the grand reform programme there was no effective strategy to buy-off opposition to reforms other than the assumption that foreign aid inflows will cushion the adjustment costs. With the mighty hurry to implement reform, the government basically played into the hands of the opponents of reforms. Thus electricity, railway, health reforms, all backfired without any achievements (Kelegama 2006: 42–43).

---

[24] Daily News, 19 July 2002. '36 Laws to be Passed in August, September'.
[25] Statement by the IMF staff rep, 3 September, 2002.

Regaining Sri Lanka

By the time negotiations with the LTTE began in September 2002, the government was holding parallel negotiations with the IMF for the PRGF. Following further progress on the peace negotiations with the LTTE in December 2002, the IMF approved a $567 million PRGF/EFF credit in April 2003, and the World Bank simultaneously approved a $125 million Poverty Reduction Strategy Credit (PRSC) (World Bank 2003b). Both were based on financing a programme of accelerated reforms of which the key highlights were labour market de-regulation, strengthening property rights in land markets, privatising the power and banking sector, and rationalising the civil service. Approval of concessional finance from the IMF/World Bank then opened the gates for $4.5 billion in further donor aid pledged at the Tokyo donor conference of June 2003.

The make-over of the IMF's Extended Structural Adjustment Facility (ESAF) into the PRGF in 1999 brought into being a new set of standardised procedures and processes that had to be followed. Application for a PRGF loan from the IMF required recipient countries to prepare and submit a detailed Poverty Reduction Strategy Paper (PRSP). The PRSP approach was introduced largely in response to two widespread criticisms that had emerged of the market reform based lending programmes of the IMF and World Bank. Firstly, recipient countries and governments were being forced to implement top-down market reform policies designed and imposed from Washington. Secondly, these reforms had negative social consequences, and were not adequately sensitive to poverty alleviation.

Consequently, the new PRSP approach required a much more comprehensive and technically rigorous approach to poverty analysis. It also required the strategy to be 'country-driven, promoting broad based participation of civil society'.[26] As the IMF describes:

> the principle of broad public participation and greater country ownership is central to the PRGF ... PRGF-supported programs reflect more closely each country's poverty reduction and growth priorities.[27]

With these stated aims in mind, the reality of the PRSP formulation in Sri Lanka is instructive, not just to understand how it contributed to destabilising

---

[26] IMF (2005), Poverty Reduction Strategy Papers – A Factsheet, September 2005.
[27] IMF (2006), The Poverty Reduction and Growth Facility – A Factsheet, August 2006.

the peace agenda, but also as a case-study of how its key design features on process and content were so transparently circumvented and undermined. Between March and December 2002, the UNF government commissioned the drafting of a comprehensive economic master-plan called *Regaining Sri Lanka* (RSL). As with the contents of the cease-fire agreement or the progress with the peace process, very little information about this document was divulged to the public, parliament, or even many members of the government. It was ultimately submitted to the IMF and World Bank in December 2002 as the PRSP.

The lead author of the RSL was Jim Robertson, a US national who had worked with the prime minister a decade earlier under the Premadasa government. The RSL was drafted by a small team of hand-picked technocrats housed within the newly created Ministry of Policy Development and Implementation.[28] Under the auspices of the new ministry, the RSL staff was deliberately isolated from the politicised bureaucracy who could have leaked or influenced its content. Indeed, its lead author described how 'None of us working felt any direct [political] pressure'.[29] Milinda Moragoda later described the secrecy and political insulation as a necessary condition for success: the government did not want the RSL document to get embroiled in the political process, until such time it dovetailed with political developments in the peace process.[30] The process of drafting the RSL involved inputs in committees that included academics, technical experts, and the corporate sector. As Chandra Jayaratne, then chairman of the Ceylon Chamber described,

> There was a significant degree of input [from the business sector]. ... You just asked for something and it was given. ... When we saw RSL, we thought our dreams are coming true.[31]

The joint Bank-Fund review of the PRGF and PRSC described the RSL as:

> a strong and aggressive proposal to remove the existing policy induced and structural constraints that inhibit private sector activity in the way of changing the role of the state (IMF 2003).

---

[28] Interview, Sarasalie Fonseka, Colombo, 27 July 2006, M.Sarvananthan, Colombo, 24 August 2006, Jim Robertson.

[29] Interview, Jim Robertson.

[30] Comments at the CPA-Berghof conference 'Peace and Development: The Road to Tokyo', Colombo 26 – 27 April 2003.

[31] Interview, Chandra Jayaratne, Colombo, 7 August 2006.

The RSL laid out a comprehensive medium term framework of infrastructure construction, privatisation, land and labour market reforms, and a private sector led growth strategy. But given the new requirements under the PRGF/PRSP process, many of these provisions had to be reworded as contributions towards poverty alleviation. The mechanics of doing so involved grafting onto the RSL an earlier document on poverty alleviation with a requisite section on poverty analytics that had been drafted under the previous government. Beyond the emphasis on poverty, the document also had to endure some measure of consultation. This was not a task that its framers enjoyed, and as the lead author confided:

> One of the fundamental problems with the PRSP's process is that the Bank and the Fund have fooled themselves into thinking that they require the whole thing to go through a consultative process.[32]

Indeed, the RSL document did not have any adequate measure of public input or consultation in its drafting. When it was eventually released in the domestic realm, it quickly became very controversial. Through the rest of the life of the government, and even after that, opposition politicians, trade unionists, and civil society activists singled out the RSL as a doctrinaire manual of market reformist excess. It was viewed as emblematic of the secretive and non-inclusive nature of the government's policy formulation process, and its subservience to the agenda of the private sector and the donors. In February 2003, as the World Bank and IMF considered Sri Lanka's application for a PRGF facility, a coalition of 72 trade unions and civil society groups addressed a letter to them, charging:

> We categorically state that the Government of Sri Lanka has failed to carry out even this minimal consultation with the people, and that the proposals have been worked out in total isolation. ... We, acting on behalf of the people, totally reject the proposals contained in the PRSP.[33]

Despite this, the joint WB–IMF review of the PRSP recommended that Sri Lanka's application for a PRGF be approved in March 2003. Moreover, the reviewers surprisingly found cause to *applaud* the widespread nature of the consultation that it was based upon:

---

[32] Interview, Jim Robertson.

[33] Statement by the Alliance for the Protection of National Resources and Human rights (ANRHR), 18 February 2003.

The extent of consultation that is embodied in Sri Lanka's PRSP 'Regaining Sri Lanka' is commendable and is in fact one of the strengths of the document. A large number of stakeholders, including the government, academia, research organisations, non-government and community organisations, the private sector, trade unions, and donors were consulted at various stages of the document's preparation (IMF 2003).

Similarly, the World Bank's 2003 Country Assistance Strategy for Sri Lanka, written in the immediate aftermath of the PRGF approval makes several unfounded references to the 'broad', 'widespread', and 'island-wide' nature of the 'stakeholder consultations':

> During the past four years, the administration has engaged in broad stakeholder consultations to reach consensus on a medium to long term strategy for faster and sustained economic development and poverty reduction. ... The island-wide consultative process also mobilised views of key stakeholders (World Bank 2003a:11).

While it is unclear at what level this misleading evaluation was authored and tolerated, it is extraordinary to note that the World Bank would just two years later, reverse its view on this matter, and report the opposite to be true. That is, in the first review of the PRSP, written after the collapse of the UNF government and its reform agenda in 2005, the Bank found not only that there had actually been *inadequate* consultation, but that this might have been a critical cause of its failure.

> In general, program implementation could have benefited from wider and deeper consultations with stakeholders, especially civil society and within government.[34]

In the meanwhile, the content and formulation of the RSL document soon became problematic domestically. The secrecy behind its formulation left the document exposed to criticism from a wide number of social and political constituencies, with very few people left capable of, or inclined to, defend it. By seeking to depoliticise economic policy, it effectively lacked the political buy-in or ownership of any domestic political constituency except the corporate sector. By drafting such a putatively technocratic document, deliberately insulated from wider input, or even from contact with and feedback from ruling party

---

[34] World Bank (2005), p.12.

members and government ministers, the document came to reflect a very narrowly held economic vision. As the general secretary of one of the largest trade union federations described:

> There were no consultations with the trade unions. The UNP was more disciplined, but it was not transparent. There was no dialogue with stakeholders, so everyone was suspicious.[35]

Style and Substance

Many of the retrospective evaluations of the RSL, and its role in the larger failure of the government have grudgingly admitted a failure to communicate. The World Bank describes how:

> The rationale for certain 'politically-sensitive' reforms was not adequately explained through a more systematic communications strategy. For example, it appears that public opinion on welfare reform turned negative because initial cuts in the number of Samurdhi [welfare] beneficiaries were perceived as arbitrary and politically-motivated (World Bank 2005:12).

Similarly, asked to identify the cause of the UNF government's election defeat in April 2004, virtually every respondent from within that government and the corporate sector invoked a 'failure to communicate'. A leading UNP figure described:

> The agenda was alright, but the main problem was communication. People wanted something for nothing. Our people are not educated enough to understand what we are trying to do.[36]

Others sympathetic to the agenda, but outside the government, were more forthright in identifying issues of substance over style:

> The people expected great things from peace – but the life of poor people did not change. The peace dividend did not trickle down. UNP failed completely in communicating their message, in selling peace to the majority. In the north, peace brought about positive change, but in the south, there was no change

---

[35] Interview, Leslie Devendra, Colombo, 9 April 2007.
[36] Interview, Malik Samarawickrema.

as such. People saw the rich getting richer, etc. That plus the UNP's poor marketing, corruption, etc., cost them the election.[37]

The former secretary to the prime minister, Bradman Weerakoon, was one of the few within the power circle to go beyond issues of communication. He described how the government concentrated on the positive economic news from indicators such as the buoyant stock exchange, low inflation, or GDP growth, and failed to understand that this did not reflect improvements in the lives of most people.

> Subsidies were cut, welfare going down. There were no jobs, or the only jobs were in the private sector. This is something that was not quite seen. The enthusiasm was to move forward as fast as you can.... It was too hard, too unresponsive to the demands and needs of people.[38]

When confronted with these issues in person, Ranil Wickremasinghe's responses were telling:

RV: Did the government at any point feel that there was a contradiction between the peace agenda and the market reform agenda? Was there a need to calibrate the two agendas more carefully?

RW: Not at all.

RV: In retrospect, would you say that the peace agenda of the 2002–2004 period was perhaps too ambitious, or the reform agenda too ambitious, and in that sense, would a more cautious agenda have been more prudent? With the benefit of hindsight, do you have any regrets about the policies your government pursued, or about any aspect of its actions during their period in power?

RW: No.

RV: [upon further repeating the last question and rephrasing it several times in order to elicit a more detailed response]

RW: The Government did not fall because of our policies – it fell because our policies did not have enough time to kick in.[39]

Indeed, many members of the former government saw the peace process and market reforms as synergistic, and mutually dependent on each other

---

[37] Interview, Neela Marikkar.

[38] Interview, Bradman Weerakoon, Colombo, 24 August 2006.

[39] Interview, Ranil Wickremasinghe, Colombo, 22 September 2006.

for success. The World Bank actually went further, to assert – without any justification, and in the face of their own evidence to the contrary in other countries – that the fragile post-conflict scenario actually presented a unique window of opportunity to implement 'difficult' market reforms. 'There are good prospects for addressing key economic and social reforms in such a situation even those that have proven difficult in the past' (World Bank 2003a: 16).

Two years later, the World Bank's post-hoc review of the PRSC came close to reversing this position. Without necessarily recognising it as such, they argued instead that difficult reforms should perhaps have been implemented more gradually and sequenced better:

> The past experience also suggests that more attention needs to be given to the sequencing of reforms. The PRSC program was perhaps too overloaded with 'politically-sensitive' reforms, i.e., public sector, welfare, labor and land reforms, and a more phased approach may have been more manageable (World Bank 2005: 14).

This unusual and unjustified optimism that difficult market reforms would succeed in the midst of an equally difficult peace process was eventually tempered only by the considerably different reality that transpired – the collapse of the government, and the failure of both the peace process and the reform agenda. The election campaign of March–April 2004 is frequently interpreted as a resounding verdict by the Sinhala Buddhist majority against the peace process. Indeed, the scale of the LTTE's cease-fire violations and violent provocations had by then already become cause for widespread concern.

But the sparse evidence that is available suggests that there was more at stake. Sinhala Buddhist rural voters were well aware of the fact that a defeat for the UNF would inevitably be a setback for the peace process, a situation that they were not indifferent to. The militarisation of rural Sinhala Buddhist society paradoxically created strong incentives for supporting the peace process from families who were well aware that a return to war would once again put their childrens' lives at risk.

Reporters sent to cover the 2004 election campaign in rural districts frequently found that the public sector hiring freeze and the removal of the fertiliser subsidy were the two most important issues raised. 'No one has got jobs in the past two years', said one respondent from Ratnapura district.[40] At the same time, they

---

[40] Sunday Times, 21 March, 2004. 'Burdened by Life, but Happy to be Alive'.

recognised the benefits the peace process, and were 'happy to be alive'. Residents of the southern districts of Hambantota, Matara and Galle, which voted overwhelmingly against the UNF, similarly complained that 'the government has done little recruiting in the past two years', and that in a difficult agricultural year, the cost of fertilisers had more than doubled.[41]

Emblematic of the dilemma facing the majority community was this plea from a village voter in a border district of Anuradhapura vulnerable to attack by the LTTE: 'We don't want another war. But we also want our economic problems solved.'[42]

In other words, there was widespread relief and appreciation of the benefits of the peace process, and these voters did not lightly choose to risk a return to war. But the UNF's own agenda of linking peace with economic reforms appears to have pushed many who were supportive of peace to vote against it.

This is of course, not to deny the existence of a considerable protest vote against the UNF/UNP's handling of the peace process, the extent to which the LTTE's conduct created widespread anxieties, and the growth of a more strident Sinhala nationalist constituency which opposed the peace process on principle and voted against it from the very beginning. But this constituency is in itself quite small, and has only sustained political momentum and electoral strength when fortified by, and conjoined to, a populist economic protest agenda. In the April 2004 elections, the UNF/UNP provided exactly such an agenda. Having fused peace to market reform, the relatively small opposition to the peace process was magnified and made electorally viable by a new and growing opposition to the market reform agenda.

Conclusions

The frustrations of the business community with the previous government, their historical association and links with the UNP, and the articulation of a set of a 'business for peace' demands, beginning in the 1998–99 period are critical to understanding the nature of the peace process that later emerged in Sri Lanka. Effectively, the peace agenda emerged as part of the articulation and realisation of the material interests of Sri Lanka's corporate sector, as just one component of an ambitious programme of market reforms in pursuit of an accelerated private-sector led development strategy. When the peace

---

[41] *Sunday Times* 7 March 2004, 'Which Way South'.
[42] *Sunday Times* 29 February 2004, 'Reaping Votes on Farmers Woes'.

process entered the political realm through the UNP and came to fruition upon its election to power in December 2001, it remained subject to the same economistic rationale, and came tethered to the same group of issues.[43]

The embededdness of the peace process within such an economic rationale and the social constituency of its inspiration and sponsorship had important consequences for its sustainability. The government's heavily market-reform laden economic agenda enjoyed a very narrow social constituency of support; and indeed, generated considerable opposition and hostility. In addition, their simultaneous pursuit of fiscal austerity to secure desperately needed financing from the IMF meant that not only was there little in the way of a peace dividend to distribute, but there were instead cutbacks on subsidies and employment opportunities that disproportionately affected the rural Sinhalese poor. The inherent unpopularity of this economic agenda was compounded by the secrecy and lack of consultation in its formulation.

It is of course impossible to decipher the precise individual voter calculus that led to the UNP's election defeat in April 2004. But the evidence does suggest that the majority community did not blithely vote to terminate the peace process, and that a considerable component of the anti-UNP vote was on economic grounds. As a veteran trade unionist described:

> [on the peace process], even the left was praising Ranil. But his dealings with the west [on the Iraq war], the market economy, the absence of any social component to the reforms brought him down. Ranil lost the people because of the reforms.[44]

---

[43] This argument has been laid out in Bastian (2005).
[44] Interview, T.M.R. Rassideen, Colombo, 5 April 2007.

8 | Sectarian Socialism

Between 2001 and 2004, the *Janatha Vimukthi Peramuna* (JVP) emerged at the vanguard of a broad campaign of opposition to the peace process underway between the UNP-led government of Ranil Wickremasinghe and the LTTE. In the months after the signing of the ceasefire agreement in February 2002, the JVP articulated a powerful and coherent ideo-political programme of opposition to the internationally-sponsored peace process, and its foreign sponsors, which it propagated energetically and relentlessly. It successfully capitalised on the growing momentum of economic discontent against the UNF's market reform policies and used its growing influence in the union movement to instigate a series of public sector strikes in hospitals and trains in late 2003 and early 2004. The JVP played a decisive role in mobilising and coalescing public opinion against the peace process, and in bringing about its collapse.

After the 2004 parliamentary election, the JVP's influence as a stubborn and uncompromising coalition partner within the new United Peoples Freedom Alliance (UPFA) government contributed to the failure of all subsequent attempts over the following two years to re-ignite the peace process. The JVP posed impossible pre-conditions to be met before agreeing to talks, refused to tolerate any agreement with the LTTE over joint post-tsunami aid distribution in early 2005, and backed the successful presidential campaign of Mahinda Rajapaksa on a platform explicitly opposed to the peace process. From early 2006 onwards, the JVP openly promoted a military solution to the conflict, goading the government to resume the war that finally resumed in July–August 2006.

This chapter examines the role of the Janatha Vimukthi Peramuna (JVP) in the collapse of the 2001–2004 peace process, and draws on this as an entry point to a broader historical exploration of the JVP as a phenomenon, and to the central themes raised in this book. The material in this chapter must be viewed in close connection to that on the UNP in the previous chapter, which is in many ways, its mirror image. The evolution of the JVP's anti-peace process agenda occurred in parallel to, and in the context of, the same circumstances within which the UNP developed its pro-peace agenda. This chapter draws on primary materials from the JVP's own literature, field interviews with a variety of JVP and non-JVP personalities, newspaper coverage of their activities over the period 1993–2004, secondary literature on the JVP, and data on its union and organisational strength from several sources.

Death and Rebirth

The Janatha Vimukthi Peramuna (JVP) occupies a unique position in the Sri Lankan political landscape as an icon of 'anti-systemic' rage and youth radicalism.[1] Formed in the 1966/67 period as a small splinter group that emerged out of The Communist Party (Peking), itself a small splinter group, the JVP had, by 1971, grown rapidly to gain tens of thousands of young cadres, almost entirely of rural, Sinhala Buddhist origins. In April 1971, the JVP launched an armed rebellion to overthrow the state, but it was quickly suppressed (Alles 1977, Kearney 1975, Arasaratnam 1972, Kearney 1975, Jiggins 1975), with thousands of cadres killed or jailed. The JVP survived repression and jail in the mid-1970s, and re-emerged by the early 1980s as the third largest political force in the south, after the UNP and SLFP.

In the mid-1980s, the JVP went underground once again, and, in 1987, launched a second, far more violent and protracted armed insurgency that almost brought the government to its knees by early 1989 (Gunasekara 1998, Chandraprema 1991, Gunaratna 1990, Attanayake 2001, Moore 1993). This, in turn, invited a far more brutal and exterminationist response from the state security forces and shadowy pro-state militia groups, who, over the second half of 1989, hunted down and summarily executed tens of thousands of JVP cadres and sympathisers. Between 1990 and 1993, the JVP appeared to have disappeared entirely, and many believed that it would never re-emerge. One of the few historical accounts of the 1987–90 insurgency, written immediately after its defeat, would confidently predict (wrongly) that the JVP would never rise again:

---

[1] The use of the term 'anti-systemic' here follows Jagath Senaratne's definition of the JVP as anti-government, anti-state, anti-ruling class, and anti-'alternative left-wing power centres'. See Senaratne 1987: 104–105.

Among the remnants, there are of course some people who harbour delusions of building up the JVP once more. But this is a pipe dream. ... After what they did in 1987–90, they will never again be able to build up a mass following. Somawansa Amarasinghe [the sole surviving central committee member] is still alive and at large. This too has no significance (Chandraprema 1991: 310).

But within five years, the JVP sprang back to life, and once again established itself as a viable electoral contender. Starting with just one parliamentary seat in 1994, the JVP won ten seats in 2000, 16 in 2001, and 39 in 2004. As with the two previous episodes in 1971 and 1987–89, the JVP's third coming in 1994–2006 culminated in a furious blaze of activity that changed the course of Sri Lanka's history. In doing so, it also led to a cycle of decline, transformation, and re-invention. As a post-script to the narratives and episodes in the JVP's evolution described here, it is also important to point out that the JVP suffered a serious decline in its fortunes after its peak in the 2004–06 period. The party suffered two splits, with a more Sinhala nationalist oriented group departing in 2008 under Wimal Weerawansa, and a more socialist, university-student oriented group leaving in 2012 to form the Frontline Socialist Party (FSP). While the specifics of its post-2004 life remain outside the purview of this chapter, the broader circumstances of the party's crisis under the Mahinda Rajapaksa period are briefly addressed in the next chapter.

The JVP's second re-emergence in the mid-1990s proved to be an extremely complicated and challenging task. Tens of thousands of activists and sympathisers had been captured and killed between late 1989 and early 1990. This included virtually the entire national and district level leadership, including their iconic founder-leader Rohana Wijeweera himself, along with 41 of the 42 members of the central committee. The only surviving member of the central committee, Somawansa Amarasinghe, had escaped to exile in Paris, and was struggling to re-establish his leadership over the party and ownership of its brand-name against a number of rival factions, including one headed by Wijeweera's brother-in-law.[2] As a result, the scattered local remnants of the JVP, who remained underground in a state of paralysis and fear, were reluctant to re-emerge into the open. Many had actually been in hiding for an entire decade, as the party had been proscribed since August 1983. The new

---

[2] See *Sunday Times*, 31 July 1994, 'Five Groups Fight for Control of JVP'. Interviews, Wijitha Herath, Gampaha, 28th August 2006, Wasantha Samarasinghe, Colombo, 2nd September 2006.

leader, Somawansa Amarasinghe, himself felt compelled to remain in exile in London, and moved back to Sri Lanka only in 2004, a full decade after the party resumed a legal overground existence.

As with the new UNP leader Ranil Wickremasinghe in the same period, the newly re-created JVP after 1994 was constantly forced to explain that it had indeed made a clean break with its recent violent past. Party leaders and activists found themselves having to refute numerous rumours and accusations that they were secretly re-arming for another rebellion, and suspected that such allegations were planted in the media to serve as the pretext for a renewed phase of repression. However, even with these handicaps and anxieties, the JVP nevertheless bounced back quickly. Between 1997 and 1999, the JVP managed to establish its presence as a mainstream force in local and provincial councils, which it contested vigorously and with increasing success. In most contests, the JVP polled between 5% and 10% of the vote – a return to the levels achieved in the last election it had competed, in 1982.[3] This immediately placed it in third position behind the two main parties, and significantly ahead of all the other smaller, non-minority-based parties. Under Sri Lanka's system of modified proportional representation, this modest vote share nevertheless often translated into a meaningful number of elected representatives, and occasionally, the ability to shift the balance of power.

Much of the JVP's growth in this period related to the specific circumstances of the PA government of President Chandrika Kumaratunga, and the compromises that it sought to strike with respect to economic policy and the ethnic question. For the first time since the rise of the two party system in the mid-1950s, the two main parties had, in the mid-1990s, achieved a substantial degree of convergence in their agendas. The remaining differences between them on major issues were largely a matter of emphasis, tactics, competence, and personalities, rather than principle and direction. But as a direct consequence of this consensus, there was also now an increasingly open and viable space on both the economic left for opposition to the market reforms, and on the Sinhala nationalist right for mobilisation directed at preserving the unitary state and opposition to the devolution of powers along ethnic lines. With the executive presidency in the grasp of elite reformists, this new space for populist opposition to reforms was increasingly manifest in the legislature, and the JVP stood ready to capture and capitalise on the SLFP's lost votes.

---

[3] The JVP had competed in the 1982 District Development Council (DDC) elections and in the 1982 presidential elections before their 1983 proscription.

Marxism and the National Question

As suggested in the two prior chapters, the fundamental analytical enigma of the JVP lies in explaining the ideological and social origins of its hybrid Marxist–Sinhala nationalist persona, and in the connection between these two components. A flexible allegiance to two different ideologies has allowed the JVP to tactically bend from one to the other as the political circumstances demand, and to recruit and mobilise as an authentic representative of both doctrines. This also provided command not only over its natural social base among educated rural Sinhala Buddhist youth (most visibly among university undergraduates), but also allowed it to mobilise and draw in supporters from the trade union movement, and from those agitated on the national question.

The JVP's Leninist party structure and its strict norms of discipline and collective decision-making provided an unparalleled organisational strength. Its dedicated cadre base remained active, conducting constant house-to-house visits and performing acts of public service such as tsunami relief even well beyond the election season. The JVP remained one of the few parties with a constant supply of idealistic young 'full-timers' willing to sacrifice their own careers for a life as a party organiser. In all these respects, the JVP is entirely different in comparison to the other parties, who remain weakly institutionalised, are moribund between elections, and have an entrenched culture of personality-driven politics, clientelism, and indiscipline.

The most critical of these assets that Marxism provided the JVP was the ability to convincingly present its Sinhala nationalism and opposition to ethnic conflict resolution as inspired by ideals of justice, liberation, and equality, rather than by ethnic exclusivism, militarist revanchism or religious zealotry. The JVP angrily and vociferously denied the charge that it was chauvinist,[4] and there was little in their official literature or statements that could be described as arousing overt anti-Tamil sentiment. The JVP has long advocated equal rights for all communities in Sri Lanka and has recognised that Tamils historically suffered discrimination and even violence.

The JVP's 2001 election manifesto, which otherwise bristled with hostility to the upcoming peace process, nevertheless promises to 'ensure equality and democracy to all nationalities, ethnicities and people of different religious faiths, rejecting all forms of chauvinism and tribalism'.[5] The manifesto also pledges

---

[4] For example, see interview with Tilvin Silva: The Hindu, 4 May 1999, 'We Are No Chauvinists'.

[5] JVP 2001 Parliamentary Elections Manifesto.

to rehabilitate Tamils who were displaced by the 1983 riots. As such, although the JVP did pursue an agenda that was little different in substance from Sinhala nationalism, such a characterisation was not self-evident and needed to be carefully qualified. The JVP was certainly not a Sinhala supremacist or exclusivist party, and has not advocated or participated in violence against the minorities. This distinguishes it from the more brash Sinhala nationalism of the Sinhala Urumaya (SU) and its successor, the Jathika Hela Urumaya (JHU), or indeed, the more aggressive Sinhala nationalist groups such as the Bodu Bala Sena (BBS), who are openly sectarian advocates for the Sinhala Buddhists, and have been associated with provocative and inflammatory campaigns against virtually all the other religious and ethnic minorities.

Indeed, the direct target of the JVP's hostility was not the Tamil population at large, but Tamil nationalism as an ideo-political project, which calls for a substantial measure of regional self-government, if not independent statehood, for the island's north and east. As a result of the JVP's ideological *weltanshauung*, and the socialisation of its leading cadres in a socially parochial, 'Sinhala only' environment, the party displayed a complete blind-spot for Tamil nationalism, and it remained a topic that party leaders often found bewilderingly difficult to engage with at any level. Take for example, the following exchange between an audience member and the officiating JVP cadre at a seminar sponsored by the party on the national question in 1997:

> [question by audience member]: 'Can you succinctly describe your solution to the ethnic conflict in this country?'
>
> 'Socialism', answered one of the JVP leaders unequivocally and crisply.
>
> 'What should the Tamil people do until socialist rule is established in the country?' asked another person in the seminar crowd.
>
> 'The Tamils also have to struggle for socialism until then' replied the JVP.[6]

In its campaign against the peace process, the JVP characterised Tamil nationalism as an undemocratic, chauvinistic movement of ethnic exclusivism, promoted by a terrorist organisation, and deeply implicated in a neo-colonialist enterprise by foreign powers to divide and re-conquer the island. The JVP's outlook on Tamil nationalism during the peace process remained heavily influenced by a thesis developed in the mid-1980s by the party's founder-leader Rohana Wijeweera (1986). In an extended polemical engagement within the

---

[6] Midweek Mirror, 16 April 1997, 'JVP Fails to Convince'.

Marxist tradition on the national question, Wijeweera argued that the right to self-determination was not absolute in Leninism: support for a given nationalist movement was conditional on its juxtaposition to world imperialism and to its strategic value to the communist movement.

At certain historical moments, nationalist movements can be progressive, democratic, and liberatory. But at other times, they can be distinctly dangerous, whether as the refuge of reactionary parochial elites, or as the handmaiden of predatory imperialist forces seeking to divide and re-colonise the third world. Tamil nationalism, he argued, (referring primarily to Tamil Nadu's Dravida movement, and by extension, Sri Lanka's Tamil Eelam movement), was in the latter category, and deserved to be opposed on grounds of principle.

> Actually the aim of the DMK movement is completely in line with the aim of US imperialism and their plan of action. It is very clear that US imperialism gives importance for the active expression of the agitation and struggle of the DMK movement for an independent Dravidian land again, after the partial success it has had in generating separatist movements in the north-eastern, eastern, north-western and western, northern India, and the support and aid it has been able to mobilise from countries outside the borders like Pakistan, China and Bangladesh. Should Sri Lanka be partitioned on the boundaries of nationality, should an independent Tamil Eelam state be established it would provide a catalyst for this aim. Therefore it can be a secret to nobody why US imperialism and everybody who wants to break up India have such an interest in the Tamil Eelam movement (Wijeweera 1986).

Beyond the casual and misleading conflation between Indian and Sri Lankan Tamil nationalisms, and the questionable interpretation of Lenin, Wijeweera's work marks an important departure from the other currents of Marxist thought in Sri Lanka. This tradition of radical liberalism and empathy for minority nationalities has historically brought the mainstream (non-JVP) Marxist left into a position of broad sympathy with Tamil nationalism as the democratic expression of a historically discriminated minority. Wijeweera instead argued that Tamil nationalism, through its alleged complicity with imperialism, was a dangerous and reactionary threat.

It is in the context of this assessment, and a growing ethnic war in the mid-1980s that the JVP adopted a radical Sinhala nationalist *deshapremi* (patriotic) agenda in the mid-1980s, and entered into a suicidal confrontation with the state over Indian intervention in 1987. By its own (belated) admission, the JVP was responsible for killing some 6,000 people in 1987–89 in what was ultimately a vast campaign of assassination, strikes, and public intimidation. When ultimately roused into action, the state security forces hunted down and killed almost the entire leadership and tens of thousands of cadres and supporters.

This characterisation of Tamil nationalism as imperialist proxy continued to inform the JVP through the 1990s and formed the substantive framework around which its opposition to the foreign-mediated peace process was constructed in 2001–2004. In effect, the JVP was not itself an open advocate for the exclusive rights of the Sinhala majority, and even maintained a rhetorical denunciation of Sinhala chauvinism. However, through its tireless opposition to even the most moderate versions of the Tamil nationalist agenda, and by implicitly accepting and advocating political positions that were indistinguishable from the Sinhala nationalist mainstream, the JVP effectively became its foremost spokesperson. On the basis of their actions, the JVP was viewed by large sections of Sri Lankan society, and particularly by the Tamil community, as a Sinhala nationalist organisation. But nevertheless, internally, the self-legitimation of the JVP draws upon Wijeweera's formulation that opposition to Tamil nationalism arises not from an oppressive majoritarian impulse to dominate a vulnerable minority, but from an underlying commitment to social liberation, ethnic harmony, and anti-imperialism.

How does the JVP's Sinhala nationalism relate to the rest of the Sri Lankan Marxist tradition? There are two axes along which this relationship can be calibrated. Firstly, in terms of the grand left-right economic polarity of capitalism versus socialism, the JVP is part of the 'new' left, that emerged as radical off-shoots of the more sedentary 'old' left of the Communist Party (CP) and the Lanka Sama Samaja Party (LSSP). The JVP rejected the parliamentary reformism and historic compromises of the old left, instead projecting a more Jacobinite vision of revolutionary socialism. This of course belies the fact that many of these sharp differences have become irrelevant over time, as the JVP itself became a party of parliamentary socialism after 1994. However, at critical points in time after 1994, when the CP and LSSP were coalition partners in power, the JVP was positioned distinctly to the left of those parties.

Secondly, and perhaps more importantly, the difference between the JVP and the Marxist tradition can also be viewed in terms of their approach to the 'national question'. Despite having frequently compromised with Sinhala nationalist forces for electoral expendiency, the non-JVP Marxist parties are traditionally the most minority-friendly entities in the Sri Lankan political spectrum. In most cases, and going back to their founding in the mid-1930s, their leadership consisted mostly of radicalised urban middle class, English-speaking intellectuals. In their prime, during the 1950s–1970s, the old left parties contained a sizeable contingent of Tamils among their leadership, cadre, fellow-travellers, and mass fronts.[7] Since the 1980s, the CP and LSSP have been enthusiastic supporters of a devolved power-sharing mechanism to address the aspirations of the Tamils, while some Marxist parties such as the NSSP have advocated the Tamils' right to self-determination.

In contrast, the JVP has historically been composed overwhelmingly of non-elite Sinhala Buddhists, both at the rank and file and leadership level, and have often been completely against any measures to decentralise powers to the Tamil north and east. Indeed, most of the traditional left parties have long questioned the JVP's ideological credentials, accusing it of being closet Sinhala nationalists in Marxist clothing. Batty Weerakoon, who was general secretary of the Lanka Sama Samaja Party (LSSP) during the 1990s, described the JVP as 'a petty bourgeois party with Marxist slogans. They have communal politics only.'[8] Bala Tampoe of the Ceylon Mercantile Union, an old left-oriented trade union that has lost ground to the JVP's Inter Company Employees Union (ICEU), was characteristically blunt and scathing in his assessment: 'The JVP are completely degenerated Marxists. In fact they know nothing about Marxism, and are straight forward Sinhala chauvinists.'[9] D.W. Subasinghe, who heads the trade union wing of the Communist Party remarked similarly, 'JVP is petty bourgeois, and semi-peasant, not working class. Their growth is on the national question, not on working class issues.'[10]

The JVP was widely held to lack the intellectual depth and statesmanlike bearing of the senior ideologues of the old left. The party was accused of having no base in the working class, and was ridiculed for its shallow and weak grasp of Marxist theory that had led it to flirt eclectically and erratically with Maoism, Che Guevarism, and Trotskyism. One of the JVP's oldest critics from the Marxian left tradition, Dayan Jayatilleka, characterised them as a Pol-Potist force espousing a 'malignant, midget Marxism – a dwarfed, distorted, debased, caricatured Marxism' (Jayatilleka 1995).

---

[7] Although the overwhelming bulk of MPs and votes for the CP or LSSP were from the Sinhalese south.

[8] Interview, Batty Weerakoon, Colombo, 9 April 2007.

[9] Interview, Bala Tampoe, Colombo, 27 July 2006 and 6 September 2006.

[10] Interview, D.W.Subasinghe, Colombo, 8 August 2006.

James Jupp's description of the JVP in the 1970s is in many ways typical of those within or sympathetic to the left tradition, who wish to establish how the JVP represents a fundamental disjuncture with the rest of the Marxist left; he says that 'the JVP was virtually uninfluenced by the sophisticated and cosmopolitan approach of the LSSP' (Jupp 1978:307). Later, he explains that 'to the established left the most obnoxious feature of the JVP was its eclectic and nationalist ideology' (Jupp 1978:314). Unlike the LSSP or CP, the JVP leaders were not members of the westernised middle class, were far less articulate in English, and were mostly of humble, rural origins. Their schooling in Marxist theory was weak, and they had no international connections to speak of.

Impatience with the JVP's ideological fusion of Marxism and Sinhala nationalism is not limited to the Marxist side. Among Sinhala nationalists of the *Jathika Chinthanaya* school, such as Dr. Gunadasa Amarasekera, or Professor Nalin De Silva, there is sympathy for the JVP, but also impatience with its continuing allegiance to Marxism. As Amarasekera explained very frankly:

> Within the JVP there is a deep feeling for nationalism. I think their understanding of Marxism is not very deep. Marxism is a mask to make it look respectable: Lenin, Mao and so on. Don't misunderstand; they are fine fellows who love this country and come from the grass-roots. At some stage in the past they had to have this mask. This is when it was very fashionable, sophisticated, etc. Now it is very discredited. I tell them, throw this bloody mask away. But a volte face is not possible. They must [would have to] openly say that they are not Marxist. They would have to disown their [dead] leader Rohana Wijeweera, a bloody fool of a Marxist.[11]

But these important differences between the Marxist and Sinhala nationalist traditions notwithstanding, it is impossible to understand the JVP's hybrid ideology without reference to the way the mainstream Sri Lankan communist movement had itself become increasingly tainted by association with Sinhala nationalism since the 1950s. In the interests of maintaining and leveraging their electoral relevance, both the old left parties drifted into coalitions within openly Sinhala nationalist governments, hoping to use their cabinet positions as a vehicle to bring a left-wing agenda to bear in government policy, and also to introduce a voice of moderation to counteract the Sinhala nationalism of their allies. What happened more often is that the CP and LSSP were forced into

---

[11] Interview, Gunadasa Amarasekera, Colombo, 8 April 2007.

defending policies that they had earlier stood against, and found that Sinhala nationalism was creeping into their own organisations. James Jupp describes this process within the LSSP in the early 1960s:

> For nearly six years the LSSP leaders resisted the Sinhala Only tide, facing abuse, violence and defection in the process. … Within the largest of the Marxist parties there was a constant disciplinary problem created by the tension between adhering to a demanding ideological position and functioning within a society which was making that position electorally untenable (Jupp 1978: 103).

Similarly, when Robert Kearney interviewed LSSP leaders in the 1960s and 1970s, to understand their increasing collaboration with the Sinhala nationalism that they had earlier fought against, the answers he received were essentially the very same factors that the JVP would pick up on a generation later: (i) that there was a progressive element to Sinhala nationalism; (ii) the fact that it was electorally unbeatable:

> [T]he Sinhalese resurgence had galvanised the masses and created the genuine mass movement of the contemporary period. The movement expressed deeply felt popular aspirations and contained 'progressive' features, particularly as it represented the class revolt of the Sinhalese-educated rural masses against the English-educated classes, as well as containing 'reactionary' divisive and obscurantist features. In the existing circumstances, the Samasamajists claimed, the strength of the movement was so great that opposition to it was futile and progress was possible only by associating with it and guiding it into progressive channels (Kearney 1973: 432).

But the JVP's adherence to Marxism is not merely an ideological sleight of hand to mask its inner chauvinist core. Neither is it the case that the mixture of these two tendencies represents an uneasy marriage or macro-level coalition arrived at between two distinct factions, for it occurs at a far more molecular level, and is as such impossible to disentangle. In supplanting the 'old left' parties from the late 1960s onwards, the JVP became heir to an established tradition of grass-roots collaboration and cross-pollination between the popular radical idiom of Marxism and Sinhala nationalism. It is for this reason that the JVP represents what is referred to as the 'children of 1956' (Roberts 1989b: 72). The populist upsurge in 1956 represented the first coming together of an electoral alliance of Sinhala nationalists and Marxists. The JVP represents the child of that union: a corporeal fusion of Marxism and Sinhala nationalism that exhibits both characteristics in seamless combination. As JVP leader

Somawansa Amarasinghe himself described upon returning to Sri Lanka in early 2004, 'We love this country. Before we became Marxists, we were patriots'.[12] The JVP, he held, 'did not import Marxism in its outdated raw form but infused certain Marxist elements with the indigenous Sinhala Buddhist culture, the result of more than 2000 years of an unbroken civilisation that existed'.[13]

'The Principal Socialist Party in the Country'

One of the JVP's most important achievements in its third phase was to emerge as a party of organised labour, in command of a large trade union base. This in itself was an entirely new development for the JVP. The Employers Federation of Ceylon (EFC)'s annual member survey shows that the ICEU, which had no branches in any of the more than 400 surveyed companies in 1997, became the fastest growing union in subsequent years, and had captured 16% of all unionised employees by 2002. The Labour Secretariat records show that ICEU membership grew from 9,747 to 35,116 between 2000 and 2005.[14] This had not been the case previously with the JVP, and much of its growth occurred at the expense of unions that had historically been under the influence of political parties of the 'old left', the Communist Party (CP) and the Lanka Sama Samaja Party (LSSP).[15]

At the time that this occurred, in the late 1990s, these left parties were in power as coalition partners in the PA government of President Chandrika Kumaratunga. This is also the period when some of the most ambitious privatisations of public sector enterprises were conducted, including the massive plantation sector, Sri Lankan Airlines, and Sri Lanka Telecom. For the most part, the organised labour movement was deeply opposed to the economic reform agenda, and grew increasingly frustrated at the complicity of their traditional intellectual and political leaders in the CP and LSSP in

---

[12] Business Today, 27 February 2004, Interview of Somawansa Amarasinghe by Lucien Rajakarunanayake.

[13] Asian Tribune, 20 January 2004, Interview of Somawansa Amarasinghe by Walter Jayawardhana.

[14] I am grateful to Mr. D.M.S.Dissanayake, Commissioner of Labour for providing access to this data in August 2006.

[15] Lanka Sama Samaja Party (1996), *The Tasks Ahead:Lanka Sama Samaja Party & the P.A. Government: Documents, Statements, Press Releases of the LSSP, 1994–1996*. Colombo: Lanka Sama Samaja Party.

its implementation. The reality was that despite being coalition partners in government, these two parties were marginal to economic policy formulation and were powerless to affect the pace or direction of the reforms. The LSSP's press releases and party statements of the time are replete with grave ambivalence and much hand-wringing on issues of subsidy withdrawals, privatisation, and the renewal of the emergency provisions.[16] One LSSP leader confessed to the media:

> We are against privatisation, but everybody thinks that we are in favour of privatisation. When our party members went to express their protest about the privatisation of the Steel Corporation we were told that it was no use joining protest campaigns after agreeing to it at cabinet level.[17]

Workers from unions attached to pro-government parties were constantly frustrated at the inability of their leadership to translate cabinet level influence into tangible benefits, and began looking for more radical alternatives. It is under these circumstances that the JVP managed to make significant inroads into the union movement for the first time in their history, largely out of defections from other left wing-led unions. As a JVP trade union leader described 'Our growth was from other unions, not from newly unionised'.[18] One rival union leader described the JVP's strategy as an 'aggressive, unethical stance towards building up unions'.[19]

Emblematic of this trend is a news report from May 2000 of how an LSSP-affiliated union quickly shut down two acrimonious strikes involving over 1,000 workers following the promulgation of new emergency regulations. Following this, 'Workers resigned en masse from the [LSSP union] in protest over its betrayal of the strike and formed another union affiliated to the Janatha Vimukthi Peramuna (JVP)'.[20] As the leader of the CP's trade union wing lamented:

> Our leadership in the unions was compromised as pro-government. They [JVP] had a different image. They are better organised. Their cadres are committed, and all over the country.[21]

---

[16] LSSP (1996).

[17] Sunday Times, 27 July 1997, 'LSSP to Quit Cabinet'.

[18] Interview, Wasantha Samarasinghe, Colombo, 2 September 2006.

[19] Interview, Gerald Lodwyk, Colombo, 9 April 2007.

[20] WSWS, 'Sri Lankan unions abruptly end two long-running strikes', 30 May 2000.

[21] Interview, D.W. Subasinghe, Colombo, 8 August 2006.

Wasantha Samarasinghe, who was general secretary of the JVP's private sector trade union federation, the Inter Company Employees Union (ICEU), claimed that his union contained 100,000 members in 492 branches as of 2006, mostly from large corporates, hotels, and manufacturing enterprises.[22] Not unsurprisingly, the leaders of non-JVP unions and left party activists interviewed were all, without exception, hostile to the JVP and singled them out for strong criticism. Bala Tampoe, an elder statesman of the trade union movement who had acted as lawyer to the JVP in the 1970s said: 'They are not interested in building working class organisations. They just want a vote bank.'[23] Leslie Devendra of the SLFP affiliated Sri Lanka Nidahas Sevaka Sangamaya (SLNSS) said 'I think their influence in the trade unions is very sad for this country. Their style of militancy is very bad for the trade union movement and for the country.'[24] M.R. Shah of the non-partisan Ceylon Bank Employees Union (CBEU) charged them with being 'disruptive elements in the working class'.[25]

As the JVP general secretary Tilvin Silva described :

[The CP and LSSP] betrayed the working classes who for more than half a century had depended on them. After accepting portfolios in the capitalist governments, they have lost both their independence and the confidence of the people. We have come into fill this gap and are today the principal socialist party in the country.[26]

Marxism with Indubitably Sinhalese Characteristics

Between early 2000 and late 2005, the JVP assumed the position of the leading Sinhala nationalist organisation in the country in the context of shaping and leading the opposition to the Norway-mediated peace process. The JVP vociferously opposed any attempt to politically resolve the ethnic conflict, whether through negotiations and a political settlement with the LTTE, or even through an internally generated package of state reform and devolution independent of the LTTE. This position was articulated in terms of a fairly

---

[22] Interview, Wasantha Samarasinghe.
[23] Interviews, Bala Tampoe, Colombo, 27 July 2006 and 6 September 2006.
[24] Interview, Leslie Devendra, Colombo, 9 April 2007
[25] Interview, M.R. Shah, Colombo, 28 September 2006.
[26] Sunday Times, 6 April 1997, 'We are the Third Force in the Country Now – Tilvin'.

standard Sinhala nationalist narrative: any attempt to disturb the 'unitary character' of the Sri Lankan state would be a step towards the division of the country.

From March 2000 onwards, the JVP initiated a long campaign against the introduction of Norwegian mediators.[27] A few months later in August 2000, it was once again in the forefront of nationwide protests against President Kumaratunga's new constitution and devolution proposals. In the aftermath of the December 2001 elections, it was the JVP, rather than the dispirited SLFP, that remained energised and concentrated on coalescing and leading the opposition to the evolving cease-fire and peace process. In the following months, the JVP effectively stole a march over the other forces in opposition by taking the initiative to categorically oppose the CFA (February 2002), negotiations with the LTTE (September 2002 – March 2003), the government's interim power-sharing proposals (May–October 2003), and the LTTE's counter-proposals (November 2003). Even after the elections of April 2004, the JVP remained deeply hostile to the resumption of any negotiations with the LTTE (May 2004 – December 2004), and were instrumental in the failure of P-TOMS, the post-tsunami aid-sharing mechanism, which, in retrospect, proved to be the last meaningful engagement of the peace process (March–July 2005).

The JVP's increasing association with Sinhala nationalism in the post-2000 period did not signify an abandonment of activism on traditionally economic or class-based issues. The insecurities generated by the economic crisis of 2000–2001, and the subsequent UNF government's market reforms, provided the JVP with a growing base of support from a variety of sources, including farmers, the unemployed, and public sector workers. At an ideological and practical level, the JVP's success lay in their ability to fold these often spontaneous sources of predominantly economic opposition into component elements of an over-arching and coherent Sinhala nationalist framework. As such, opposition to economic globalisation became part of an encompassing movement of resistance against predatory neo-colonial powers, international NGOs, and international capital, all of whom were accused of conspiring to divide and recolonise the country through the peace process.

The international supporters of the UNF government and the peace process became unwitting participants in the construction and articulation of the JVP's ideo-political position by offering to release generous financial support

---

[27] Tamilnet, 13 March 2000, 'JVP to Agitate against Norway's role'.

conditional upon economic reforms and progress in the peace process. By campaigning against both the economic reforms and the peace process, and by ideologically conflating these two elements, the JVP was in effect mirroring its opponents. Just as the UNP envisaged the peace agenda as a component element of an economic development strategy based on market reforms and greater global integration, so the JVP argued that the peace process and market reforms were part of a coherent assault by a constellation of foreign forces and their domestic quislings to weaken, fragment and re-conquer the island. As Tilvin Silva, the JVP's general secretary described it:

> On the one side, the country is being sold to transnational corporations through the Regaining Sri Lanka programme while on the other, a separate state is being given to the LTTE.[28]

One factor behind the JVP's success in mobilising on both issues is that the other elements of the Sri Lankan left who could have competed for control of the economic opposition were torn between the two issues. The LSSP, CP, NSSP and the large majority of the non-JVP trade unions were deeply opposed to the government's economic agenda, but were supportive of the peace process. The government of Ranil Wickremasinghe was pursuing a number of controversial reforms on land, labour, and privatisation, but many non-JVP unions and left-parties held back from campaigning on these issues for fear of disrupting the fragile peace process.[29] On balance, they tactically prioritised peace over economic issues, and many in the Marxist left ultimately decided to support the government. In October 2003, and again in January 2004, when the government (and hence the peace process) appeared in danger of collapsing under the weight of the JVP-led campaign, the main non-JVP left parties met with Ranil Wickremasinghe and agreed to use their influence to defuse trade union pressure on the government in return for a postponement of the more controversial parts of the reform agenda such as privatisation and labour law reform.[30] In practice, very little came of this effort. The left was not strong enough to prevent the collapse of the peace process, but nevertheless laid themselves open to the charge

---

[28] Sunday Times, 21 September 2003, 'SLFP leaders more concerned about astrologers than issues – JVP leader' (interview of Tilvin Silva by Shelani Perera).

[29] Interview Vickramabahu Karunarathne, Colombo, 21 September 2006.

[30] WSWS, 8 March 2004, 'The NSSP, the "peace process" and the Sri Lankan elections', and Sunday Times, 11 January 2004, 'A Government tries to put on a Brave Face'.

of collaborating in the government's unpopular reform agenda at a time of growing worker unrest.

In contrast, the JVP was consistent and unrestrained in its opposition to the government on both peace and economic reforms. Fortuitously for the JVP, the timing of the implementation of both these agenda items also closely overlapped, so that controversial economic reform issues were introduced and debated amidst a parallel escalation of anxieties relating to the peace process. For example, in early January 2003, the government introduced four new bills on labour law reform[31] on virtually the same day that the critical fourth round of negotiations with the LTTE were initiated in Thailand. Both of these issues aroused considerable anxiety in themselves and were occasion for widespread anti-government demonstrations by a variety of different organisations. But over the course of the following week, the JVP adroitly exploited these distinct sources of tension and fused them together by bringing 25,000 people onto the streets of the capital Colombo in the biggest opposition rally against the government to date.[32]

Following this, the JVP launched a series of increasingly powerful demonstrations on an almost monthly basis that paralysed Colombo through the end of 2003. These were also accompanied by a wave of industrial action in the public sector, many in critical public services. In August–November 2003, the JVP brought anti-government sentiment to fever pitch by instigating an almost continuous sequence of high profile strikes, marches through the country, and massive demonstrations against the peace process, and a variety of other political actions in centre of Colombo.

In late September 2003, 80,000 hospital workers went on strike for 13 days, paralysing health services. As soon as they returned to work, 10,000 railway employees went on strike, causing chaos in the public transport system. Meanwhile, the JVP-affiliated Joint Union of Unemployed Graduates (JUUG) held a continuous protest outside Fort railway station for two months protesting lack of public sector jobs. Numerous other government departments and public sector companies also threatened strike action, as did farmers unions.

---

[31] Respectively, the Termination of Employment of Workmen (Special Provisions Amendment) Bill, the Industrial Disputes (Hearing and Determination of Proceedings (Special Provisions) Bill, the Industrial Disputes (Amendment) Bill and the Employment of Women, Young Persons and Children (Amendment) Bill.

[32] Tamilnet, 8 January 2003: 'Massive JVP Rally Condemns Peace Talks', Daily Mirror, 9 January 2003, 'JVP Vows to Topple Government this Year', Island, 9 January 2003, 'Norwegian-led Peace Will Lead the Country to Ruins – JVP'.

Table 8.1 | Main JVP Protests and Union Actions January 2003–February 2004

Date	Location	Strength	Cause	Organisers
8 Jan 03	Colombo	25,000	Peace/Labour	JVP
20 Feb 03	March to Colombo	50,000	CFA anniversary	JVP
10 Mar 03	Colombo	100,000	Peace process	JVP plus allies
25 Apr 03	Colombo	'thousands'	Peace process.	JVP
6 Jun 03	Colombo	10,000	Peace process	JVP
25 Jun 03	Colombo	5,000	Peace process	JVP
12 Aug 03	Colombo	thousands	Peace process	JVP
28 Aug 03	Galle–Colombo march	100,000	Peace process	JVP
16–29 Sep 03	Strike action	80,000	various	Hospital unions
22 Sep 03	Colombo	30,000	various	Hospital unions
1–3 Oct 03	Strike action	20,000	Privatisation	Railway unions
1 Oct 03	Kandy–Colombo march	100,000+	Peace process	PNM
21 Oct 03	Strike Action		Public Sector	JVP
24 Oct 03	Colombo	100,000+	Anti-govt	SLFP
7 Nov 03	Colombo	'thousands'	Peace process	PNM
19 Jan 04	Hunger Strike	10	Labour legislation	ICEU (JVP union)
25 Jan 04	Hunger Strike	12	Salary package	Hospital unions
Jan–Feb 04	Strike Action	10,000	Privatisation	Railway unions
6–9 Feb 04	Hunger Strike	13 farmers	Fertiliser subsidy	JVP farmers union

Source: Compiled from the Daily Mirror, Sunday Times, Daily News, Tamilnet, The Island.

Many of these strikes were directly instigated by the JVP through their new-found influence in the unions, with the explicit intention of destabilising the government. But there was also a considerable independent and spontaneous element, fuelled by the growing economic anxieties over issues such as privatisation and the weakening of protective labour regulations. In addition, the IMF-inspired fiscal austerity measures implemented in 2002, including the fertiliser subsidy cut and the public sector hiring freeze, had predisposed a variety of different socio-economic constituencies against the government. As one independent trade union leader – who supported the peace process – described: 'The entire work-force in the country was opposed to Ranil'.[33]

---

[33] Interview, M.R. Shah, Colombo, 28 September 2006.

The growing scale of the JVP's anti-government juggernaut in late 2003 was directed, on the one hand, at the government itself, but was also tactically directed to pressure President Chandrika Kumaratunga to use her constitutional powers to destabilise and dismiss the UNF government, dissolve parliament, and trigger fresh parliamentary elections. A new wave of strikes ensued in January 2004, just as the final negotiations were underway between the JVP and the president. There was a sudden outbreak of hunger strikes by the JVP unions protesting labour legislation outside the labour ministry, by hospital workers outside the health ministry, and by farmers against the withdrawal of the fertiliser subsidy. Finally, there was another mammoth strike that shut down the railways from 27 January to 9 February 2004. All these strikes converged on Colombo and were brought to a climax in the first week of February 2004. The instrumental and political nature of the strike wave, and the extent to which it was under the direct control of the JVP became very evident when the strikes suddenly ended on 9 February, as soon President Kumaratunga agreed to dissolve parliament and hold elections on 2 April.

Class and Nation

The apparent triumph of ethnicity over class in the post-colonial history of Sri Lanka does not imply that class is irrelevant, either as a category for political mobilisation or ideo-political analysis. Indeed, the mass appeal of Sinhala nationalism lies in the fact that it is fundamentally rooted in the dynamics of class. This is not to say that the JVP can be easily understood as a simple class phenomenon, and neither is it the case that it can be reduced to any one class, for the steady increase in its electoral support during 1994–2004 clearly signifies an expanding appeal among different social groups.

This is also not to equate the popularity of the JVP with the prevalence of poverty in the abstract sense, for the majority of those officially classified as 'the poor' have consistently not voted for the JVP (Rampton 2002). In other words, both in terms of class and poverty, it is necessary to situate the JVP not by studying class in itself, or the extent of the deprivation of their supporters per se, but by where the JVP's support bases are located and how they have evolved with respect to the class structure as a whole. As a sociological phenomenon, the JVP's support base comprise the educated rural Sinhala Buddhist population of poorer backgrounds who are the social products of the expansion of free Sinhala-medium secondary and university education. They came of age in the aftermath of the Sinhala nationalist upsurge in 1956, were nurtured in the vernacular cultural renaissance of the time, and absorbed the powerful Marxist and Sinhala nationalist anti-systemic ideo-political currents that this unleashed.

At the time of the JVP's 1971 uprising, the social background of the 10,192 insurgents who surrendered or were captured were recorded in considerable detail by the authorities, and were later published in a paper by Gananath Obeyesekere. The figures revealed by Obeyesekere are remarkable not only for the extent to which they provide a unique set of data on a large number of participants in a revolutionary movement, but for the degree of homogeneity of this group. Of those in custody, 98% were Sinhalese, 95% Sinhala Buddhist, 89% were aged under 30, and 92% were the children of farmers, labourers, plantation workers or the low grades of government service, and 86% had attended rural secondary schools.[34] The JVP's first insurgency can, as such, be accurately summarised as a movement of secondary school educated, Sinhala Buddhist youth of under-privileged rural backgrounds. In a very large number of cases, they were the children of small or middle level farmers from areas that were geographically, economically, and psychologically very peripheral to the capital Colombo.

It is within these circumstances of enduring economic, social, political, and regional exclusion, reproduced through different generations of state policy, that Sinhala nationalism finds expression as a positional stance of anti-elite protest. In post-colonial Sri Lanka, where the ruling economic and political elite has been characterised by conspicuous cultural westernisation, the articulation of class consciousness and hostility by the poorer strata seeking upward mobility has constantly reverted to an assertion of nativist authenticity and Sinhala nationalism. This is not to say that the 'elite' and 'mass' describe homogenous, static, stable, or consistent categories, for the internal differentiation within the 'mass' is a critical factor in the enduring appeal of Sinhala nationalism, and its continuous re-emergence in the political sphere. Neither are these

---

[34] Obeyesekere (1974). The descriptive statistics presented here are modified to exclude Obeyesekere's category of 'unspecified' from calculation of percentages. There are of course evident risks in using such data, the most serious of which is the possibility that it might over-represent the social categories presumed to be guilty by the police, and who were hence more actively sought out by them for capture and arrest. If the police searched out young, educated, unemployed Sinhala Buddhists for arrest, then they would clearly be over-represented in the sample. This concern is partly mitigated by the fact that only 44% of the total 10,192 were actually arrested while 56% had surrendered themselves.

divisions based on insurmountable ascriptive categories, for they occur in a context of perceived expectation of social mobility, and particularly, upward inter-generational mobility.

The critical link between class and nationalism is provided by the social democratic state, and by the enduring relevance of the state from late-colonial times in promoting the class transition of upwardly mobile rural communities. The materiality of nationalism is thus intimately connected to the fact that the state is the largest material benefactor in society; and that Sinhala nationalism is an ideology that connects the people to the state. By providing education and welfare, protecting and promoting domestic entrepreneurs, and generating direct employment opportunities, the social democratic state became the vehicle by which the lives of the rural poor could be completely and permanently transformed.

Sri Lanka's social democratic state, which went through a long phase of expansion from the 1940s to the 1970s, has, since the 1980s, experienced periodic phases of compression. After the early 1990s, the only part of the state that grew consistently was the military. The war in effect, preserved the social democratic features of the state and many of the functions of poverty reduction and upward social mobility that it earlier performed. Considering that many aspects of social policy have been encroached upon by non-governmental organisations and foreign aid donors during this period, there was an erosion of the public service component of the state and a proportional increase in the military role of the state. In rural (Sinhalese) Sri Lanka, the military has, since the 1990s, performed an important function in employment provision to the collapsing small-holder rural economy. Chapter 5 shows that the military had become the single largest employer of rural youth, accounting for as many as half of all cash-paying jobs in some areas. The preservation of the militarised social democratic state is thus one of the central impulses that continues to provoke Sinhala nationalism. It provided the ideological and social context within which the JVP re-emerged into electoral relevance in the 1990s.

Sinhala nationalism therefore forms part of the socio-political assertion of a certain segment of the 'mass' for whom nationalism is effectively an ideological expression of their material claims upon the social democratic state: a claim that is widely viewed as righteous and legitimate, and that emanates from a system of moral regulation. Amidst the juggernaut of market de-regulation, privatisation and the systematic neglect and under-funding of the state sector, the re-assertion of Sinhala nationalism by a party of populist Marxism, the dogged opposition to the devolution of the state's powers, and the widespread appeal of an anti-globalisation ideology all point in the same direction. They characterise the desperate strategies of those close to the bottom of the ladder to preserve and protect the social democratic state, in which lies their only realistic chance of emerging from a life of poverty, and of improving their life chances for themselves and their coming generations.

Sinhala nationalist mobilisation is thus not necessarily an alternative to class, but is, in many ways, a reversion to class mobilisation through more successful means. It mobilises class-based grievances, but not by appealing systematically to class at all, or by appealing to the working class as such, or even to the most depressed or disadavantaged groups. Instead, it taps into the tremendous vats of discontent from a variety of under-privileged groups in Sinhalese society for whom the preservation of the shrinking social democratic state is a matter of desperate urgency. Lacking independent wealth, they continue to depend on state provision of education, health, and employment to sustain themselves and to maintain their standard of living. And it is through the ideological apparatus of Sinhala nationalism, deeply inflected with economic populism, that opposition to the diminution of the state – whether through market reform or devolution – emerges conflated, though maybe not in an entirely coherent manner, into the political realm. In other words, the JVP succeeded where other Marxists failed, by mobilising class through the symbols and moral idiom of the nation. Similarly, they successfully projected themselves as the defenders of the nation in terms of their authentic roots in class politics.

9 | Conclusions: Elites, Masses and the Rajapaksa Presidency

In May 2017, construction workers building Colombo's new Shangri La hotel reported the discovery of human skeletal remains under the site. For a brief period, work was paused. Discomfort and embarrassment served to interrupt the forward march of development, as people wondered what might have been uncovered, and what it might lead to. Who were these people? How did they die? How did their bodies come to be buried in that spot? The ten acre piece of land in question was previously the headquarters of the Sri Lankan army, and had been the nerve-centre of military operations during the civil war. Were these the bodies of those who had gone missing or who disappeared in that period?

Shortly after the end of the war in 2009, the army was relocated in order to release this prime piece of real estate facing the Arabian sea and Galle Face Green for commercial development. The Hong Kong-based Shangri La group which purchased it had reportedly invested US$600 million to transform the site into a majestic and exclusive property development with a hotel, luxury apartments, and a shopping mall.

Upon the discovery of the human remains, an investigation was announced. In the meanwhile, construction work resumed and was completed within six months. The Shangri La hotel was ceremonially opened by the president in November 2017. No further information on the investigation was released, or is likely to emerge, so that the discovery of the bodies under this temple to affluence and futurism remains only as a macabre metaphor – a glimpse of the way in which development is being used to bury the conflict and consign it to the past. This task may not be easy: with over 65,000 complaints of missing people that have accumulated in various commissions of enquiry over the course of the war, there are possibly many more such skeletons to be uncovered in the years to come.

In this book, development and conflict have been articulated in terms of the dynamics of two separate spheres. On the one hand, as Cowen and Shenton

(1996) explain, there are the 'immanent' processes by which real world socio-economic transformations affect the dynamics of nationalist consciousness, ethnic politics, and the course of the civil war. On the other, there is the realm of the 'intentional' – the way that particular representations of these immanent dynamics are distilled into knowledge and cast into policy. The study of 'intentional' development and conflict is polarised between radically different perspectives on its intentions and possibilities. Firstly, there is an optimistic and positivist view that dominates in the world of policy formulation in ministries and aid agencies: development can – if it is planned, researched, and executed appropriately – prevent, mitigate, and reverse conflict. The fact that it often fails in this ambition is put down to flawed implementation, or inadequate design. Secondly, there is a pessimistic and suspicious view in the critical social science literature: development amounts to a projection of power or ethnic domination, so that behind a façade of well-intentioned technicality lies an instrumental agenda that is based on control and domination.

These ideas and understandings of development and nationalism are all relevant, and many of the chapters in this book speak to and draw on them. But what often emerges is that in themselves, these are often incomplete and inadequate. They suggest intentionality and first order causality, whereas the effects described in this book show how some of the most important connections between development, nationalism, and conflict have been unintentional, unforeseen, contingent outcomes from causal links that are not direct. In other words, it is not necessary to presume that development policy was inherently nationalist and conflictual, in the sense that it was formulated by chauvinistic demagogues, or that it was implemented by bigoted or insensitive bureaucrats (although both factors were far from absent). The dynamics of the conflict, socio-economic change and development policies were so tightly interwoven as to make it meaningless to disaggregate them in order to achieve two commonly posed historical counter-factual scenarios: firstly, that if not for the outbreak of the conflict, Sri Lanka would have achieved the same level of prosperity as Dubai or Singapore; secondly, and seemingly contrarily, that faster economic growth could have prevented the outbreak of conflict in the first place.

Nevertheless, despite their shortcomings in terms of theory and causality, these founding formulations on development, nationalism, and conflict are still significant as widely shared narratives and representations. Their significance can be understood in a different way: as the rationale through which real world agents view this relationship to work. That is, neither the positivist optimism (that development can reverse conflict) nor the instrumentalist suspicion (that it is a projection of power) necessarily amount to adequate or coherent alternatives in themselves. What makes them important is that they constitute the cognitive basis upon which people – governments, policy makers, political actors, and political subjects – understand development and conflict to be connected. It is in this way that they explain the motives and actions of people and influence real world outcomes. The task, thus, is not of choosing between being economic naïvete and political paranoia, or of charting some tortuous middle path of compromise between them, but to find an analytical vantage point and an inter-disciplinary sensibility that can recognise and engage with them both.

Sinhala nationalism has been explored here primarily in terms of two fundamental aspects and levels: its social character, and its inner cognitive framework. In this chapter, there is an extension into another element: institutions. Chapters 2 and 3 start with the social character, exploring the historical context in which Sinhala nationalism became a mass political phenomenon. That is, Sinhala nationalism is situated within a template of 'elite–mass' politics at a time of electoral expansion and socio-economic transformation. Sinhala nationalism became widely influential as a political ideology at a time when rapid political and economic transformation brought the material fortunes and aspirations of a large part of the population under the ambit of the expanding state. The analysis in chapter 3 follows one important avenue of social change and upward mobility: the transition from peasant proprietors to state employment. Under conditions of deteriorating peasant agriculture in the 1930s, education and government employment provided a vehicle for upward mobility in income and social status. The slow but steady increase in the popularity and viability of this mechanism in the first half of the 20th century was strictly limited by its high opportunity cost and by the availability of English language secondary schools. Nevertheless, it remained heavily sought after and had – even as early as the 1930s – started provoking signs of tension along Sinhala–Tamil lines.

By the mid-1950s, the expansion of free secondary education, combined with the demographic effects of malaria eradication, vastly and suddenly expanded this pathway of upward mobility. In an increasingly competitive situation where the aspirations for state employment were clearly incommensurate with the availability of such jobs, Sinhala nationalism was embraced and, in turn, defined, by those segments of the population described by Ivor Jennings: 'the sons of small cultivators, minor officials, shop-keepers, and the lower middle-class groups generally' (1954: 344). That is, Sinhala nationalism became inscribed as the way in which equal and rightful entitlement – or what amounts to prioritised treatment – from the state could be claimed by virtue of membership in a community of Sinhala Buddhists.

There are two important implications of framing Sinhala nationalism within this historical and socio-economic basis. Firstly, its association with lower ranked social groups, and their frustrated ambitions to upward mobility has meant that Sinhala nationalism is embedded with a powerful anti-elite, counter-hegemonic, redistributive moral core. Secondly, the fact that Sinhala nationalism has remained an enduring and central feature of the Sri Lankan political landscape implies that it draws sustenance from the constant reproduction of the same kinds of social processes and frustrations. Both of these factors emerge again in chapter 5, where the role of state employment in upward mobility and poverty alleviation through military employment is re-examined under conditions of market reform.

Given that inequality had increased, incomes were stagnant, and employment opportunities for educated Sinhalese youth had shrunk, it would appear that the circumstances of the 1990s provided fertile ground for a resurgence of political turmoil and social instability; particularly given that there existed a widely available vernacular vocabulary of anti-state economic protest within the canon of Sinhala nationalism. Indeed, chapter 8 describes how the JVP's ideo-political mix of Sinhala nationalism and Marxism placed it in a uniquely advantageous position to capture the mounting insecurity among small-holder farmers, industrial workers, the urban lower-middle class, and the large swathe of the population that depends critically on the state for basic services, livelihoods, and life chances. However, the economic repercussions of the war also provided the means whereby these tensions were contained and cushioned. By providing tens of thousands of secure, stable, pensionable government jobs to educated rural youth, who otherwise had no other means of security or upward mobility, the war in the north perversely bought a measure of social peace and well-being to the poorest communities in the south.

The significance of this social transition and social welfare in building and sustaining support for Sinhala nationalism can be judged in the light of its influence during the peace process, and in the electoral verdict of April 2004. Chapter 7 describes how conditions of economic crisis and fiscal austerity forced the government to suspend public sector recruitment during the early months of the peace process. During the two year-long peace process, the size of the public sector dropped by 20%, and the government's privatisation programme threatened to extend this much further. The elections of April 2004 captured the growing sense of economic insecurity that the government aroused, and the opposition exploited this well, offering to restore the fertiliser subsidy, and to increase government employment for the educated unemployed.

In chapters 2 and 4, the analysis of Sinhala nationalism shifted from the socio-economic side to the ideo-political. Sinhala nationalism not only provided the island's majority community with a single shared collective identity and a sense of collective aspiration, but also a broader moral framework. That is, it constitutes a system of governing and regulating electoral politics in the defence of a set of core values, goals, and ideals of supreme veneration. In its content, Sinhala nationalism contains strong ideas about the valid and legitimate role of the state in society. This includes the protection of peasant agriculture, public health and education, redistributive social justice, and the prioritisation of the material, cultural, and spatial claims of the Sinhala Buddhists vis-à-vis other lesser claimants.

The existence of such a strongly defined and widely held conception of state legitimacy has had serious consequences for the project of ethnic conflict resolution or market-driven development. Any government that wished to pursue these reforms would effectively be confronting what the Sinhala Buddhist public widely considered to be the implicit social contract between the rulers and the ruled. The first such state reform project, directed towards addressing the ethnic conflict and achieving a lasting reconciliation with the Tamil minority, broadly comes under the category of 'de-Sinhalising' the state. An important component of such reforms is the devolution of powers from Colombo towards the Tamil-dominated areas of the north and east. The second such project of state reform is the economic agenda of market liberalisation, which basically involves a dismantling of redistributive policies, the privatisation of state enterprises, and the deregulation of state control over the factors of production: land, labour and capital. It implies a substantial withdrawal of the state from the central economic role it came to play during the 1950s–70s.

Chapter 4 went on to describe how a new elite-driven counter-populist agenda of state reform took shape and became strategised under J. R. Jayewardene's UNP in the 1970s. Jayewardene had a keen appreciation for the fact that his economic agenda ran counter to the economic morality of nationalism, and needed to find new ways to win consent. In addition to rolling back the space for populist electoral democracy through the executive presidency, he camouflaged his reform agenda under an exaggerated performance of Buddhist religiosity and populist development schemes infused with the imagery of

Sinhala nationalism. In effect, he sought to pre-emptively capture control of the symbols and language of resistance that might be used against him. However, there were two important shortcomings of this approach that made Jayewardene a prisoner, and then, a victim, of his own strategy.

Firstly, the UNP's assumption of an explicit and exaggerated Sinhala Buddhist identity led to the growing alienation and radicalisation of the Tamils, and played a direct role in the escalation to civil war. Secondly, having let loose the genie of Sinhala nationalism, he found it impossible to keep control of it. Instead, it grew, became dangerous, and gained a life of its own, preventing him from making even the modest concessions that might have either resolved the conflict or legitimised the parliamentary Tamil opposition. As a result, when he was ultimately forced to accept an Indian-imposed solution in 1987, it unleashed all that he had struggled to contain in the unprecedented violence of the second JVP insurgency. The implications are that a market-reforming government in Sri Lanka is in an inherently weak position to implement a solution to the ethnic conflict.

Chapter 4 introduces one of the central features of the Sri Lankan political party system in the way that it has evolved under the influence of Sinhala nationalism since 1956, one which has complicated the resolution of the conflict since then. The left–right axis, as it has emerged in mature liberal democratic party systems and in other regions of South Asia, is commonly defined so that the 'left' and the 'right' as defined by economic redistribution and ethnic minority rights is consistent. The 'right' generally signifies economic and cultural conservatism in terms of privileging the dominant position of the wealthy and the dominant cultural/religious group. Similarly, the 'left' signifies the opposite on both counts, signifying economic redistribution and ethno-cultural equality. The orientation of the party system along such lines in India, Pakistan, and Bangladesh, for example, is anchored primarily by the position of the Indian National Congress, the Pakistan People's Party, and the Awami League respectively, as the mainstream parties that have historically positioned themselves consistently to the left on both issues

However, this situation stands perfectly reversed in the Sri Lankan political spectrum, where the party that stands furthest to the right in economic terms (UNP) is historically the furthest to the left of the mainstream spectrum on issues of ethnic and religious minorities. The SLFP that emerged in 1956, and to an even more extreme extent, the JVP which emerged in 1971, represent parties that are significantly to the left of the UNP in economic policy, but to the right in terms of the ethnic question.

The two polar elements of the Sri Lankan political system have consequently comprised a configuration that I have termed 'cosmopolitan capitalists' versus 'sectarian socialists'. The UNP that emerged in the decade after its formation in 1947 was composed of, and clearly espoused the interests of, a wealthy, urban, westernised capitalist elite. In contrast, their socio-political challengers assumed the form of their mirror image on both fronts: that is, as anti-cosmopolitans and anti-capitalists on a fairly consistent one-dimensional array such that the degree of Sinhala nationalism (and implicit anti-minoritism) broadly correlated with the extent of 'leftism' in economic terms. With the SLFP standing roughly half way between these two extremes on both issues, the three main parties in the Sri Lankan political spectrum can be situated along a continuum on these issues.

The existence of this cross-polarity has been a recurrent source of political instability whenever the balance of forces between the party in power and that in opposition has conformed closely to it. This factor came into play in the periods of 1954–1956, 1987–89, and 2002–2004. It has invariably resulted in a marked deterioration of ethnic relations and has worsened or complicated the ability of the government to resolve the ethnic conflict. In contrast, the assumption of a strongly Sinhala nationalist government that simultaneously pursues more egalitarian economic policies has typically led to an increased alienation of the minorities and the growth of Tamil nationalist sentiment. This was the case during 1956–64, 1970–77, and in the 2005–14 period.

The increasing awareness of these problems within the Sri Lankan political establishment has, since 1977, led to the crafting of coalitions that have sought to avoid these extreme and destabilising positions on the spectrum. The governments of J.R. Jayewardene (1977–89), Ranasinghe Premadasa (1989–93), and Chandrika Kumaratunga (1994–2001) consciously sought to position themselves in ways that confounded this divide, co-opting elements from both left and right and pursuing policies that might appease both constituencies in the hope of achieving greater political stability. To some extent, these presidencies succeeded in their early years of power, but found that their eclectic strategies eventually aroused the opposition of *both* Tamil and Sinhala nationalisms over time, with each one finding ample grounds for anger and outrage in the government's conduct.

It is in the context of the failure of this politics of the middle way, and the persistence of the war, that Sri Lankan politics has after 2001 reverted to the more extreme stances of the left–right cross-polarity. The government of Ranil Wickremasinghe (2001–2004) pursued market reforms without recourse to the populist symbolism or reckless public spending that had greased the path of previous market reformers from his own party. At the same time, he adopted the most generous, and accommodating stance of any Sri Lankan government thus far towards the resolution of the ethnic conflict. But in doing so, he effectively placed his government in the same trap of 'cosmopolitan capitalism' that his predecessors Jayewardene and Premadasa had struggled hard to emerge from. By conflating market reforms and peace, the UNP-led government of 2001–2004 gave powerful impetus to the JVP to lead an equally conflated opposition programme of opposing both these elements in a coordinated, composite programme of nationalist/Marxist opposition.

Some elements of the UNF's market reform and fiscal austerity programme were particularly unpopular, such as the withdrawal of the fertiliser subsidy, and a public sector hiring freeze. But perhaps more substantial than these individual budgetary line items was the larger strategic failure of statecraft. As discussed in chapters 6–8, these projects were not strategised and packaged in the way that previous UNP governments had done to win consent for them; that is, with offsetting development programmes, and performances of nationalist authenticity. As a consequence, it mobilised a traditional two-pronged nationalist populist opposition that fused the economic and the ethnic.

Elites, Masses and the Rajapaksa Presidency

The collapse of the UNF government in 2004 brought about the rise of Mahinda Rajapaksa. Rajapaksa, who had been a cabinet minister under Chandrika Kumaratunga, was appointed as leader of the opposition in 2002, became prime minister in 2004, and won the presidential election in 2005. He subsequently won a second term as president in 2010 before losing to Maithripala Sirisena in his bid for a third term in 2015. The nine-year presidency of Mahinda Rajapaksa from 2005 to 2014 was historic and fateful for Sri Lanka, not just because it brought the war to an end, but also because of his approach to the presidency, statecraft, economic development, international relations, ethnic relations, and governance institutions. Can the Rajapaksa presidency be situated in terms of the framework advanced in this book – that is, in terms of the 'elite–mass' confrontation and the rival projects of state reform that they represent?

In order to do that, it is first necessary to situate what Rajapaksa represents within the larger project of Sri Lanka's executive presidency, and to explain the presidency itself in terms of this framework. The shift from a Westminster-style parliamentary system to a semi-presidential or premier-presidential system came about with J.R. Jayewardene's 1978 constitution. It has remained the subject of intense controversy ever since. In substantial terms, the executive presidency must be seen as a response by Sri Lanka's elite to the tumultuous transformations of 1956, and as an attempt to reverse what they viewed as the chaotic and dangerous experience of mass electoral democracy.

As with Sinhala nationalism, the existence of an elite–mass confrontation is not an invention of the modern period, but assumed its present form in the context of universal franchise and electoral politics. As described in chapter 2, the native Ceylonese elite of that period strongly resisted expanding the franchise to their social inferiors, and predicted that it would lead to chaos.

Nevertheless, universal franchise did happen, and colonial Ceylon gradually transitioned into the era of mass electoral politics. In 1948, Ceylon was granted independence under dominion status, as Donoughmore was superseded by the new Soulbury constitution that provided a more conventional Westminster-style superstructure. In the decade that followed, mass electoral politics profoundly destabilised the sedate and clubby world of elite-dominated politics. The political enfranchisement of the adult population transformed the nature of electoral competition, providing new incentives that guided the behavior of political aspirants. By the mid-1940s the government had initiated a range of transformative social welfare schemes such as subsidised food, free education and free public health services, which changed life for the better for the large majority that had hitherto been deprived of these (Jayasuriya 2010). As a result, by the early 1960s Sri Lanka was being described as an unusual and precocious development miracle. Between 1946 and 1963, while it remained one of the poorest countries in the world, the infant mortality rate dropped from 141 per 1000 to 56 per 1000, and life expectancy rose from 43 to 63 years. The adult literacy rate, which was already comparatively high in 1946 at 58%, rose quickly to 72% by 1963 (Isenman 1980). These improvements also occurred in the absence of anything like a near-commensurate increase in economic growth, so that in terms of these human development measures, Sri Lanka had burst into a league of countries that were a factor of between five and ten times wealthier in terms of income.

At the same time, it is not possible to ignore the many negative features that were also intrinsic to this process, and which would vindicate the apprehensions, however condescending they may seem in retrospect, of the Donoughmore-era elites. Universal suffrage, granted abruptly to an impoverished rural population who had never actually asked for it, was quickly exploited and captured –

first, by dominant social groups, and later by populist demagogues. Electoral competition fuelled and channelled a growing tide of ethno-nationalism, bringing the Sinhalese and Tamils into frontal political confrontation that eventually escalated into civil war. Stanley Tambiah's evocative description of 'ethnic fratricide' did not result from or cause the 'dismantling of democracy' but, on the contrary, emerged out of the normal exercise of electoral politics, or what has been described as the 'illiberal consequences of liberal institutions' (Spencer 2008).

In economic terms, the consequences of electoral democracy led Joan Robinson, the Cambridge economist, to famously remark that 'Ceylon has tasted the fruit before she has planted the tree' (Robinson 1959: 41). That is, it led to an unsustainable growth in welfare expenditure, so the productive sectors of the economy were heavily taxed to fund not long-term investments, but unproductive consumption subsidies. Emblematic of the economic and political dysfunctionality of the time was the institution of the rice subsidy and its quick elevation to the status of a political 'holy cow'. Introduced initially as a war-time measure, the subsidy grew to occupy 20% of all government expenditures and became electorally impossible to withdraw, even when the government was in fiscal distress.

With the general strike, or 'hartal' of 1953, the Sinhala-only language act of 1956, ethnic riots in 1958, and the assassination of the then prime minister by a monk in 1959, the democratic dystopia of mob rule appeared to have come frighteningly to life. Even though many surviving members of that native elite were actually at the helm, and were themselves deeply complicit in presiding over and politically profiting from these tumultuous events, they nevertheless viewed the unfolding political and economic chaos with evident concern and distaste. In distress, they desperately sought to find means to reverse these excesses, and to push the populist genie back into the bottle.

One early attempt that demonstrated the desperation that had gripped the *ancien regime* was the failed 'colonel's coup' of 1962. The main conspirators of this plot to depose the government of Mrs Sirimavo Bandaranaike were a group of senior military and police officers whose educational, social and religious background (they were for example, almost entirely Christian), and family connections linked them closely to the erstwhile colonial-era social and economic elite. It emerged only much later that three of the most senior members of that very elite – former prime minister Sir John Kotelawala, opposition leader Dudley Senanayake, and president, Sir Oliver Goonetileke – were complicit in the plot, and were to have stepped forward to assume control.

In seeking to understand the motivations behind the plot, David Horowitz's interviews with the officers revealed a familiar set of anxieties of that social stratum with the new political environment. They described 'politicians pandering to the mob', 'unrest', 'strikes', 'no discipline', 'danger from the left' (Horowitz 1980: 77). Fatefully for the subsequent history of democracy in Sri Lanka, the 1962 coup was uncovered and stopped in time. Moreover, Dudley Senanayake's complicity in the plot was not uncovered until after his death in 1973, by which time he had been re-elected and had served another full term as prime minister (De Silva & Wriggins 1994: 113–120).

The other, far more historically successful plan, emanating from largely the same impulse, and the brainchild of a leading politician from the same economic and social elite, was the Gaullist semi-presidential system. Conceived, nurtured and executed almost single-handedly by J.R. Jayewardene himself, the broader unspoken compulsion that guided this project was, as with the *coup d'etat*, one of protecting political decision-making from the heat of electoral pressures. The sources of Jayewardene's inspiration are uncertain (he first broached the idea in a speech in 1966), but in substance, it was evidently modelled on the French Fifth Republic. Jayewardene was also clearly in awe of the impressive economic successes achieved by his more authoritarian Asian contemporaries, and Lee Kuan Yew's Singapore was often held up as a paragon to behold and emulate. Finally, Sri Lanka's embrace of the presidential system also occurred at a time in the 1960s and 1970s, when several former British colonies facing similar crises of governability under the Westminster system – such as Ghana, Nigeria and Uganda – switched to a presidential system.

The problem at hand with the Westminster system is that the executive is formed out of, and remains embedded within, the legislature. It is thus inherently unstable and vulnerable to the daily ebb and flow of political drama. The shifting loyalties of individual legislators place the executive under the constant threat of sudden collapse through a confidence vote. Moreover, elections to the legislature are based on a plurality (first-past-the-post) system, in which relatively small shifts in voting percentages are magnified into exaggerated parliamentary majorities, as happened in Sri Lanka in 1956, 1960 (July), 1970, and 1977. In contrast to this, executive presidents are directly elected with a fixed term, so that the chief executive stands above and outside parliament with independent, personal authority, and is thus insulated from everyday electoral politics. The motivation behind the executive presidency was thus to hold back the tide of mass electoral politics, and create the institutional means to implement deep state reforms on economic management and ethnic relations, which were in themselves counter-populist and electorally unfeasible. Donald Horowitz describes that 'its principal purpose was to create a political executive with a fixed term that would permit the incumbent to make unpopular decisions' (Horowitz 1980: 77). Put plainly, the presidency was an attempt to recalibrate the elite–mass equation in favour of elites.

In its early years, the presidency was relatively more successful and helped to bring about a structural economic transformation; although in doing so, the more authoritarian aspects of the presidency required a performance of Buddhist authenticity as well as a vast expansion of public sector investment projects as described in chapter 4. In terms of legislation and constitutional amendments, Jayewardene benefited greatly from the parliamentary super-majority (140 of 168 seats) inherited as a relic of the previous constitution and the 'first-past-the-post' system. This allowed him not just to introduce the new constitution, but to pass 16 subsequent constitutional amendments in the artificially elongated decade-long (from 1978 to 1988) life of that parliament. No such super-majority, or indeed, even a simple majority, would be available any more under the new proportional representation voting system that he introduced.

After it first came into effect with the parliamentary election of 1989, the structure of legislative representation and the ratio of party strength in Sri Lanka changed completely. Proportional representation created deeply fragmented parliaments out of which presidents would struggle to piece together fragile multi-party coalitions. Constitutional amendments became a rarity and only three were passed in the 27 years from 1989 to 2016.

Parliament itself was, unlike the president, not protected by a fixed term (until the 19th amendment in 2015), and as such constantly remained much closer to the popular pulse, and vulnerable to defections, confidence votes, by-elections, dissolution, and fresh elections. The new voting system improved the representative quality of parliament in several dimensions, making it more democratic and giving smaller parties and dispersed ethnic communities a commensurate share of legislative decision-making power. But in doing so it also served to constrain the powers of every president after Jayewardene, requiring them to share power and make special concessions with numerous small coalition partners.

As a result, the legislature increasingly became the vehicle through which mass electoral politics found expression, and constrained the power of the presidency. Over the course of Chandrika Kumaratunga's two terms as president (1994–2005), the project of the executive presidency envisioned by Jayewardene gradually came undone as the pendulum of power swung towards parliament. Under the 'co-habitation' period of 2001–04, the executive presidency was reduced to the ornamental position of a Westminster-style figurehead while a hostile prime minister took firm control of the executive and formed a government.

It is under these adverse circumstances that Rajapaksa won the election of November 2005 and assumed a weakened presidency that depended on supported from a slim parliamentary majority composed of powerful coalition partners. Rajapaksa's first term as president was dominated by the last phase of the civil war, and by his quest to stabilise his hold on power by building a pliant legislative majority – and he was fortunate on both counts. A steady drumbeat of military victories in the east, and, later, the north did much to buttress his personal popularity with the core Sinhalese electorate, and this assisted greatly in his campaign to divide and conquer parliament. Between 2006 and 2008, Rajapaksa cleverly wielded both carrots-and-sticks to win over small parties and defectors to his coalition. The most important such 'carrot' that he held was the ability to create new ministerships to reward legislators, and there was an unprecedented expansion in the number of ministers and ministries in this period. By winning over a large number of defectors from the opposition UNP, including some of its senior leaders such as Milinda Moragoda and Karu Jayasuriya, he was able to end his parliamentary dependence on the mercurial JVP and its contingent of 37 MPs.

However, in addition to sharp political acumen and a grasp of tactics, the deeper strategic approach that Rajapaksa deployed was to wrest the mantle of populist nationalism away from parliament and to embrace it openly himself. Rajapaksa's election campaign in 2005, backed by the JVP and JHU, was based largely on Sinhala nationalist opposition to the then peace process and to the 2002 Norwegian-mediated cease-fire agreement. In addition, his election manifesto pledged to end the economic reforms of the Ranil Wickremasinghe government. In its place, he not only promoted a more open and triumphalist Sinhala nationalism and Sinhalisation, but he also demonstratively opposed the market reform agenda.

Unlike the four previous episodes of war in the north and east, when government forces aimed largely to contain the LTTE, or to pressure them into negotiations, Rajapaksa pursued an explicitly exterminationist military campaign of destroying the LTTE outright. This naturally also implied a greater willingness to accept the civilian death toll that would result, and to resist international pressure and media criticism. Between August 2006 and

May 2009, government forces steadily pushed the LTTE back and regained control of its territory in the east coast and Wanni. By early 2009, the LTTE had lost its administrative capital, Killinochi, and was encircled within a small pocket of land in the north-eastern coast of Mullaitivu district. The final showdown that ensued between the two sides in this area became intensely complicated by the presence of a massive train of displaced Tamil civilians, numbering an estimated 200,000. The civilians had followed the retreating LTTE from across the Northern province into their shrinking area of control, and had, by January 2009, effectively become trapped – sandwiched and sandbagged between the two armies.

As the standoff between the two sides stretched out over the next four months, there was heavy diplomatic pressure on Rajapaksa to negotiate a surrender, permit humanitarian relief, and protect the civilians by demarcating 'no-fire zones'. Rajapaksa vigorously fended off all such efforts at increased outside scrutiny and intervention, viewing demands for civilian protection with suspicion as part of a hidden agenda to rescue the encircled LTTE leadership from imminent defeat and death. Foreign aid workers and un-embedded journalists were ordered out of the war zone. The LTTE itself, despite facing overwhelming odds, refused to surrender until the very end, or indeed, to make provision for the safe evacuation of the civilians, who included many of the families of the LTTE leadership. The internationalisation of the humanitarian crisis in early 2009 was also spurred by the activism of the million-strong Sri Lankan Tamil diaspora, who launched a series of massive street demonstrations across the world from London to Toronto expressing support for the LTTE, and calling for an international humanitarian intervention to rescue the civilians.

Solidarity for the LTTE and anguish for the humanitarian crisis was evident in the politically sensitive southern Indian state of Tamil Nadu, and was heightened by the Indian general election campaign, which happened to coincide with the last few weeks of the military stand-off in April–May 2009. The war finally ended on 18 May 2009, when the Sri Lankan army over-ran the LTTE's remaining positions, killing its leader Velupillai Prabhakaran. In the final months of the war during January–May 2009, virtually all of the LTTE's remaining leadership and cadres were killed or captured. A large number of Tamil civilians were also killed during these last months, while the survivors were interned in and 'filtered' through camps for several months afterwards.

Rajapaksa's crushing victory over the LTTE, bringing the 26-year-old war to an end, gave him enormous prestige and public support in the Sinhala south. Presidential elections were brought forward by nine months to capitalise on this, and Rajapaksa was comfortably re-elected with a 58% vote share in January 2010, defeating his rival the former army commander Sarath Fonseka. A few months later, his UPFA coalition expanded its majority to 144 seats out of 225 in the parliamentary elections, bringing him within reach of the two-thirds majority required for constitutional amendments.

Having thus successfully reasserted the power of the presidency, Rajapaksa dedicated his second term to a nationalist vision of economic development. The *Mahinda Chintana* document made a commitment to achieving an 8% annual growth rate, and to double the per capita Gross Domestic Product. Rajapaksa not only maintained a safe rhetorical distance from any market reforms, but declared the neoliberal era in Sri Lanka to have ended with his election in 2005. Indeed, most economic reforms were suspended in those nine years from 2005 to 2014. In place of market reforms and their association with a Western-oriented comprador capitalism, the post-war government's public declarations indicated an economic development regime that resembled East Asian models of authoritarian, state-directed, catch-up developmentalism. In practice, it displayed three distinctive features.

Firstly, it signified the reversion to 'hardware' over 'software', with the prioritisation of ports, airports, and expressways, including in many war-affected areas in the north and east. In contrast, there was a conscious de-prioritisation, and even hostility to 'software', the kind of smaller, village-level projects of community development, microfinance, or local peacebuilding, frequently implemented by NGOs rather than states, which had gained greater prominence since the 1990s.

Secondly, it signified a shift away from Western countries and Western development aid. Many Western countries had been closely involved in the 2002–05 peace process and became highly critical of the Rajapaksa government. In turn, Rajapaksa viewed Western-funded development projects, particularly those in the north and east, with suspicion as nodes of subversion, and subjected them to an increasing burden of surveillance and control. In their place, China emerged as Rajapaksa's preferred source of external finance and support, with Chinese public sector firms constructing some of the most important and high profile projects including the Hambantota port and the Katunayake expressway.

Third, it signified an understanding of post-war transformation in which the end of the war was equated with the end of the conflict. As with many Sinhala nationalists, the Rajapaksa government's developmental approach to conflict resolution contained the idea that there was actually no ethnic conflict as such, or indeed any genuine Tamil grievances that required state reform. Instead, the conflict was seen in terms of a terrorist threat, fuelled by regional under-development, and exploited by opportunistic Tamil politicians. As a result, and also in order to preserve its popularity with the Sinhalese electorate, Rajapaksa was resistant to the idea of recognising, engaging with, or addressing Tamil grievances through state reforms and through any process of accountability.

During his entire nine-year period in power, Rajapaksa effectively refused to take any meaningful steps to arrive at a political resolution of the ethnic conflict. Instead, from the All Parties Representative Committee (APRC) of 2006 to the implementation of the Lessons Learnt and Reconciliation Committee (LLRC) of 2011, Rajapaksa wantonly undid whatever he had grudgingly done. His government accelerated economic and infrastructure development in the north and east, using these funds as a political weapon with which to cultivate links of patronage and support among Tamils, and thus to undermine the appeal of ethnic Tamil political mobilisation.

At the same time, the market-reform project as a whole was suspended during these years. There were no further privatisations, but a minor expansion in the public sector during a brief period in 2011 when 37 under-performing private sector enterprises were nationalised. Between 2004 and 2015, the total number of people in state employment increased by 21% to 1.1 million (Sri Lanka Labour Force Survey annual report 2015). Premachandra Athukorala explains that the main drivers of economic growth in the post-war period were not the internationally connected segments of tourism, garments, and financial services, as had been the case since the 1980s, but were the multiplier effects of large domestic public-sector infrastructure projects, in the construction, transport and utilities sectors. He notes, 'These sectors accounted for over 70% of the total increment in GDP'. Moreover, he shows that foreign direct investment was largely directed at the domestic market-oriented industries such as food and beverages, and that 'a large number of export-oriented firms have closed down their operations' (Athukorala 2016: 28).

It is of course entirely debatable whether this actually amounts to a rollout of socialism or a rollback of neoliberalism in substance, because the broad framework of economic policy remained largely unchanged. Moreover, neoliberalism itself is such a flexibly defined and over-deployed term that it can be analytically indeterminate (Venugopal 2015). Arguably, the primary economic impulse directing the actions of the Rajapaksa government and his family members in key positions of power was more about personal enrichment from the control of state resources than any sustained ideological commitment to reversing market reforms. Nevertheless, the Rajapaksa period was one where the optics and rhetorics of anti-neoliberalism were carefully projected and sustained.

In rejecting the elite-led counter-populist state reforms relating to ethnic relations and the economy, Rajapaksa stabilised his presidency by starving his opponents, including the JVP, of the necessary moral oxygen and political space to mobilise against him. At first glance, Rajapaksa's approach resembled that of J.R. Jayewardene in many ways. He used a combination of muscular authoritarianism, Sinhala nationalist politics, and a nationalist developmental vision to gain a commanding position over the political landscape. However, the comparisons must end there. The three previous executive presidents – Jayewardene, Premadasa, and Kumaratunga – had, at various times, been charged with *conceding* to economic populism, and *pandering* to ethnic chauvinism, the implication being that these were necessary tactical evils of the political game that they were forced to endure and perform for reasons of expediency, and perhaps even against their own better judgment. Politics was in this sense, understood by its protagonists to be a game in which elites used bread and circuses to distract the hungry, wild masses in order to get on with the business of government undisturbed.

Rajapaksa, instead, championed an agenda of cultivating mass popularity and immersing himself in mass politics in a far more transparent way without it being used in the pursuit of any hidden elite-driven agenda – other than perhaps self-enrichment. Opposition to market reforms, and the cultivation of Sinhala nationalism was, under Rajapaksa, not a means to an end, a tiger to be ridden, or a fig leaf to lend legitimacy to some unpopular counter-populist agenda of state reform. Instead, it became the end-game and the agenda in itself. In doing so, the presidency was rescued from the crisis it had fallen into in the years after proportional representation was introduced. But in doing so, its rationale and logic was inverted and its founding purpose was rejected. That is, whereas the presidency was designed to shield the executive from the heat of day-to-day electoral vulnerability, and from ethnic nationalist and welfarist outbidding, these tendencies eventually overwhelmed the presidency. In order for the presidency to survive, it had to surrender to the pressures and embrace them.

All this notwithstanding, there are also important limitations and qualifications to this framework, and to this particular analysis, which must be conceded. Rajapaksa's defeat in the January 2015 presidential elections against Maithripala Sirisena signified the extent to which Sinhala nationalism and economic welfarism have diminishing returns, and can ultimately fail to sustain electoral momentum. In this particular case, a combination of anti-incumbency, and a growing public weariness with the evident abuse of power by the Rajapaksa family became an important election issue. That said, Rajapaksa still carried a clear majority of around 55 percent of Sinhala Buddhist votes in the election, and lost power largely because of the overwhelming numbers of religious and ethnic minorities (Catholics, Tamils and Muslims) who voted against him. For their part, the opposition was also careful to minimise the role of Sinhala nationalism as an election issue by placing Maithripala Sirisena, himself a Sinhala Buddhist of rural origins as their candidate, and by featuring an important Sinhala nationalist party, the *Jathika Hela Urumaya* (JHU) in their coalition.

Bibliography

Official Documents and Government Publications

Administration Report of the Commissioner of Examinations (annual)
Administration Report of the Director of Agriculture (annual)
Administration Report of the Director of Education (annual)
Administration Report of the Director of Health Services (annual)
Administration Report of the General Treasury (annual)
Administration Report of the Government Agent for the Northern Province
Administration Report of the Rubber Controller (annual)
Administration Report of the Tea Controller (annual)
Census of Agriculture 1952, 1962, 1973
Census of Ceylon 1901, 1911, 1921, 1931, 1946, 1953
Census of Government and Local Government Employees 1951
Census of Population 1963, 1971
Central Bank of Ceylon Annual Report.
Central Bank of Ceylon, Consumer Finance Survey (CFS), 1953, 1963, 1973, 1978/79, 1981/82, 1986/87, 1996/97.
Department of Agriculture (various), Cost of Cultivation of Agricultural Crops. Socio-Economic Planning Centre, Peradeniya.
Department of Census and Statistics (previously Statistics and Office Systems), The Ceylon Blue Book (annual) 1898–1938.
Department of Elections (various)
Final Report on the Economic Survey of Rural Ceylon 1950–51. Sessional Paper XI, 1954.
Government of Sri Lanka (2002), Regaining Sri Lanka: Vision and Strategy for Accelerated Development. Colombo: Mimeo.
Hansard (various)
Labour Force Survey (various).
Ministry of Finance (1951), Economic and Social Development 1926–50.
Planning Secretariat (1955), Six-Year Programme of Investment 1954/55 to 1959/60.
Report of the Delimitation Commission, 1976.
Report of the Kandyan Peasantry Commission, Sessional Paper XVIII, 1951.
Report of the Salaries and Cadres Commission, Sessional Paper III, IV, 1961.
Report of the Salaries and Cadres Commission, Sessional Paper III, IV, 1974.
Statistical Abstract (annual), 1949–2010.

Aid Donor Documents

Asian Development Bank. 2001. *Perceptions of the Poor: Poverty Consultations in Four Districts in Sri Lanka. Final Report.* Manila.

International Labour Organisation. 1971. *Matching Employment Opportunities and Expectations: A programme of Action for Ceylon.* Geneva.

International Monetary Fund. 2002. *Country Report 02/86: Sri Lanka: First and Second Reviews Under the Stand-By Arrangement and Requests for Waiver of Performance Criterion and for Extension of the Arrangement.* Washington D.C.

International Monetary Fund. 2003. *Sri Lanka Joint Staff Assessment of the Poverty Reduction Strategy Paper. IMF Country Report 03-106.* Washington D.C.

World Bank. 1953. 'The Economic Development of Ceylon.' Report of a mission organised by the International Bank for Reconstruction and Development at the request of the Government of Ceylon. Baltimore: Johns Hopkins Press.

World Bank. 1986. *The World Bank and Sri Lanka: Review of a Relationship. World Bank Report no. 6074.* Washington D.C.

World Bank. 1995. *Sri Lanka Poverty Assessment. World Bank Report no.13431-CE.* Washington D.C.

World Bank. 2000. *Sri Lanka: Recapturing Missed Opportunities. Poverty Reduction and Economic Management. World Bank Report No. 20430-CE.* Washington D.C.

World Bank. 2001. *Sri Lanka Country Assistance Evaluation. Operations Evaluation Department. World Bank Report No. 21771.* Washington D.C.

World Bank. 2002. *Economic Reform Technical Assistance Project, Project Appraisal Document. World Bank Report No: 25066.* Washington D.C.

World Bank. 2003a. *Country Assistance Strategy for the Democratic Socialist Republic of Sri Lanka, 2003–2006.* Colombo.

World Bank. 2003b. *Programme Document for Poverty Reduction Support Credit I. Report No. 25937-CE.* Washington D.C.

World Bank. 2004. *Project Performance Reassessment Report. Sri Lanka: Third Mahaweli Ganga Development Project (Credit 1166-CE). Report No.: 29489.* Washington D.C.

World Bank. 2004. *Sri Lanka: Development Policy Review. World Bank Report no. 29396-LK.* Washington D.C.

World Bank. 2005. *Implementation Completion Report for Sri Lanka PRSC I. World Bank Report 33919.* Washington D.C.

Newspapers and Periodicals

Daily Mirror (DM), 1996–2004
Midweek Mirror (MM), various.
Ceylon Daily News, & Daily News (CDN), 1953–56, 1977–83, 1996–2004
Daily Resume (English translation of vernacular newspapers), 2000–2004
Sunday Times (ST), 1996–2004
JVP news clipping file, 2000–2004 (ICES Colombo library).
JVP news clipping file, 1994–2002 (Wijewardene Memorial Media library).

Red Power (monthly), 1996–2002
Tamilnet, 1998–2004
LMD magazine 2000–2004
The Hindu (Chennai), various.
Business Today (various)

Pamphlets

Buddhist Committee of Inquiry. 1956. 'The Betrayal of Buddhism: An Abridged Version of the Report of the Buddhist Committee of Inquiry.'
LSSP. 1996. 'The Tasks Ahead: Lanka Sama Samaja Party & the P.A. Government : Documents, Statements, Press Releases of the LSSP, 1994–1996.' Colombo: Lanka Sama Samaja Party.
JVP. 2001. Parliamentary Elections Manifesto (Five Year Plan to Build up the Nation?)

Secondary Literature

Abeysekara, A. 2002. *Colors of the Robe: Religion, Identity and Difference*. Columbia, S.C.: University of South Carolina Press.
Akram-Lodhi, H. 1987. 'Class and Chauvinism in Sri Lanka'. *Journal of Contemporary Asia* 17(2): 160–86.
Alles, A.C. 1977. *Insurgency, 1971: An Account of the April Insurrection in Sri Lanka*. Colombo: Published by author.
Amarasinghe, R. 1999. *Revolutionary Idealism and Parliamentary Politics: A study of Trotskyism in Sri Lanka*. Colombo: Social Scientists Association.
Amunugama, S. 1985. 'Anagarika Dharmapala (1864–1933) and the transformation of Sinhala Buddhist organisation in a colonial setting.' *Social Science Information* 24 (4): 697–730.
Amunugama, S. 1991. 'Buddhaputra or Bhumiputra? Dilemmas of Modern Sinhala Buddhist Monks in Relation to Ethnic and Political Conflict.' *Religion* 21: 115–39.
Anderson, B. 1983. *Imagined Communities: Reflections on the Spread and Origin of Nationalism*. London: Verso.
Anonymous. 2013. 'Cementing Hegemony.' *Economic and Political Weekly* 48 (34): 22-26.
Arasaratnam, S. 1972. 'The Ceylon Insurrection of April 1971: Some Causes and Consequences.' *Pacific Affairs* 45 (3): 356–71.
Argenti-Pillen, A. 2003. *Masking Terror: How Women Contain Violence in Southern Sri Lanka*. Philadelphia: University of Pennsylvania Press.
Arunatilake, N., S. K. Jayasuriya, and S. Kelegama. 2001. 'The Economic Cost of the War in Sri Lanka.' *World Development* 29 (9): 1483–1500.
Ashton, S. R. 1999. 'Ceylon', in *The 20th Century*. Edited by J. Brown et al. Vol. 4 of *The Oxford History of the British Empire*. Oxford: Oxford University Press.
Athukorala, P. and S. Jayasuriya. 1994. *Macroeconomic Policies, Crises and Growth in Sri Lanka, 1960–90*. Washington, D.C.: World Bank.

Attanayake, A. 2001. *Sri Lanka: Constitutionalism, Youth Protest and Political Violence.* Colombo: Published by author.

Balasingham, A. 2004. *War and Peace: Armed Struggle and Peace Efforts of Liberation Tigers.* London: Fairmax.

Ball, N. 1983. 'Defense and Development: A Critique of the Benoit Study.' *Economic Development and Cultural Change* 31 (3): 507-24.

Banks, M. 1961. 'Caste in Jaffna.' In *Aspects of Caste in South India, Ceylon, and North-West Pakistan*, edited by E. Leach, 61-77. Cambridge: Cambridge University Press.

Barro, R. J. 1991. 'Economic Growth in a Cross Section of Countries.' *Quarterly Journal of Economics* 106 (2): 407-43.

Barron, T. J. 1988. 'The Donoughmore Commission and Ceylon's national identity.' *Journal of Commonwealth & Comparative Politics* 26 (2): 147-57.

Baran, P. and P. Sweezy. 1966. *Monopoly Capital.* New York: Monthly Review Press.

Bartholomeusz, T. J. 2005. *In Defense of Dharma: Just-War Ideology in Buddhist Sri Lanka.* London: Routledge.

Bass, D. 2012. Everyday Ethnicity in Sri Lanka: Up-Country Tamil Identity Politics. London: Routledge.

Bastian, S. 1990. 'Political Economy of Ethnic Violence in Sri Lanka: The July 1983 Riots.' In *Mirrors of Violence: Communities, Riots and Survivors*, edited by V. Das. New Delhi: Oxford University Press.

Bastian, S. 2005. 'The Economic Agenda and the Peace Process.' *Asia Foundation Sri Lanka Strategic Conflict Assessment.* Colombo: The Asia Foundation.

Bastin, R. 1997. 'The Authentic Inner Life: Complicity and Resistance in the Tamil Hindu Revival'. In *Sri Lanka: Collective Identities Revisited*, edited by M. Roberts, Vol. 1. 385-438. Colombo: Marga Institute.

Bauer, E., C. Bigdon, and B. Korf. 2003. 'Development Projects in Complex Emergencies – the Case of Trincomalee, Sri Lanka.' In *Building Local Capacities for Peace: Rethinking Conflict and Development in Sri Lanka*, edited by M. Mayer, D. Rajasingam-Senanayake and Y. Thangarajah, 177–195. New Delhi: Macmillan.

Bauman, Z. 1989. *Modernity and the Holocaust.* London: Polity.

Bayly, C. A. 1988. *Indian Society and the Making of the British Empire.* Cambridge: Cambridge University Press.

Benoit, E. 1978. 'Growth and Defense in Developing Countries.' *Economic Development and Cultural Change* 26 (2): 271–87.

Berdal, M. 2005. 'Beyond Greed and Grievance – and not too soon.' *Review of International Studies* 31 (4): 687–98.

Billig, M. 1995. *Banal Nationalism.* London: Sage Publications Ltd.

Biyanwila, J. 2003. 'Trade Unions in Sri Lanka Under Globalisation: Reinventing Worker Solidarity.' PhD Thesis, University of Western Australia.

Blackburn, A. M. 2010. *Locations of Buddhism: Colonialism and Modernity in Sri Lanka.* Chicago: University of Chicago Press.

Blattman, C. and E. Miguel. 2010. 'Civil War.' *Journal of Economic Literature* 48 (1): 3–57.

Bond, G. D. 1992. The Buddhist Revival in Sri Lanka: Religious Tradition, Reinterpretation and Response. New Delhi: Motilal Banarsidass.

Bose, S. 1994. *States, Nations, Sovereignty: Sri Lanka, India and the Tamil Eelam Movement.* New Delhi, London: Sage Publications.

Bose, S. 2002. 'Flawed Mediation, Chaotic Implementation: The 1987 Indo-Sri Lankan Peace Agreement', in *Ending Civil Wars: The Implementation of Peace Agreements*, edited by S. J. Stedman, D. Rothchild, E. M. Cousens, 631–59. Boulder, Colorado: Lynne Rienner.

Brass, P. R. 1991. *Ethnicity and Nationalism: Theory and Comparison.* Newbury Park, California: Sage Publications.

Brow, J. 1988. 'In Pursuit of Hegemony: Representations of Authority and Justice in a Sri Lankan Village.' *American Ethnologist*, 15 (2): 311–27.

Brow, J. 1990a, 'Nationalist Rhetoric and Local Practice: the Fate of the Village Community in Kukulewa.' In *History and the Roots of the Conflict*, edited by J. Spencer, 125–44. London: Routledge.

Brow, J. 1990b. 'The Incorporation of a Marginal Community within the Sinhalese Nation.' *Anthropological Quarterly* 63 (1): 7–17.

Brow, J. 1997. *Demons and Development: The Struggle for Community in a Sri Lankan Village.* Tucson: University of Arizona Press

Brubaker, R. 1996. *Nationalism Reframed: Nationhood and the National Question in the New Europe.* Cambridge: Cambridge University Press.

Brubaker, R. 1999. 'The Manichean Myth: Rethinking the Distinction between "Civic" and "Ethnic" Nationalism.' In *Nation and National Identity: The European Experience in Perspective*, edited by H. Kriesi, K. Armingeon, H. Siegrist, and A. Wimmer, 55–71. Zurich: Ruegger.

Burke, A. and A. Mulakala. 2005. *Donors and Peacebuilding. Sri Lanka Strategic Conflict Assessment 2005.* Colombo: Asia Foundation.

Bush, K. 1999. 'The Limits and Scope for the Use of Development Assistance Incentives and Disincentives for Influencing Conflict Situations. Case Study: Sri Lanka.' Paris: OECD-DAC (Informal Task Force on Conflict, Peace and Development Co-operation).

Bush, K. 2003. *The Intra-Group Dimensions of Ethnic Conflict in Sri Lanka.* New York and Basingstoke: Palgrave Macmillan.

Chandraprema, C. A. 1991. *Sri Lanka, the Years of Terror: The J.V.P. Insurrection, 1987–1989.* Colombo: Lake House.

Collier, P. 1998. 'On the Economic Consequences of Civil War.' *Oxford Economic Papers* 50 (4): 563–73.

Collier, P. et al. 2003. *Breaking the Conflict Trap: Civil War and Development Policy.* Oxford: Oxford University Press.

Coperahewa, S. 2012. 'Purifying the Sinhala Language: The Hela Movement of Munidasa Cumaratunga (1930s–1940s).' *Modern Asian Studies* 46 (04): 857–91.

Cowen, M. and R. Shenton. 1996. *Doctrines of Development.* London: Routledge.

Cramer, C. 2006. *Civil War Is Not a Stupid Thing: Accounting for Violence in Developing Countries.* London: Hurst.

De Jong, K., M. Mulhern , N. Ford , I. Simpson , A. Swan , S. van der Kam. 2002. 'Psychological Trauma of the Civil War in Sri Lanka,' *The Lancet* 359: 1517–18.

De Mel, N. 2007. *Militarising Sri Lanka: Popular Culture, Memory and Narrative in the Armed Conflict*. London: Sage.

De Silva, C. R. 1984. 'Sinhala-Tamil Relations and Education in Sri Lanka: The University Admissions Issue.' In *From Independence to Statehood: Managing Ethnic Conflict in Five African and Asian States*, edited by R. B. Goldmann and A.J. Wilson, 125–46. London: Pinter

De Silva, J. 1997. 'Praxis, Language and Silences – The July 1987 Uprising of the JVP in Sri Lanka.' In *Collective Identities Revisited*, Vol. 2, edited by M. Roberts, 163–98. Colombo: Marga Institute.

De Silva, K. M. 1998. *Reaping the Whirlwind: Ethnic Conflict, Ethnic Politics in Sri Lanka*. New Delhi: Penguin India.

De Silva, K. M. and H. Wriggins. 1994. *J.R. Jayewardene of Sri Lanka: A Political Biography*. Vol. 2, *From 1956 to His Retirement*. London: Leo Cooper.

De Silva, P. 2013. 'Reordering of Postcolonial Sri Pāda Temple in Sri Lanka: Buddhism, State and Nationalism.' *History and Sociology of South Asia* 7 (2): 155–76.

De Silva, S. B. 1982. *The Political Economy of Underdevelopment*. London: Routledge.

Debray, R. 1977. 'Marxism and the National Question.' *New Left Review* 105 (Sept–Oct 1977): 25–41.

Deger, S. 1986. 'Economic Development and Defense Expenditure.' *Economic Development and Cultural Change* 35 (1): 179-96.

DeVotta. 2004. *Blowback: Linguistic Nationalism, Institutional Decay, and Ethnic Conflict in Sri Lanka*. Stanford, California: Stanford University Press.

DeVotta, N. 2005. 'From Ethnic Outbidding to Ethnic Conflict: The Institutional Bases for Sri Lanka's Separatist War.' *Nations and Nationalisms* 11 (1): 141–59.

Dharmadasa, K. N. O. 1992. *Language, Religion, and Ethnic Assertiveness: The Growth of Sinhalese Nationalism in Sri Lanka*. Ann Arbor: University of Michigan Press.

Di Lampedusa, G. T. 2008. *Il Gattopardo*. Milano: Feltrinelli.

Duffield, M. 2001. *Global Governance and the New Wars*. London: Zed.

Duffield, M. 2006. *Development, Security and Unending War: Governing the World of Peoples*. Cambridge: Polity.

Dunham, D. and S. Kelegama. 1997. 'Does Leadership Matter in the Economic Reform Process? Liberalisation and Governance in Sri Lanka, 1989–93.' *World Development* 25 (2): 179–90.

Dunham, D. and S. Jayasuriya. 2000. 'Equity, Growth and Insurrection: Liberalisation and the Welfare Debate in Contemporary Sri Lanka.' *Oxford Development Studies* 28 (1): 97–110.

Dunham, D. and S. Jayasuriya. 2001. 'Liberalisation and Political Decay: Sri Lanka's Journey from a Welfare State to a Brutalised Society,' ISS Working Paper 352, The Hague.

Escobar, A. 1995. *Encountering Development: The Making and Unmaking of the Third World*. Princeton, New Jersey: Princeton University Press.

Faini, R., P. Annez and L. Taylor. 1984. 'Defense Spending, Economic Structure, and Growth: Evidence among Countries and over Time.' *Economic Development and Cultural Change* 32 (3): 487-98.

Farmer, B. 1957. *Pioneer Peasant Colonisation in Ceylon*. London: Oxford University Press.

Farmer, B. 1965. 'The Social Basis of Nationalism in Ceylon.' *The Journal of Asian Studies*, 24 (3): 431–39.

Ferguson, J. 1994. *The Anti-Politics Machine: 'Development,' Depoliticisation, and Bureaucratic Power in Lesotho*. Cambridge: Cambridge University Press.

Fernando, T. 1973. 'Elite Politics in the New States: The Case of Post-Independence Sri Lanka.' *Pacific Affairs* 46 (3): 361–83. doi: 10.2307/2756574.

Field, G. M. 2014. 'Music for Inner Domains: Sinhala Song and the Arya and Hela Schools of Cultural Nationalism in Colonial Sri Lanka'. *The Journal of Asian Studies* 73 (04): 1043–58.

Fitzgerald, V., F. Stewart, and M. Wang. 2001. 'An Overview of the Case Studies.' In *War and Underdevelopment*, edited by F. Stewart and V. Fitzgerald, 104–48. Oxford: Oxford University Press.

Forrest, D.M. 1967. *A Hundred Years of Ceylon Tea: 1867–1967*. London: Chatto and Windus.

Foucault, M. 1979. *Discipline and Punish: the Birth of the Prison*. Harmondsworth: Penguin.

Gamburd, M. 2004. 'The Economics of Enlisting: A Village View of Armed Service.' In *Economy, Culture, and Civil War in Sri Lanka*, edited by D. Winslow and M. Woost, 151–67. Bloomington, Indiana: Indiana University Press.

Gellner, E. 1964. *Thought and Change*. London: Weidenfeld & Nicolson.

Gellner, E. 1983. *Nations and Nationalism*. Ithaca, New York: Cornell University Press.

Ghosh, P. 2003. *Devolution versus Nationalism: The Devolution Discourse in Sri Lanka*. New Delhi: Sage.

Gombrich, R. and G. Obeyesekere. 1988. *Buddhism Transformed: Religious Change in Sri Lanka*. Princeton, New Jersey: Princeton University Press.

Goodhand, J. 2001. *Aid, Conflict and Peace Building in Sri Lanka*. London: Conflict, Security and Development Group, King's College.

Goodhand, J. 2006. *Aiding Peace? The Role of NGOs in Armed Conflict*. New York: International Peace Academy.

Goodhand, J. 2010. 'Stabilising a Victor's Peace? Humanitarian Action and Reconstruction in Eastern Sri Lanka.' *Disasters* 34 (s3), S342–S367.

Goodhand, J., B. Klem, D. Fonseka, D. Keethaponcalan, and S. Sardesai. 2005. *Aid, Conflict & Peace building in Sri Lanka 2000–2005*. Colombo: Asia Foundation.

Goodhand, J., N. Lewer and D. Hulme. 2000. 'Social Capital and the Political Economy of Violence: the Case of Sri Lanka.' *Disasters* 24 (4): 390–406.

Götz, N. 2015. '"Moral Economy": Its Conceptual History and Analytical Prospects.' *Journal of Global Ethics* 11 (2): 147–62.

Government of Sri Lanka. 2002. *Regaining Sri Lanka: Vision and Strategy for Accelerated Development*. Colombo.

Greenfeld, L. 1992. *Nationalism: Five Roads to Modernity*. Cambridge, MA: Harvard University Press.

Greenfeld, L. 2001 *The Spirit of Capitalism: Nationalism and Economic Growth*. Cambridge, Massachusetts: Harvard University Press.

Grobar, L. M. and S. Gnanaselvam. 1993. 'The Economic Effects of the Sri Lankan Civil War.' *Economic Development and Cultural Change* 41 (2): 395–405.

Gunaratna, R. 1990. *Sri Lanka: A Lost Revolution? The Inside Story of the JVP.* Kandy: Institute of Fundamental Studies.

Gunasekara, P. 1998 *Sri Lanka in Crisis: A Lost Generation – The Untold Story.* Colombo: S. Godage & Brothers,

Gunasingam, M. 1999. *Sri Lankan Tamil Nationalism: A Study of its Origins.* Sydney: MV Publications.

Gunasinghe, N. 1984. 'Open Economy and Its Impact on Ethnic Relations in Sri Lanka.' In *Sri Lanka, the Ethnic Conflict: Myths, Realities & Perspectives,* edited by The Committee for Rational Development, 197–213. New Delhi: Navrang.

Gunasinghe, N. 1985. 'Peasant Agrarian Systems and Structural Transformation in Sri Lanka.' In *Capital and Peasant Production: Studies in the Continuity and Discontinuity of Agrarian Structures in Sri Lanka,* edited by C. Abeysekera. Colombo: Social Scientists Association.

Gunasinghe, N. 1996. 'Land Reform, Class Structure and the State in Sri Lanka: 1970–77.' In *Newton Gunasinghe: Selected Essays,* edited by S. Perera. Colombo: Social Scientists Association.

Gunatilaka, R. and D. Chotikapanich. 2006. 'Inequality Trends and Determinants in Sri Lanka 1980–2002: A Shapley Approach to Decomposition. Business and Economics.' Working Paper 6/06, Monash University.

Gunawardena, C. 1979. 'Ethnic Representation, Regional Imbalance and University Admissions in Sri Lanka.' Comparative Education 15 (3)[Special Number (4): Disparities and Alternatives in Education]: 301–12.

Gunawardena, R.A.L.H. 1985. 'The People of the Lion: Sinhala Consciousness in History and Historiography.' In *Ethnicity and Social Change in Sri Lanka,* 55–107. Colombo: Social Scientists Association.

Haggard and Kaufman . 1992. *The Politics of Economic Adjustment.* Princeton, New Jersey: Princeton University Press.

Herbst, J. 1993. *The Politics of Reform in Ghana.* Berkeley: University of California Press.

Herring, R. 1987. 'Economic Liberalisation Policies in Sri Lanka: International Pressures, Constraints and Support.' *Economic and Political Weekly* 22 (8): 325–33.

Herring, R. 1994. 'Explaining Sri Lanka's Exceptionalism: Popular Responses to Welfarism and the Open Economy.' In *Free Markets & Food Riots,* edited by J. Walton and D. Seddon, 253–87. New York: Blackwell.

Hettige 2000. 'Economic Liberalisation, Qualifications and Livelihoods in Sri Lanka'. *Assessment in Education* 7 (3): 325–33.

Hewamanne, S. 2008. *Stitching Identities in a Free Trade Zone: Gender and Politics in Sri Lanka.* Philadelphia: University of Pennsylvania Press.

University of Ceylon. *History of Ceylon.* Vol. 3. Peradeniya: University of Ceylon Press.

Höglund, K. and C. Orjuela. 2012. 'Hybrid Peace Governance and Illiberal Peacebuilding in Sri Lanka.' *Global Governance* 18 (1): 89–104.

Horowitz, D. 1980. 'Coup Theories and Officers' Motives: Sri Lanka in Comparative Perspective.' Princeton, New Jersey: Princeton University Press.

Horowitz, D. 1989. 'Incentives and Behaviour in the Ethnic Politics of Sri Lanka and Malaysia.' *Third World Quarterly* 10 (4): 18–35.

Horowitz, D. L. 1990. 'Comparing Democratic Systems.' *Journal of Democracy* 1 (4): 73–79.

Hroch, M. 1985. *Social Preconditions of National Revival in Europe: A Comparative Analysis of the Social Composition of Patriotic Groups Among the Smaller European Nations.* Cambridge: Cambridge University Press.

International Institute of Strategic Studies, The. 1980–2005. *The Military Balance.* London.

International Crisis Group. 2012. 'Sri Lanka's North II: Rebuilding Under the Military.' *Asia Report No. 220.* Colombo/Brussels: International Crisis Group.

International Labour Organisation. 1971. *Matching Employment Opportunities and Expectations: A programme of Action for Ceylon.* Geneva.

Isenman, P. 1980. 'Basic Needs: the Case of Sri Lanka.' *World Development* 8 (3): 237–58.

Ismail, Q. 1995. 'The Antinomies of Elite Muslim Self-Representation in Modern Sri Lanka.' In *Unmaking the Nation: The Politics of Identity and History in Modern Sri Lanka*, edited by P. Jeganathan and Q. Ismail, 55–105. Colombo: Social Scientists Association.

Jayanntha, D. 1992. *Electoral Allegiance in Sri Lanka.* Cambridge: Cambridge University Press.

Jayasuriya, J. E. 1969. *Education in Ceylon Before and After Independence: 1939–1968.* Colombo: Associated Educational Publishers.

Jayasuriya, L. 2013. *Taking Social Development Seriously: The Experience of Sri Lanka.* New Delhi: Sage.

Jayatilleka, D. 1995. *Sri Lanka: The Travails of a Democracy, Unfinished War, Protracted Crisis.* New Delhi: Vikas Publishing House/International Centre for Ethnic Studies.

Jayawardeena, L.R.U. 1963. 'Supply of Sinhalese Labour to Ceylon Plantations, (1830–1930): A Study of Imperial Policy in a Peasant Society.' PhD thesis, Cambridge University.

Jayawardena, K. 1971. 'The Origins of the Left Movement in Sri Lanka.' *Modern Ceylon Studies* 2 (5): 195–221.

Jayawardena, K. 1987. 'The National Question and the Left Movement in Sri Lanka.' *South Asia Bulletin* 7 (1–2): 11–22.

Jayawardena, K. 2000. *Nobodies to Somebodies: The Rise of the Colonial Bourgeoisie in Sri Lanka.* Colombo: Social Scientists Association.

Jayawardena, K. 2003. *Ethnic and Class Conflict in Sri Lanka: The Emergence of Sinhala-Buddhist Consciousness 1883–1983.* Colombo: Sanjiva Books.

Jayawardena, L., A. Maaslund and P. N. Radhakrishnan. 1987. *Stabilisation and Adjustment Programmes and Policies: Case Study of Sri Lanka.* Helsinki: WIDER.

Jayewardene, J. R. 1992. *Men and Memories.* New Delhi: Vikas.

Jayaweera, S. 1973. 'Education Policy in the Early Twentieth Century,' in *History of Ceylon*, Vol. 3, edited by K. M. de Silva, 461–75. Peradeniya: University of Ceylon Press Board.

Jeganathan, P. 1995. 'Authorising History, Ordering Land: The Conquest of Anuradhapura.' In *Unmaking the Nation: The Politics of Identity and History in Modern Sri Lanka*, edited by P. Jeganathan and Q. Ismail, 106–36. Colombo: Social Scientists Association.

Jeganathan, P. 1998. 'Violence as an Analytical Problem: Sri Lankanist Anthropology after July 1983.' *Nethra: Journal of International Centre for Ethnic Studies* 2 (4): 7–47.

Jeganathan, P. and Q. Ismail (eds). *Unmaking the Nation: The Politics of Identity and History in Modern Sri Lanka*. Colombo: Social Scientists Association.

Jenkins, R. 1999. *Democratic Politics and Economic Reform in India*. Cambridge: Cambridge University Press.

Jennings, I. 1951. *The Economy of Ceylon*. London: Oxford University Press.

Jennings, I. 1954. 'Politics in Ceylon Since 1952.' *Pacific Affairs* 27 (4): 338 –52.

Jiggins, J. 1979. *Caste and Family in the Politics of the Sinhalese, 1947–1976*. Cambridge: Cambridge University Press.

Jupp, J. 1978. *Sri Lanka – Third World Democracy*. London: Frank Cass.

Kadirgamar, A. 2013. 'The Question of Militarisation in Post-war Sri Lanka.' *Economic and Political Weekly* 48 (7): 42-46.

Kanapathipillai, V. 1990. 'July 1983: The survivors' experience.' In *Mirrors of Violence. Communities, Riots and Survivors in South Asia*, edited by V. Das, 321–44. New Delhi: Oxford University Press.

Kapferer, B. 2011. Legends of People, Myths of State: Violence, Intolerance, and Political Culture in Sri Lanka And Australia. Oxford and New York, Berghahn Books.

Karunatilake, H. N. S. 1987. *The Economy of Ceylon*. Colombo: Centre for Demographic and Socio-Economic Studies.

Kearney, R. 1967. *Communalism and Language in the Politics of Ceylon*. Durham, NC: Duke University Press.

Kearney, R. 1971. *Trade Unions and Politics in Ceylon*. Berkeley: University of California Press.

Kearney, R. 1973. 'The Marxist Parties of Ceylon.' In *Radical Politics in South Asia*, edited by P. Brass and M. Franda, 401–40. Cambridge, Massachusetts: MIT Press.

Kearney, R. 1975. 'Educational Expansion and Political Volatility in Sri Lanka: The 1971 Insurrection.' *Asian Survey* 15 (9): 727–44.

Kearney, R. and B. Miller. 1987. *Internal Migration in Sri Lanka and its Social Consequences*. Boulder, Colorado: Westview Press.

Kearney, R. and J. Jiggins 1975, 'The Ceylon insurrection of 1971.' *Commonwealth & Comparative Politics* 13 (1): 40–64.

Keen, D. 2006. *Endless War? Hidden Functions of the War on Terror*. London: Pluto.

Keen, D. 2008. *Complex Emergencies*. London: Polity

Kelegama, S. 2000. 'Development in Independent Sri Lanka: What Went Wrong?' *Economic and Political Weekly* 35 (17): 1477–90.

Kelegama, S. 2005. 'Transforming Conflict with an Economic Dividend: The Sri Lankan Experience.' *The Round Table* 94 (381): 429-42.

Kelegama, S. 2006. *Contemporary Economic Issues: Sri Lanka in the Global Context*. Colombo: Sri Lanka Economic Association.

Kemper, S. 1980. 'Reform and Segmentation in Monastic Fraternities in Low Country Sri Lanka.' *The Journal of Asian Studies* 40 (1): 27–41.

Kemper, S. 1990. 'J.R. Jayewardene, Righteousness and Realpolitik.' In *Sri Lanka: History and the Roots of the Conflict*, edited by J. Spencer. London: Routledge.

Kemper, S. 1991. *The Presence of the Past. Chronicles, Politics, and Culture in Sinhala Life.* Ithaca, New York: Cornell University Press.

Kemper, S. 2015. *Rescued from the Nation: Anagarika Dharmapala and the Buddhist World.* Chicago: University of Chicago Press.

Kent, D. W. 2015. 'Preaching in a Time of Declining Dharma: History, Ethics and Protection in Sermons to the Sri Lankan Army.' *Contemporary Buddhism* 16 (1): 188–223.

Klem, B. 2014. 'The Political Geography of War's End: Territorialisation, Circulation, and Moral Anxiety in Trincomalee, Sri Lanka.' *Political Geography* 38: 33–45.

Kohn, H. 1961. *The Idea of Nationalism: A Study in its Origins and Background.* New Brunswick, NJ: Transaction Publishers.

Korf, B. 2004. 'War, Livelihoods and Vulnerability in Sri Lanka.' *Development and Change* 35 (2): 275–95.

Korf, B. 2006. 'Dining with Devils? Ethnographic Enquiries into the Conflict-Development Nexus in Sri Lanka.' *Oxford Development Studies* 34 (1): 47–64.

Korf, B. 2009. 'Cartographic Violence: Engaging a Sinhala kind of Geography.' In *Spatialising Politics: Culture and Geography in Postcolonial Sri Lanka*, edited by C. Brun and T. Jazeel. New Delhi : Sage India.

Kulatunga, S. T. and R. W. Lakshman. 2013. 'Responding to Security Threats: Livelihoods under Protracted Conflict in Sri Lanka.' *Disasters* 37 (4): 604–26.

Kumarasingham, H. 2013. *A Political Legacy of the British Empire: Power and the Parliamentary System in Post-Colonial India and Sri Lanka.* London: I. B. Taurus.

Kumarasingham, H. 2014. 'Elite Patronage over Party Democracy–High Politics in Sri Lanka Following Independence.' *Commonwealth & Comparative Politics* 52 (1): 166–86.

Kymlicka, W. 2001. *Politics in the Vernacular: Nationalism, Multiculturalism, and Citizenship.* Oxford: Oxford University Press.

Li, T. M. 2007. *The Will to Improve: Governmentality, Development, and the Practice of Politics.* Durham, NC: Duke University Press.

Lindberg, J. 2012. 'The Diversity and Spatiality of Rural Livelihoods in Southern Sri Lanka: Access, Poverty, and Local Perceptions.' *Norsk Geografisk Tidsskrift* 66 (2): 63–75.

Liyanage, S. 2004. 'Coping with Vulnerability among the Families of Soldiers in a Context of Demobilisation: Perspectives on Post-Conflict Peace Building.' In *Poverty and Social Conflict in Sri Lanka: Integrating Conflict Sensitivity into Poverty Analysis*, edited by R. Asirwatham and P. Thalaysingham. Colombo: Centre for Poverty Analysis and IMCAP.

Lynch, C. 1999. 'The "Good Girls" of Sri Lankan Modernity: Moral Orders of Nationalism and Capitalism.' *Identities Global Studies in Culture and Power* 6 (1): 55–89.

Lynch, C. 2007. *Juki Girls, Good Girls: Gender and Cultural Politics in Sri Lanka's Global Garment Industry*. Ithaca, NY: Cornell University Press.

Malalgoda, K. 1973. 'The Buddhist-Christian Confrontation in Ceylon, 1800–1880.' *Social Compass* 20 (2): 171–200.

Malalgoda, K. 1976. *Buddhism in Sinhalese society, 1750–1900: A Study of Religious Revival and Change*. Berkeley, California: University of California Press.

Manogaran, C. 1987. *Ethnic Conflict and Reconciliation in Sri Lanka*. Honolulu: University of Hawaii Press.

Manor, J. 1978. 'The Failure of Political Integration in Sri Lanka (Ceylon).' *Journal of Commonwealth and Comparative Politics* 17 (1): 21–46.

Manor, J. 1989. *The Expedient Utopian: Bandaranaike and Ceylon*. Cambridge: Cambridge University Press.

Marga Institute, International Alert, National Peace Council. 2001. *Cost of the War: Economic, Socio-Political and Human Cost of the War in Sri Lanka*. Colombo.

Matthews, B. 1982. 'District Development Councils in Sri Lanka.' *Asian Survey* 22 (11): 1117–34.

Matthews, B. 1988. 'Sinhala Cultural and Buddhist Patriotic Organisations in Contemporary Sri Lanka.' *Pacific Affairs* 61 (4): 620–32.

McGilvray, D. B. 1998. 'Arabs, Moors and Muslims: Sri Lankan Muslim Ethnicity in Regional Perspective.' *Contributions to Indian Sociology* 32 (2): 433–83.

Meyer, E. 1992. '"Enclave" Plantations, "Hemmed-in" Villages and Dualistic Representations in Colonial Ceylon. *The Journal of Peasant Studies* 19 (3-4), 199-228.

Moore, M. 1985. *The State and Peasant Politics in Sri Lanka*. Cambridge: Cambridge University Press.

Moore, M. 1990. 'Economic Liberalisation Versus Political Pluralism in Sri Lanka.' Modern Asian Studies, 24 (2): 341–83.

Moore, M. 1992a. 'Sri Lanka: A Special Case of Development.' In *Agrarian Change in Sri Lanka*, edited by J. Brow and J. Weeramunda, 17–40. New Delhi: Sage Publications.

Moore, M. 1992b. 'The Ideological History of the Sri Lankan Peasantry.' In *Agrarian Change in Sri Lanka*, edited by J. Brow and J. Weeramunda, 325–56. New Delhi: Sage Publications.

Moore, M. 1997. 'Leading the Left to the Right: Populist Coalitions and Economic Reform.' *World Development* 25 (7): 1009–28.

Moore, M. 1998. 'Ethnicity, Caste, and the Legitimacy of Capitalism.' In *Sri Lanka: Collective Identities Revisited*, Vol. 2, edited by M. Roberts, 61–102. Colombo: Marga.

Muggah, R. 2008. *Relocation Failures in Sri Lanka: A Short History of Internal Displacement and Resettlement*. London: Zed Books.

Munck, R. 1986. *The Difficult Dialogue: Marxism and Nationalism*. London: Zed.

Nairn, T. 1977. *The Break-up of Britain: Crisis and Neo-Nationalism*. London: NLB.

Narayan, A. and N. Yoshida. 2005. *Poverty in Sri Lanka: The Impact of Growth with Rising Inequality. Report No. SASPR-8*: Washington, D.C.: World Bank.

Nelson, J. 1990. *Economic Crisis and Political Choice*. Princeton: Princeton University Press.

Nigel, J. 2009. 'Livelihoods in a Conflict Setting.' *Norsk Geografisk Tidsskrift-Norwegian Journal of Geography 63* (1): 23–34.

Nissan, E. 1989. 'History in the Making: Anuradhapura and the Sinhala Buddhist Nation.' *Social Analysis* 9 (25): 64–77.

Nissan, E. and R. L. Stirrat. 1990. 'The generation of communal identities.' In *History and the Roots of the Conflict*, edited by J. Spencer, 19-44. London: Routledge.

O'Sullivan, M. 1999. *Identity and Institutions in Ethnic Conflict: The Muslims of Sri Lanka.* DPhil thesis, University of Oxford.

O'Sullivan, M. 2001. 'Sri Lanka: Civil Strife, Civil Society, and the State 1983–1995.' In *War and Underdevelopment*, edited by F. Stewart and V. FitzGerald, 176-219. 2 Vols. Oxford: Oxford University Press.

Oberst, R. 1985. 'Democracy and the Persistence of Westernized Elite Dominance in Sri Lanka.' *Asian Survey* 25 (7): 760–72.

Obeyesekere, G. 1970. 'Religious Symbolism and Political Change in Ceylon.' *Modern Ceylon Studies* 1 (1): 43–63.

Obeyesekere, G. 1974. 'Some Comments on the Social Backgrounds of the April 1971 Insurgency in Sri Lanka (Ceylon).' *Journal of Asian Studies* 33 (3): 367–84.

Obeyesekere, G. 1979. 'The Vicissitudes of the Sinhala-Buddhist identity Through Time and Change.' In *Collective Identities, Nationalisms and Protest in Modern Sri Lanka*, edited by M. Roberts. Colombo: Marga Publications.

Obeyesekere, G. 1984. 'The Origins and Institutionalisation of Political Violence.' In *Sri Lanka in Change and Crisis*, Vol. 1, edited by J. Manor, 355–84. London: Croom Helm.

Ofstad, A. 2002. 'Countries in Violent Conflict and Aid Strategies: The Case of Sri Lanka.' *World Development* 30 (2): 165–80.

Oliver, H. 1957. *Economic Opinion and Policy in Ceylon.* London: Cambridge University Press.

Osmani, S.R. 1994. 'Economic Reform and Social Welfare: The Case of Nutrition in Sri Lanka.' *American Economic Review* 84 (2): 291–96.

Paris, R. 1997. 'Peacebuilding and the Limits of Liberal Internationalism.' *International Security* 22 (2): 54–89.

Paris, R. 2004. *At War's End: Building Peace after Civil Conflict.* Cambridge: Cambridge University Press.

Peebles, P. 1982. *A Handbook of Historical Statistics.* Boston, Massachusetts: G. K. Hall.

Peebles, P. 1990. 'Colonisation and Ethnic Conflict in the Dry Zone of Sri Lanka.' *Journal of Asian Studies* 49 (1): 30–55.

Peebles, P. 2001. *The Plantation Tamils of Ceylon.* London: Leicester University Press.

Peers, D. 2007. 'Gunpowder Empires and the Garrison State: Modernity, Hybridity, and the Political Economy of Colonial India, circa 1750– 1860.' *Comparative Studies of South Asia, Africa and the Middle East* 27 (2): 245-258.

Peiris, G. H. 1996a. 'Agrarian Change and Agricultural Development in Sri Lanka.' In *Economic Development and Social Change in Sri Lanka: A Spatial and Policy Analysis*, edited by P. Groves, 111–66. New Delhi: Manohar.

Peiris, G. H. 1996b. *Development and Change in Sri Lanka: Geographical Perspectives.* New Delhi: Macmillan.

Pfaffenberger, B. 1990. 'The Political Construction of Defensive Nationalism: The 1968 Temple-Entry Crisis in Northern Sri Lanka.' *Journal of Asian Studies* 49 (1): 78–96.

Pieris, R. 1956. *Sinhalese Social Organisation.* Colombo: Ceylon University Press Board.

Ponnambalam, S. 1981. *Dependent Capitalism in Crisis: The Sri Lankan Economy, 1948–1980.* London: Zed.

Ponnambalam, S. 1983. *Sri Lanka: National Conflict and the Tamil Liberation Struggle.* London: Zed.

Przeworski, A. 1991. *Democracy and the Market: Political and Economic Reforms in Eastern Europe and Latin America.* Cambridge, Cambridge University Press.

Pye, L. 1962. 'Armies in the Process of Political Modernisation.' In *The Role of Military in Underdeveloped Countries,* edited by J. J. Johnson, 80-89. New Jersey: Princeton University Press.

Race & Class. 1984a. 'The Mathew Doctrine.' *Race & Class* 26 (1): 129–38.

Race & Class. 1984b. 'Sri Lanka's Week of Shame: An Eyewitness Account.' *Race & Class* 26 (1): 39–50.

Rambukwella, H. 2012. 'Reconciling What? History, Realism and the Problem of an Inclusive Sri Lankan identity.' ICES Research Paper No. 3, International Centre for Ethnic Studies.

Rampton (2003), 'Sri Lanka's Many Headed Hydra: The JVP, Nationalism and the Politics of Poverty', *in Poverty Issues in Sri Lanka.* Colombo: CEPA, IMCAP, SLAAS.

Rampton, D. and A. Welikala. 2005. *The Politics of the South. Part of the Sri Lanka Strategic Conflict Assessment 2005.* Colombo: The Asia Foundation.

Rasaratnam, M. 2016. *Tamils and the Nation: India and Sri Lanka Compared.* London: Hurst.

Roberts, M. 1973a. 'Elite Formation and Elites, 1832–1931.' In *History of Ceylon,* Vol. 3, edited by K. M. De Silva, 263–84. Peradeniya: University of Ceylon Press.

Roberts, M. 1973b. 'Aspects of Ceylon's Agrarian Economy in the Nineteenth Century.' In *History of Ceylon,* Vol 3, edited by K. M. De Silva, 146–64. Peradeniya: University of Ceylon.

Roberts, M. 1974. 'Problems of Social Stratification and the Demarcation of National and Local Elites in British Ceylon.' *Journal of Asian Studies* 33 (4): 549–77.

Roberts, M. 1978. 'Ethnic Conflict in Sri Lanka and Sinhalese Perspectives: Barriers to Accommodation.' *Modern Asian Studies* 12 (3): 353–76.

Roberts, M. 1979. 'Stimulants and Ingredients in the Awakening of Latter-day Nationalisms.' In *Collective Identities, Nationalisms and Protest in Modern Sri Lanka,* Vol. 1, edited by M. Roberts, 267–92. Colombo: Marga Publications.

Roberts, M. 1982. *Caste Conflict and Elite Formation: the Rise of a Karava Elite in Sri Lanka, 1500–1931.* Cambridge: Cambridge University Press.

Roberts, M. 1989a. 'Apocalypse or Accommodation? Two Contrasting Views of Sinhala–Tamil Relations in Sri Lanka.' *South Asia* 12 (1): 67–83.

Roberts, M. 1989b. 'The Political Antecedents of the Revivalist Elite within the MEP Coalition of 1956.' In *K.W. Goonewardena Felicitation Volume*, edited by De C. R. Silva and S. Kiribamune, 185–220. Peradeniya University

Roberts, M. 1994. *Exploring Confrontation. Sri Lanka: Politics, Culture and History.* Chur, Switzerland: Harwood Academic Publishers.

Roberts, M. 2001. *Primordialist Strands in Contemporary Sinhala Nationalism in Sri Lanka: Urumaya as Ur*, Vol. 20 of *A History of the Ethnic Conflict in Sri Lanka.* Colombo: Marga Institute.

Roberts, M. 2004. *Sinhala Consciousness in the Kandyan Period, 1590s to 1815.* Colombo: Vijitha Yapa Publications.

Roberts, M. and L.A. Wickremaratne. 1973. 'Export Agriculture in the Nineteenth Century.' In *University of Ceylon History of Ceylon*, Vol. 3, edited by K. M. de Silva, 89–118. Peradeniya: University of Ceylon Press Board.

Robson, D. 1983. 'Aided Self-Help Housing in Sri Lanka.' ODA Report. London: Her Majesty's Stationery Office.

Rogers, John D. 1994. 'Post-Orientalism and the Interpretation of Pre-modern and Modern Political Identities: The Case of Sri Lanka.' *Journal of Asian Studies* 53 (1): 10–23.

Rogers, John D. 2004. 'Early British Rule and Social Classification in Lanka.' *Modern Asian Studies* 38 (3): 625–47.

Russell, J. 1982. *Communal Politics under the Donoughmore Constitution 1931–47.* Colombo: Tisara Prakasakayo Ltd.

Ryan, B. 1953. *Caste in Modern Ceylon: The Sinhalese System in Transition.* New Brunswick: Rutgers University Press.

Ryan, B. 1961. 'Status, Achievement, and Education in Ceylon,' *The Journal of Asian Studies* 20 (4): 463–76.

Samarakone, P. [pseudonym]. 1984. 'The Conduct of the Referendum.' In *Sri Lanka in Change and Crisis*, edited by J. Manor, 84–117. London: Croom Helm.

Samarasinghe, S. 1984. 'Ethnic Representation in Central Government Employment and Sinhala–Tamil Relations in Sri Lanka: 1948–1981.' In *From Independence to Statehood: Managing Ethnic Conflict in Five African and Asian States*, edited by R.B. Goldmann and A. J. Wilson, 173–84. London: Pinter.

Samaraweera, V. 1973. 'Land Policy and Peasant Colonisation, 1914–1948, in *University of Ceylon History of Ceylon*, Vol. 3, edited by K. M. de Silva, 446–60. Peradeniya: University of Ceylon Press Board.

Samaraweera, V. 1980. 'Sri Lankan Marxists in Electoral Politics, 1947–77.' *Journal of Commonwealth and Comparative Politics* 18 (3): 308–24.

Samaraweera, V. 1981. 'Land, Labor, Capital and Sectional Interests in the National Politics of Sri Lanka.' *Modern Asian Studies* 15 (1): 127–62.

Sanmugathasan, N. 1972. *A Marxist Looks at the History of Ceylon.* n.p.

Saravanamuttu, P. 2003. 'Sri Lanka: The Best and Last Chance for Peace?' *Conflict, Security, Development* 3 (1): 129–38.

Sarvananthan, M. 2008. 'Economy of the Conflict Region of Sri Lanka: From Embargo to Repression.' East West Center, Policy Studies 44.

Satkunanathan, A. 2015. 'The Executive and the Shadow State in Sri Lanka.' In *Reforming Sri Lankan Presidentialism: Provenance, Problems and Prospects*, edited by A. Welikala, 370-98. Colombo: Centre for Policy Alternatives.

Schonthal, B. 2016. *Buddhism, Politics and the Limits of Law: The Pyrrhic Constitutionalism of Sri Lanka*. Cambridge: Cambridge University Press.

Scott, David, and C. Geertz. 1990. 'The Demonology of Nationalism: On the Anthropology of Ethnicity and Violence in Sri Lanka.' *International Journal of Human Resource Management* 19 (4): 491–510.

Scott, J. 1985. *Weapons of the Weak: Everyday Forms of Peasant Resistance*. New Haven, Yale University Press

Senaratne, J. 1997. *Political Violence in Sri Lanka 1977–1990: Riots, Insurrections, Counterinsurgencies, Foreign Intervention*. Amsterdam: VU University Press.

Seneviratne, H. L. 1999. *The Work of Kings: The New Buddhism in Sri Lanka*. Chicago: University of Chicago Press.

Shastri, A. 2004a. 'The Economy in Conditions of Intense Civil War: Sri Lanka 1994–2000,' in *Economy, Culture, and Civil War in Sri Lanka*, edited by D. Winslow and M. Woost, 73–94. Bloomington, Indiana: Indiana University Press.

Shastri, A. 2004b. 'The United National Party of Sri Lanka: Reproducing Hegemony.' In *Political Parties in South Asia*, edited by S. Mitra, M. Enksat and C. Spiess, 236–58. Westport, Connecticut: Praeger.

Shastri, A. 2005. 'Channelling Ethnicity Through Electoral Reform in Sri Lanka.' *Journal of Commonwealth and Comparative Politics* 43 (1): 34–60.

Singer, M. 1964. *The Emerging Elite: A Study of Political Leadership in Ceylon*. Cambridge, Massachusetts: MIT Press.

Sirivardana, S. 1986. 'Reflections on the Implementation of the Million Houses Programme.' *Habitat International* 10(3): 91–108.

Smith, A. 1991. *National Identity*. London: Penguin Books.

Smith, A. D. 2009. *Ethno-symbolism and Nationalism: A Cultural Approach*. New York: Routledge.

Smooha, S. 2002. 'The Model of Ethnic Democracy: Israel as a Jewish and Democratic state'. *Nations and Nationalism* 8 (4): 475-503.

Snodgrass, D. 1966. *Ceylon: An Export Economy in Transition*. Illinois: Richard D. Irwin.

Snodgrass, D. 1999. 'The Economic Development of Sri Lanka: A Tale of Missed Opportunities.' In *Creating Peace in Sri Lanka: Civil War and Reconciliation*, edited by R. Rotberg, 89–107. Washington, D.C.: Brookings Institution Press.

Somasundaram, D. 1998. *Scarred Minds: The Psychological Impact of War on Sri Lankan Tamils*. London: Sage.

Sørbø, G., Goodhand, J., Klem, B., Nissen, Ada, E., Selbervik, H. 2011. 'Pawns of Peace: Evaluation of Norwegian Peace Efforts in Sri Lanka, 1997-2009.' Oslo: Norwegian Agency for Development Cooperation.

Southwold-Llewellyn, S. 1994. 'The Creation of an Outsiders' Myth: The Mudalali of Sri Lanka.' In *The Moral Economy of Trade: Ethnicity and the Development of Markets*, edited by H. D. Evers and H. Schrader, 175–97. London: Routledge.

Spencer, J. 1990a. *A Sinhala Village in a Time of Trouble: Politics and Change in Rural Sri Lanka*. New Delhi: Oxford University Press.

Spencer, J. 1990b. 'Collective Violence and Everyday Practice in Sri Lanka.' *Modern Asian Studies* 24 (3): 603–23.

Spencer, J. 1993. 'Anthropology and the politics of socialism in rural Sri Lanka.' *Socialism: Ideals, Ideologies, and Local Practice* 31: 117–31.

Spencer, J. 2002. 'The Vanishing Elite: the Political and Cultural Work of Nationalist Revolution in Sri Lanka.' In *Elite Cultures: Anthropological Perspectives*, edited by C. Shore and S. Nugent, 91–109. London: Routledge.

Spencer, J. 2008. 'A Nationalism without Politics? The Illiberal consequences of Liberal Institutions in Sri Lanka.' *Third World Quarterly* 29 (3): 611–29.

Sriskandarajah, D. 2003. The Returns of Peace in Sri Lanka: The Development Cart before the Conflict Resolution Horse?. *Journal of Peacebuilding & Development* 1 (2), 21–35.

Sriskandarajah, D. 2005. 'Socio-economic Inequality and Ethno-political Conflict: Some Observations from Sri Lanka.' *Contemporary South Asia* 14 (3): 341–56.

Stalin, J. V. 1945 [1913]. *Marxism and the National Question*. Moscow: Foreign Languages Publishing House.

Stedman, S. J. and D. Rothchild. 1996. 'Peace Operations: From Short-Term to Long-Term Commitment.' *International Peacekeeping* 3 (2): 17–35.

Stedman, S. J., D. Rothchild, E. M. Cousens. 2002. *Ending Civil Wars: The Implementation of Peace Agreements*. Boulder, Colorado: Lynne Rienner.

Stein, B. 1985. 'State Formation and Economy Reconsidered.' *Modern Asian Studies*, 19 (3): 387-413.

Stern, J. 1984. 'Liberalisation in Sri Lanka: A Preliminary Assessment.' mimeo, Harvard Institute of International Development.

Stewart, F., and E. V. K. Fitzgerald. 2001. *War and Underdevelopment*. Oxford: Oxford University Press.

Stokke, K. 1997. 'Authoritarianism in the Age of Market Liberalism in Sri Lanka.' *Antipode* 29 (4): 437–55.

Stokke, K. 1998. 'Sinhalese and Tamil Nationalism as Post-Colonial Political Projects from "Above", 1948-1983.' *Political Geography* 17 (1): 83-113.

Strathern, A. 2007. *Kingship and Conversion in Sixteenth-century Sri Lanka*. Cambridge: Cambridge University Press.

Strauss, M. 1951. 'Family Characteristics and Occupational Choice of University Entrants as Clues to the Social Structure of Ceylon.' *The University of Ceylon Review* 9 (2): 129-41.

Tambiah, S. J. 1955. 'Ethnic Representation in Ceylon's Higher Administrative Services, 1870–1946.' *University of Ceylon Review* 13 (2, 3): 113–34.

Tambiah, S. J. 1986. *Sri Lanka: Ethnic Fratricide and the Dismantling of Democracy*. Chicago: University of Chicago Press.

Tambiah, S. J. 1992. *Buddhism Betrayed: Religion, Politics and Violence in Sri Lanka*. Chicago: University of Chicago Press.

Taylor, C. 2004. *Modern Social Imaginaries*. Durham NC and London: Duke University Press.

Teitelbaum, E. 2007. 'Can a Developing Democracy Benefit from Labour Repression? Evidence from Sri Lanka.' *Journal of Development Studies* 43 (5): 830–55.

Tennekoon, S. 1988. 'Rituals of Development: The Accelerated Mahaveli Development Program of Sri Lanka.' *American Ethnologist* 15 (2): 294–310.

Thiranagama, S. 2011. *In my Mother's House: Civil War in Sri Lanka.* Philadelphia, PA: University of Pennsylvania Press.

Thompson, E. P. 1971. 'The Moral Economy of the English Crowd in the Eighteenth Century'. *Past & Present* 50 (1): 76-136.

Tilly, C. 1975. 'Reflections on the History of European State-Making.' In *The Formation of National States in Western Europe*, edited by C. Tilly, 3-83. Princeton, NJ: Princeton University Press.

Tonnesson, S. and H. Antlov. 1996. 'Asia in Theories of Nationalism and National Identity.' In *Asian Forms of the Nation*, edited by S. Tonnesson and H. Antlov, 1-39. London: Routledge.

Uvin, P. 1998. *Aiding Violence: The Development Enterprise in Rwanda.* Sterling, VA: Kumarian Press.

Uyangoda, J. 2000. 'The Inner Courtyard: Political Discourses of Caste, Justice and Equality in Sri Lanka.' *Pravada* 6 (9-10): 14–19.

Uyangoda, J. 2002. 'Sri Lanka's Conflict: Complexities in a Negotiated Settlement.' In *Competing Nationalisms in South Asia*, edited by P. Brass and A. Vanaik, 195–249. New Delhi: Orient Longman.

Uyangoda, J. 2003. 'Social Conflict, Radical Resistance and Projects of State Power.' In *Building Local Capacities for Peace: Rethinking Conflict and Development in Sri Lanka*, edited by M. Mayer, D. Rajasingham-Senanayake and Y. Thangarajah, 37–64. Delhi: Macmillan India.

Uyangoda, J. 2011. 'Travails of State Reform in the Context of Protracted Civil War in Sri Lanka.' In *Liberal Peace in Question: Politics of State and Market Reform in Sri Lanka*, edited by K. Stokke and J. Uyangoda, 35–62.

Uyangoda, J. and M. Perera. 2003. *Sri Lanka's Peace Process 2002: Critical Perspectives.* Colombo: Social Scientists Association.

Van der Horst, J. 1995. *Who is He, What is he Doing: Religious Rhetoric and Performances in Sri Lanka during R. Premadasa's Presidency (1989–1993).* Amsterdam. VU University Press.

Vanden Driesen, I. H. 1997. *The Long Walk : Indian Plantation Labour in Sri Lanka in the Nineteenth Century.* New Delhi: Prestige Books.

Venkatesan S, and T. Yarrow. 2012. *Differentiating Development: Beyond an Anthropology of Critique.* Oxford, UK/New York: Berghahn.

Venugopal, R. 2006. 'Sri Lanka: The Global Dimensions of Conflict.' In *Globalisation, Violent Conflict and Self-Determination*, edited by E. V. K. FitzGerald, F. Stewart and R. Venugopal, 225–46. Basingstoke: Palgrave Macmillan.

Venugopal, R. 2015. 'Neoliberalism as concept.' *Economy and Society* 44 (2): 165-87.

Washbrook, D. 1988. 'Progress and Problems: South Asian Economic and Social History c.1720-1860.' *Modern Asian Studies* 22 (1): 57-96.

Weber, M. 1978. *Economy and Society: An Outline of Interpretive Sociology.* Berkeley: University of California Press.

Weerakoon, B. 1992. *Premadasa of Sri Lanka: A Political Biography.* New Delhi: Vikas.

Weerakoon, B. 2004. *Rendering Unto Caesar: A Fascinating Story of One Man's Tenure Under Nine Prime Ministers and Presidents of Sri Lanka.* New Delhi: Sterling

Weerakoon, D. 2004 'The Influence of Development Ideology in Macroeconomic Policy Reform Process.' In *Economic Policy in Sri Lanka: Issues and Debates,* edited by Kelegama, 54–70. Colombo: Vijitha Yapa.

Weeratunga, N. 2010. 'Being Sadharana: Talking About the Just Business Person in Sri Lanka.' In *Ordinary Ethics: Anthropology, Language And Action,* edited by M. Lambek, 328–50. New York City: Fordham University Press.

Weerawardana, I.D.S. 1960. *Ceylon General Election 1956.* Colombo: Gunasena.

Welikala, A. 2015. *Reforming Sri Lankan Presidentialism: Provenance, Problems and Prospects.* Colombo: Centre for Policy Alternatives.

White, H. and G. Wignaraja. 1992. 'Exchange Rates, Trade Liberalisation and Aid: The Sri Lankan Experience.' *World Development* 20 (10): 1471–80.

Wickizer, V.D. 1951. *Coffee, Tea and Cocoa: An Economic and Political Analysis.* Stanford: Stanford University Press.

Wickramasinghe, N. 1995. *Ethnic Politics in Colonial Sri Lanka, 1927–1947.* New Delhi: Vikas.

Wickremeratne, L. A. 1973a. 'Economic Development in the Plantation Sector, 1900–1947.' In *History of Ceylon*, Vol. 3, edited by K. M. de Silva, 428–45. Peradeniya: University of Ceylon Press Board.

Wickremeratne, L. A. 1973b. 'The Emergence of a Welfare Policy, 1931–48.' In *History of Ceylon*, Vol. 3, edited by K. M. de Silva, 476–88. Peradeniya: University of Ceylon Press Board.

Wijeyeratne, R. de S. 2013. *Nation, Constitutionalism and Buddhism in Sri Lanka.*: Routledge.

Wijeweera, R. 1986. *Solution for Tamil Eelam Struggle.* http://www.jvpsrilanka.com. Accessed 1 September 2006.

Wilson, A. J. 1980. *The Gaullist System in Asia: The Constitution of Sri Lanka (1978).* London: Macmillan Press.

Wilson, A. J. 1988. *The Break-up of Sri Lanka: The Sinhalese–Tamil Conflict.* London: Hurst.

Wilson, A. J. 2000. *Sri Lankan Tamil Nationalism: Its Origins and Development in the Nineteenth and Twentieth Centuries.* London: Hurst.

Wilson, P. 1975. *Economic Implications of Population Growth. Sri Lanka Labour Force: 1946–81.* Canberra: Australian National University.

Woodward, S. 2002. 'Economic Priorities for Successful Peace Implementation.' In *Ending Civil Wars: The Implementation of Peace Agreements,* edited by S. Stedman, D. Rothchild, and E. Cousens, 183–215. Boulder, Colorado: Lynne Rienner.

Woost, M. 1993. 'Nationalising the Local Past in Sri Lanka: Histories of Nation and Development in a Sinhalese Village.' *American Ethnologist* 20 (3): 502–21.

Wriggins, W. Howard. 1960. *Ceylon: Dilemmas of a New Nation*. Princeton: Princeton University Press.

Yack, B. 1996. 'The Myth of the Civic Nation.' *Critical Review*, 10 (2): 193–211.

Yiftachel, O. 2006. *Ethnocracy: Land and Identity Politics in Israel/Palestine*. Philadelphia, PA: University of Pennsylvania Press.

Yiftachel, O. and A. Ghanem. 2004. 'Understanding "Ethnocratic" Regimes: The Politics of Seizing Contested Territories. *Political Geography* 23 (6): 647–76.

Zartman, I. W. 1995. *Elusive Peace: Negotiating an End to Civil Wars*. Washington: Brookings Institution Press.

Index